Victorious Substitution

Victorious Substitution

Exploring the Nature of Salvation
and Christ's Atoning Work

VEE CHANDLER

WIPF & STOCK · Eugene, Oregon

VICTORIOUS SUBSTITUTION
Exploring the Nature of Salvation and Christ's Atoning Work

Copyright © 2025 Vee Chandler. All rights reserved. Except for brief quotations in critical publications or reviews, no part of this book may be reproduced in any manner without prior written permission from the publisher. Write: Permissions, Wipf and Stock Publishers, 199 W. 8th Ave., Suite 3, Eugene, OR 97401.

Wipf & Stock
An Imprint of Wipf and Stock Publishers
199 W. 8th Ave., Suite 3
Eugene, OR 97401

www.wipfandstock.com

PAPERBACK ISBN: 979-8-3852-3741-8
HARDCOVER ISBN: 979-8-3852-3742-5
EBOOK ISBN: 979-8-3852-3743-2

VERSION NUMBER 05/16/25

All Scripture quotations, unless otherwise indicated, are taken from the Holy Bible, New International Version®, NIV®. Copyright ©1973, 1978, 1984, 2011 by Biblica, Inc.™ Used by permission of Zondervan. All rights reserved worldwide. www.zondervan.com The "NIV" and "New International Version" are trademarks registered in the United States Patent and Trademark Office by Biblica, Inc.™

For Creecy

You are the person I admire more than any other. Often in life we are blessed with one person that we want desperately to never disappoint. For me, you are that person.

And for Matthew

Your patience, and kindness, and amazing editorial skills have been some of God's best gifts to me. Without you (as you well know) this book would not be. Thank you.

Contents

Preface | ix

Introduction | xi

Part I   Atonement Theory: Is Penal Substitution the Default View? | 1

1   Theories of the Atonement | 3

2   Logical, Moral, and Theological Objections to the Penal Substitution Theory | 20

3   Exegetical Objections to the Penal Substitution Theory | 33

Part II   A Defense of the Ransom Theory | 55

4   Ransom Theory: Early Development and New Testament Support | 57

5   Luther's View and Common Objections to the Ransom Theory | 80

Part III   The Victorious Substitution Theory of the Atonement | 97

6   The Scriptural Foundations of Victorious Substitution: Sacrifice and Atonement | 99

| 7 | The Scriptural Foundations of Victorious Substitution: Substitution and Penalty | 111 |

Part IV The Christian Experience of Victorious Substitution | 131

| 8 | The Application of Atonement: A New Situation | 133 |
| 9 | How to Enter into the Victorious Life Provided through the Atonement | 163 |

Conclusion | 173

Appendix A: Romans 3:21–26: Context, Terminology, and Exegesis | 179

Appendix B: Atonement Fact versus Theory | 218

Bibliography | 223

Preface

THIS BOOK PRESENTS A theory of the Atonement that was originally written in 2012 as a slightly revised version of my PhD dissertation. This book is not complicated but a simple explanation of various theories of the Atonement with their strengths and weaknesses. The word *atonement* in Scripture means reconciliation, and "the Atonement" in the following pages specifically refers to Christ's death as the means of reconciliation between God and humankind. A careful effort is made to distinguish what Scripture reveals about what the death of Christ accomplished (fact) and why it was necessary (theory). In other words, atonement theories ask the question, Why did Jesus have to die for us to be reconciled to God? Some theories are *objective* in that they suggest Christ died to bring about a change related to God. Other theories are *subjective*, suggesting Christ died to bring about a change related to humans. God has chosen to leave some element of mystery surrounding this question; it is not directly answered in Scripture. But it is okay to think about the question, and even to speculate, as long as we make it clear when we are thinking and speculating and that we are not adding to Scripture or claiming it says something that it does not.

Introduction

WHY THE NEED FOR THIS BOOK?

THE NEW TESTAMENT PRESENTS the suffering and death of Jesus as a necessity affirmed with emphasis by Jesus himself before his death. "The Son of Man," he said, "must suffer many things and be rejected by the elders, the chief priests and the teachers of the law, and that he must be killed and after three days rise again" (Mark 8:31). And again, after his death: "Did not the Messiah have to suffer these things and then enter his glory?" (Luke 24:26). The question is wherein that necessity lay; *why* did he have to suffer and die in order that the world might be reconciled to God.

John A. T. Robinson tells of once seeing a church notice board that proclaimed, "Christ is the answer." Scribbled next to it was, "Yes, but what is the question?" This ironic query reminds us of the "problem" involved in understanding the Atonement. The great truth that Jesus saves has caused theologians across the ages to ask, "From what?"[1] Although the church has not doubted that "God was reconciling the world to himself in Christ" (2 Cor 5:19), no one theory of the Atonement has ever commanded universal support.[2] The results and sufficiency of Christ's death may be affirmed without explanation simply on the authority of Scripture and Christ himself. Indeed, some theories of the Atonement hardly seem to pass beyond mere affirmation of this sufficiency for salvation. But that does not satisfy, and ought not satisfy, Christians who are eager to give a reason for the faith that is in them. If Christ's death was indispensable

---

1. Fiddes, *Present Salvation*, 5.
2. Letham, *Work of Christ*, 174.

to the fulfillment of his redemptive purpose, the connection between his death and the reason for its necessity should be addressed.[3] To say that his death constituted a suitable way to effect reconciliation is insufficient. Understanding should be sought as to why no other way was practicable.[4]

PRESUPPOSITIONS OF THIS STUDY

In seeking to understand the Atonement, this book assumes that a discernible truth resides in Scripture and that Scripture is the inspired word of God. This assumption requires that no part of Scripture that sheds light on the Atonement be disregarded. The Bible uses several different metaphors to convey the reality of the Atonement. Therefore, an attempt must be made to harmonize these metaphors with the intent of determining how they complement one another.

This book also assumes that God has left some element of mystery in what he has chosen to make known concerning the Atonement. He has not disclosed all the details. What he has revealed can be understood and is sufficient for salvation, and the fullest knowledge of the nature of that salvation should be sought. Any theory of the Atonement must be found to be in harmony with what has been revealed about the world that God has created, the character of God, and the will of God. Although logic and reason should be wholeheartedly employed in the formulation of any atonement theory, determinations concerning the reasons for the death of Christ must be based foremost on what Scripture itself reveals, even if doing so means accepting an element of mystery.

DEFINING SOME TERMS

The doctrine of the Atonement refers to the restoration of the broken relationship between God and humankind that is accomplished by Jesus Christ. The word *atonement* is one of the few theological terms whose etymology can be readily discerned in English. It can be broken down into the three-word phrase "at-one-ment."[5] It is, then, a word signifying "setting at one," hence the removing of enmity and the healing of

---

3. H. Clark, *Cross and Eternal Order*, 103.
4. McDonald, *Atonement*, 161.
5. Peters, "Final Scapegoat," 153.

estrangement. Originally, it was a term of ordinary speech that could be found in the work of Shakespeare:[6]

> And therefore be assured, my good Lord Marshal,
> If we do now make our atonement well,
> Our peace will, like a broken limb united,
> Grow stronger for the breaking.[7]

In another example, Shakespeare's Richard II says to his two contending lords,

> There shall your swords and lances arbitrate
> The swelling difference of your settled hate.
> Since we cannot atone you, we shall see
> Justice design the victor's chivalry.[8]

That is, end your quarrel and bring peace between you.[9] English Bibles of the sixteenth and seventeenth centuries began using *atonement* to translate the Hebrew *kaphar* and the Greek *hilasmos* and *katallage*, meaning *expiation* and *reconciliation*.[10] In the developing theological vocabulary the term was thus consecrated.[11] The term has thereby come to refer to the state of reconciliation between a gracious God and estranged humanity, the state of at-one-ment accomplished through the work of the savior, Jesus Christ.

In our modern speech, the word *atonement* is not commonly used in secular contexts, but when it is used it generally implies compensation for wrong, rendered by the wrongdoer. That the words *atone* and *atonement* have changed their meaning in this way is largely due to the influence of the penal substitution theory. In this theory, Christ's death is a satisfaction for sins, a payment of a debt incurred by humankind to God.[12]

---

6. Smith, *Atonement in Light of History*, 3.
7. Shakespeare, *Henry IV*, act 4, scene 1.
8. Shakespeare, *Richard II*, act 1, scene 1.
9. Burnaby, *Christian Words*, 96.
10. Peters, "Final Scapegoat," 153.
11. Smith, *Atonement in Light of History*, 3.
12. Burnaby, *Christian Words*, 96.

THE CENTRAL QUESTION

It is clear from Scripture that the impetus for the Atonement is the love of God. But this love, as its cause, does not explain the reason or necessity for the Atonement. Why must the love of God take such a course in realizing its end and fulfilling its purpose? What makes atonement a theological issue is not only the question of why but also the question of how. How is reconciliation between God and humankind effected? The New Testament answer is that the blood sacrifice of Jesus Christ results in the forgiveness of sins and the justification of sinful people. But the problem remains: *How* does atonement work?[13] *Why* was it necessary for Christ to suffer and die in order to make reconciliation between God and humankind possible? That is the question that will guide this inquiry.

There is no absolute statement in the New Testament as to how the death of Christ brings about reconciliation between God and humankind or why it was essential.[14] For this reason there are many theories of the Atonement. These theories are all conceptual tools with which one attempts to grasp a mystery that God has not fully revealed.[15] All theories believe the Atonement to be central to the Christian faith, and all proclaim it as foundational, but they interpret the nature of this divine work quite differently, and no one theory has ever been established as the official doctrine of the church.[16]

OBJECTIVE AND SUBJECTIVE THEORIES

The concept of atonement implies something wrong between God and humankind, a barrier to be removed, an estrangement to be overcome. The debate revolves around exactly what that barrier includes. The words *objective* and *subjective* have been used to describe the difference between God's action and humanity's response. Objective means that it is God's action that brings about reconciliation. Subjective means that it is the human response to God's action that brings about reconciliation. Traditional objective theories of the Atonement have suggested some change in God resulting from the atoning work of Christ. More subjective accounts

---

13. Peters, "Final Scapegoat," 153.
14. Baillie, *God Was in Christ*, 188.
15. Fiddes, *Present Salvation*, 28.
16. Bushnell, *Vicarious Sacrifice*, xiv; Hicks, "What Did Christ Accomplish," 149; Hodgson, *Atonement*, 13.

Introduction

have laid the stress upon the power of Christ's death to produce a change in human attitudes.

Salvation requires a change in human minds and emotions, described in the Bible as repentance. Human attitudes of pride, fear, and anxiety create obstacles between God and humankind, which God, the Savior, sets out to displace. Objective views of the Atonement have also suggested that there are obstacles to reconciliation in God's own nature. While affirming that there is no reluctance on God's part to forgive and accept, it is thought that God's retributive justice must be satisfied before he can put his forgiving love into effect. Because humans are guilty sinners, an objective view maintains that a debt must be paid to "justice" before one can be pardoned, requiring a change in God in the sense that his righteous wrath is satisfied through some kind of propitiating act.

More subjective atonement theories insist that the only problem lies in human hearts and minds. While God is always willing to receive, the problem is how to remove humankind's innate hindrances and how to persuade people to respond to God's offer of love and forgiveness.[17]

One view, then, sees the Atonement as something that has been accomplished objectively for us by the Savior, Jesus Christ, and is focused on the event of his death. In his suffering and death, the divine wrath upon human sin is satisfied. The other views the Atonement as being accomplished subjectively within human existence as men and women, moved by the example of Christ in his life of obedience and self-sacrificing love, repent and live lives of obedience to God.[18]

THE SCOPE OF OUR STUDY

The history and development of the diverse atonement theories, with their various objective and subjective elements, is a fascinating study in itself. It is no small merit that each theory presented a clear and intelligible answer to the question of why Christ's death was effectual for human salvation.[19] Christian thought and experience are cumulative, and no one generation can, or should, seek to write its theology on a clean slate. In attempting to reach an understanding of the Atonement, it is helpful to study and enter into the successive efforts of Christian thinkers

---

17. Fiddes, *Present Salvation*, 27–28.
18. Hart, "Anselm," 314.
19. Smith, *Atonement in Light of History*, 173–74.

from the beginning to our own time.[20] Therefore, as background the major theories of the Atonement will be examined, along with their historical place and significance. Included will be the ransom theory of the Patristic Period, Anselm's satisfaction theory, the moral influence theory of Abelard, the penal substitution theory of the Reformers, the exemplarist theory of Socinus, and the governmental theory of Grotius.

This book, which contains four parts, presents a theory of the Atonement called the victorious substitution theory. Following a discussion of the history of atonement theory, there are three logical steps that must be taken, or conclusions that must be reached, in the process of presenting the victorious substitution theory. The first is to refute the assertion made by the penal substitution theory that Christ died in order to satisfy God's retributive justice. This involves demonstrating that although the concept of substitution is soundly based on Scripture, the acceptance of substitution does not require the acceptance of satisfaction. In other words, one can reject the conclusions of the penal substitution theory without rejecting the substitutionary nature of Christ's death. The second step is to defend the ransom, or classic, theory of the Atonement by a thorough examination of its scriptural basis. The third step is to assert that the substitutionary aspect of Christ's death has its appropriate place as part of the ransom theory and is properly related to the ransom concept.

This assertion is unique in atonement theory. The substitutionary aspect of the Atonement explains the necessity of Christ's suffering and death as the payment of the ransom price or the provision for a great exchange. Christ was humankind's substitute, bearing the penalty for, or the consequences of, our sin. God's justice, however, did not demand substitution or penalty. Rather, substitution is the provision for a necessary exchange, the ransom price that liberated human beings from the power of evil and the evil one. In other words, the substitutionary and penal aspects of the death of Christ are properly related to the cosmic struggle, which is emphasized in the ransom theory.

Finally, part 4 examines how a proper understanding of the Atonement guides the life experience of a Christian, particularly when struggling with issues of forgiveness and reconciliation relating to one's relationship with God and other people.

This study, as seen by its scope and purpose, must address several subsidiary questions and related issues, such as the meaning of the terms

---

20. Barry, *Atonement*, 14–15.

propitiation and *expiation*, an interpretation of the Old Testament sacrificial system, and an examination of the verses frequently used to support the conclusions of the penal substitution theory (Rom 3:21–26; 2 Cor 5:21; 1 Pet 3:18; Gal 3:13).

THE VALUE OF OUR STUDY

This book will attempt to understand the nature of salvation and the necessity of atonement through Christ's shed blood. An analysis of the various atonement theories clarifies that which is scriptural fact and that which is theory. Such clarification proves valuable because, too often, atonement theory is presented as fact rather than as interpretation. What Christ's life and death accomplished is not the mystery; that sins are forgiven in and through Christ's death is the plain teaching of Scripture. How forgiveness of sins is tied to Christ's death, how his death provided the means of reconciliation, may well be an impenetrable mystery. Scripture clearly and factually presents the *meaning* of Calvary. Notwithstanding, the *mechanics* of Calvary entail mystery and therefore theory.[21] To be able to distinguish between meaning, which is factual, and mechanics, which is theory, is essential.

It should be said at the outset that although it is valuable to seek to understand atonement theory and to formulate one's own theory, it is also important to remember, as C. S. Lewis said, "A man can accept what Christ has done without knowing how it works" and, "The thing itself is infinitely more important than any explanations the theologians have produced."[22]

One should also recognize and accept when dealing with a theory or an interpretation that room must be left for disagreement. A great effort will be made to distinguish between scriptural fact and interpretation of that fact. However, it is acknowledged that even in making this distinction there will be diversity of opinion.

This work hopes to make a contribution by achieving two ends: to enable its readers to (1) distinguish between fact and theory regarding the Atonement, and (2) understand the victorious substitution theory as a rational explanation of the necessity of Christ's suffering and death based on scriptural texts.

---

21. Jensen, "Forgiveness and Atonement," 141–49.
22. Lewis, *Mere Christianity*, 57–58.

PART I

Atonement Theory

Is Penal Substitution the Default View?

Part 1 examines the major theories of the Atonement and consists of an explanation of each theory and its historical place and significance. Included in this overview are the ransom theory of the Patristic Period, Anselm's satisfaction theory, the moral influence theory of Abelard, the penal substitution theory of the Reformers, the exemplarist theory of Socinus, and the governmental theory of Grotius.

Objections to the penal substitution theory are presented in four categories: logical, moral, theological, and exegetical. These objections are not directed toward an understanding of Christ's death as substitutionary or penal, but toward the theory that God's holiness or justice requires retribution as a basis for forgiving sins.

1

Theories of the Atonement

THE RANSOM THEORY: CHRIST'S DEATH AS THE PAYMENT OF RANSOM

"For nearly a thousand years many of the most eminent teachers of the Church were accustomed to represent the Death of Christ as a ransom by which we are delivered from captivity to the devil."[1] This came to be called the ransom theory of the Atonement, and because it was the standard view of the early church, it is sometimes called the classic theory.[2] It is the simplest statement of the work of Christ and was the dominant view until the twelfth century.[3] Although the church fathers (including Origen, Athanasius, Basil the Great, Gregory of Nyssa, Gregory of Nazianzus, Cyril of Alexandria, Cyril of Jerusalem, Chrysostom, and Augustine[4]) did not write extensively concerning the Atonement, they did seek to answer the question, Why did Christ come? Their answer came to be called the ransom theory of the Atonement. It emphasizes Christ's own explanation for his coming that he made at the beginning of his ministry when he quoted Isaiah's prophecy, "The Spirit of the Lord is on me, because he has anointed me to proclaim good news to the poor. He

1. Dale, *Atonement*, 358–59.
2. Aulén, *Christus Victor*, 101–2.
3. McDonald, *Atonement*, 40.
4. Aulén, *Christus Victor*, 37.

has sent me to proclaim freedom for the prisoners and recovery of sight for the blind, to set the oppressed free, to proclaim the year of the Lord's favor" (Luke 4:18). To address the question, Why did he die? the ransom theory also emphasizes Christ's own words preparing his disciples for his coming death: "The Son of Man did not come to be served, but to serve, and to give his life as a ransom for many" (Matt 20:28).

Scripture speaks of the bondage of fear (Heb 2:15; Gal 5:1; Rom 8:15, 21) and of the slavery of sin (John 8:34; Rom 6:17, 20). Of this fear and sin Satan is the author and final cause, therefore Christ's work ultimately deals with the devil himself (1 John 3:8). Only by his subduing, by meeting the demands of the situation caused by him, can there be deliverance and redemption. Only then is humankind ransomed from the forces of evil and death.[5]

The ransom theory views biblical history as a great cosmic struggle between the forces of good and evil. In this struggle Satan is seen as having established his kingdom in the earth, for Scripture says, "The whole world is under the control of the evil one" (1 John 5:19). Jesus comes to redeem humankind from the "dominion of darkness" (Col 1:13), "that by his death he might break the power of him who holds the power of death—that is, the devil" (Heb 2:14). The theory also embraces several of Paul's concepts, that humans have been "bought at a price" (1 Cor 6:20), that Jesus "disarmed the powers and authorities" and "made a public spectacle of them, triumphing over them" (Col 2:15), and that at "the end" Jesus "hands over the kingdom to God the Father after he has destroyed all dominion, authority and power. For he must reign until he has put all his enemies under his feet. The last enemy to be destroyed is death" (1 Cor 15:24–26).

Early writers such as Irenaeus and Athanasius were content to declare this conquest of the devil without speculating how the ransom worked. Irenaeus speaks of God moving against the kingdom of evil, redeeming what was originally God's. God accomplishes this redemption not by using violence but in a way that justice is not compromised. Since humankind fell of its own free will by the devil's persuasion and deception, so must its redemption be in harmony with this principle of moral freedom. Humankind was not forcefully enslaved, nor should it be forcefully freed.[6] Irenaeus sees Christ's life as a conflict with demonic powers

---

5. McDonald, *Atonement*, 138–40.
6. Irenaeus, *Ante-Nicene Fathers*, 113, 115.

that hold humankind in bondage. Christ's death is seen as a fulfillment of the Genesis 3:15 prophecy that the savior would be wounded in the heel in the process of crushing the head of the serpent.[7] The temptation narrative records Christ's first victory over the devil; the decisive blow was delivered at Calvary.[8] First John 3:8 plainly states that the reason for Christ's coming "was to destroy the devil's work." Irenaeus does not speculate, however, as to *how* the death of Christ constituted victory over Satan.[9] Likewise, Athanasius does not speculate but says that "death came to him [Christ] from the enemy action," but "the death which was inflicted upon him . . . became the glorious moment to death's defeat."[10]

As time passed the inevitable question was asked: To whom was the ransom price paid? Justin Martyr seems to have been the first to answer it categorically—to the devil. This idea was supported by the common view that since God is just in all his dealings, he would not deliver humankind by force but by a rightful conquest. Justin does not theorize, though, how by his dying Christ defeated Satan.[11]

A century later, the writings of Gregory of Nyssa (ca. 335–95) also argue that God was just in the means he chose to redeem humankind. Gregory reasons that since enslavement is humankind's own doing, its own free choice, then to deprive Satan of his captives by some arbitrary method would have been unjust.[12] Rather than take from Satan what was rightfully his, a transaction was needed. Gregory theorizes that Satan was eager to have power over Christ in exchange for the souls of humans.[13]

Augustine also maintains that God's way of redemption was just. He says that humankind was "delivered into the power of the devil" by God's permission because of God's justice.[14] The devil was then, in turn, overcome by God's plan. Augustine theorizes that Satan was the victim of his own pride, for he thought he could overcome and hold Christ. But, because Christ never sinned, Satan had no such power and Christ was liable neither to death nor Satan's control.[15] Augustine thought that since

---

7. Irenaeus, *Ante-Nicene Fathers*, 110.
8. Irenaeus, *Ante-Nicene Fathers*, 113.
9. McDonald, *Atonement*, 141.
10. Athanasius, *On the Incarnation*, 53–54.
11. McDonald, *Atonement*, 141.
12. Gregory of Nyssa, *Oratio Catechetica*, 78–79.
13. Gregory of Nyssa, *Oratio Catechetica*, 80.
14. Augustine, *On the Trinity*, 121.
15. Augustine, *On the Trinity*, 122, 124.

humankind consented to its own corruption by Satan, Satan held them by legitimate right. The penalty for sin is death, so the devil was able to inflict death on all persons. But in Christ's death there could be no penalty for sin, for he had no sin. Jesus, as he approached his death, stated that "the prince of this world is coming. He has no hold on me" (John 14:30).

In recent times the ransom theory has been reintroduced through the work of renowned Swedish theologian Gustaf Aulén in his book *Christus Victor* (1931). Aulén insists that in whatever form the theory is expressed, the dominant point is God's triumph.[16] He emphasizes that the truth underlying all speculation as to how the ransom worked is that a victorious Christ effects humankind's release from the devil's tyranny. He points out that, in speaking of his own death, Jesus said, "Now is the time for judgment on this world; now the prince of this world will be driven out" (John 12:31).

In summary, the ransom theory presents Christ's death as effecting on humankind's behalf an objective atonement in that humankind's redemption required God's action and was a costly affair.[17] It is unique among the theories of the Atonement, as it holds that the effects of Christ's death were directed neither toward God nor humankind, but that atonement was accomplished by a work directed primarily toward Satan.[18] As Scripture says, Christ came to "set the captives free," to "give his life as a ransom for many," and to "destroy the works of the devil."

THE SATISFACTION THEORY: CHRIST'S DEATH AS THE REQUIREMENT FOR RECONCILIATION

While the ransom theory dominated during the time of the early church, or the Patristic Period, the Medieval Period (eleventh through fourteenth centuries) brought about a new explanation of the Atonement.[19] During this time Anselm, the archbishop of Canterbury (1093–1109), repudiated as blasphemous the thousand-year-old idea of the death of Christ as a ransom paid to the devil. What God owed Satan, he said, was nothing but punishment for seducing humankind and usurping God's own authority.

---

16. Aulén, *Christus Victor*, 26–27.
17. McDonald, *Atonement*, 262.
18. Erickson, *Christian Theology*, 796.
19. Smith, *Atonement in Light of History*, 75.

Theories of the Atonement

Satan never had any lawful rights over humans. Although humankind deserted God he still remains their lawful sovereign.[20]

Anselm's theory is based on the idea that if a wrong is done there must be satisfaction (payback) for justice to be served. The Catholic Church had gradually developed its penitential system, which depended upon the idea that penance, as a satisfaction offered in this life, might be accepted as an alternative to the punishment of eternal death.[21] The ecclesiastical concept of satisfaction was in keeping with the legal system of the time, which was part of the feudal structure.[22] Anselm proposed an atonement theory based on what he perceived to be the demands of divine justice. His theory came to be called the satisfaction theory of the Atonement.[23] Whereas the ransom theory emphasizes the problem of evil and Satan, Anselm's theory centers around the concept of justice and accepts reparations as a substitute for criminal punishment.[24]

Humankind must either render a satisfaction to God, restoring his honor that has been offended by sin, or suffer the punishment of eternal death. Since this is impossible for humans to do, God's honor must be vindicated in the alternative way—by the punishment of sinners. But punishment in the eternal death of humankind is not what God desires. The life and death of Christ is the solution to the dilemma because it enables God to avoid punishing humans. As a perfect human who did not deserve to die, Christ offered his life to God as a satisfaction (payback) restoring to God his honor. In this way Christ pays the debt for all humankind and humans are released from punishment.

This is not penal substitution because Christ is not punished *in place* of humankind. Rather, humankind is released from punishment through satisfaction.[25] (By the time of the Reformation, the Roman view of criminal law had replaced feudal law, with no alternative to punishment if a law were broken. The only way to satisfy justice would be punishment.)[26] In Anselm's satisfaction theory Christ also is not punished *for the sins* of humankind. Punishment is the sinner's due; it cannot be and is not

---

20. Barry, *Atonement*, 143.
21. Grensted, *Doctrine of Atonement*, 122–23.
22. Grensted, *Doctrine of Atonement*, 122–23.
23. Fiddes, *Present Salvation*, 97.
24. Barry, *Atonement*, 143.
25. Fiddes, *Present Salvation*, 97.
26. Fiddes, *Present Salvation*, 97.

inflicted on Christ. Christ is not punished; rather, he makes satisfaction. He gives to God such honor as to make it possible for him to forgo the punishment of sinners without compromising his authority or lowering his dignity.

To Anselm, the atoning efficacy lies not in the death of Christ but in his life. It is his obedience and submission to the will of God throughout his entire life that honors God and makes satisfaction for the disobedience of humankind. The death of Christ is simply the last incident and climax of his obedient life.[27] The satisfaction theory of the Atonement is set forth in his book *Cur Deus Homo?* (Why Did God Become Man?). This small book attempts to prove on purely rational grounds (without scriptural proof texts) the necessity of the death of Christ. Anselm says that God, in his mercy, cannot simply forgive sinners because to do so would compromise morality. Eternal punishment is not an option because that would defeat God's purpose for humanity. Why then did God become man? Anselm answers that humans cannot make satisfaction because they are all sinful. Only God can make the necessary satisfaction. Since the sinless Christ owes no satisfaction, his voluntary self-sacrifice earns merit sufficient to secure the forgiveness of all the sins of humankind.[28]

In summary, Anselm's satisfaction theory is objective in that it holds that the Atonement is not primarily directed toward humankind, but rather emphasizes that Christ died to satisfy a principle in the very nature of God.[29] Sin is viewed in an external way as quantitative, as an item in an account book or a weight in the scales.[30] God is represented as unable to pardon humankind until the debt of sin has been cleared and the price paid.[31] Anselm's theory provides the archetype for the penal substitution theory developed during the Reformation.[32]

---

27. Smith, *Atonement in Light of History*, 83–84.
28. Anselm, *Cur Deus Homo?*, 171–72.
29. Grensted, *Doctrine of Atonement*, 120.
30. Grensted, *Doctrine of Atonement*, 81–82.
31. N. Robinson, *Jesus Christ Saves Men*, 82.
32. Barry, *Atonement*, 143.

THE MORAL INFLUENCE THEORY: CHRIST'S DEATH AS THE DEMONSTRATION OF LOVE

Although Anselm's satisfaction theory never won universal assent, it nevertheless gained sufficient approval to become the distinctive atonement doctrine of the Middle Ages. Just as during the Patristic Period there were those who disapproved of the ransom theory, so during the Medieval Period there were those who rejected the satisfaction theory. The chief protest was raised by Peter Abelard (ca. 1079–1142), a younger contemporary of Anselm. Abelard's theory is commonly called the moral influence theory of the Atonement.[33] The only agreement between Abelard and Anselm is that both repudiate the ransom theory based on the conviction that the devil has no rights over humankind.[34] Abelard also repudiates the satisfaction concept, beginning the controversy that has continued ever since.[35]

According to Abelard, the purpose of Christ's incarnation is for Christ to "illuminate the world by the light of his wisdom and kindle it to his own love."[36] Abelard emphasizes the love of God. He denies that God demands some sort of satisfaction of his justice or honor. He does not accept that some change must be wrought in God before he can forgive the sins of humankind. Rather, for there to be reconciliation, the change must take place in humanity.[37]

In order for humankind to change its ways and return to God, it must be able to trust and know God. It is this knowledge that Christ's life and death imparts. The incarnation and death of Christ serve as a demonstration to humankind of God's great love and readiness to forgive. Without the work of Christ, God can still forgive human sins, as he did during OT times and as Christ did during his time on earth.[38] Christ's life and death, however, assuage human fear and ignorance of God's nature because Christ identifies with human sufferings even to the point of death.[39]

---

33. Smith, *Atonement in Light of History*, 93.
34. McDonald, *Atonement*, 175.
35. N. Robinson, *Jesus Christ Saves Men*, 85.
36. Barry, *Atonement*, 145.
37. N. Robinson, *Jesus Christ Saves Men*, 85.
38. McDonald, *Atonement*, 175.
39. Grudem, *Systematic Theology*, 581.

The moral influence theory emphasizes the text, "God demonstrates his own love for us in this: While we were still sinners, Christ died for us" (Rom 5:8). Christ's suffering and death is the supreme proof of the forgiving love of God. Once understood, this love kindles an answering love in the heart of the sinner and brings them to God. The sinner then repents, which is all that is needed to be forgiven by God and reconciled to him.[40] There is no difficulty or hindrance in God's ability and desire to forgive. The difficulty is in humans, and it is to solve their problem that Christ came and died.[41] He did not die to procure forgiveness but to enable humans to receive it.[42] Because a change of heart on our part effects reconciliation, this is a subjective theory of the Atonement.[43]

During the Middle Ages, the moral influence theory initially did not receive widespread support. It gained popularity when it was advocated by theologians of the Enlightenment such as Horace Bushnell (1802–1876).[44] Bushnell believes the death of Jesus was not "the end or the object of his ministry . . . but was simply the bad fortune such a work . . . [encountered]."[45] He believes the death of Jesus meets the three most basic needs of humankind for reconciliation. First, humans need an openness to God or an inclination to respond when God calls them to repentance. The natural response of humans to God is like that of Adam and Eve in the garden who hid from him, afraid of him. Christ, understanding this fear, shows his concern for humans by entering into their world and dying a terrible death.[46] In this way the fear of God is removed, which is the first step toward reconciliation.[47] The second need of humans, according to Bushnell, is conviction of sin and repentance from sin. There must be a profound and genuine sense of sorrow for personal sin, which hurts God. Humans can be influenced morally more easily when they know and feel God's love for them.[48] Third, humans need inspiration and encouragement for holy living. This inspiration comes

---

40. N. Robinson, *Jesus Christ Saves Men*, 86.
41. Rashdall, *Atonement in Christian Theology*, 26.
42. Connell, "Atonement," 41.
43. Winter, "Man's Salvation," 43.
44. Yung, "Theories of Atonement," 542.
45. Bushnell, *Vicarious Sacrifice*, 130–31.
46. Bushnell, *Vicarious Sacrifice*, 154.
47. Erickson, *Christian Theology*, 788.
48. Erickson, *Christian Theology*, 788.

from the example of the life of Jesus and causes humans to be recreated or born anew.[49]

The moral influence theory does not assume Christ's death as an absolute necessity. It attempts not to answer the question, Why must Christ die? but rather, Why did Christ die? The answer given is that God, through Christ, provides a dramatic and tragic gesture that calls and inspires humankind.[50]

In summary, in the moral influence theory the purpose of Christ's death is its subjective influence upon the mind of the sinner. It is seen as a demonstration of God's love, which, when comprehended by humans, kindles in their hearts the response of love for God, in turn leading to repentance. The only barrier to the forgiveness of sins is the impenitence of the sinner.[51] God is ready to forgive every sinner who repents, but his justice prevents him from forgiving an impenitent sinner.[52] When humans respond to God's love in repentance and faith, reconciliation takes place.[53] Humans are redeemed, then, not by the death of Christ, but by their response to it.[54]

THE PENAL SUBSTITUTION THEORY: CHRIST'S DEATH AS GOD'S DEMAND FOR JUSTICE

A variation of Anselm's satisfaction theory, developed during the Reformation, is called the penal substitution theory. Before the Reformation only hints of a penal theory can be found.[55] The theory, sometimes called the forensic or judicial view, was developed formally by Melanchthon and is "the orthodox understanding of the Atonement held by evangelical theologians."[56] Its chief characteristic is that the righteousness or justice of God demands the punishment of sinful humans.[57] Calvin was

---

49. Erickson, *Christian Theology*, 788.
50. G. Clark, *Atonement*, 115.
51. Hicks, "What Did Christ Accomplish," 152.
52. Hicks, "What Did Christ Accomplish," 155.
53. Hicks, "What Did Christ Accomplish," 153.
54. Crawford, "Parable of the Atonement," 6.
55. Grensted, *Doctrine of Atonement*, 19.
56. Grensted, *Doctrine of Atonement*, 204; Grudem, *Systematic Theology*, 579.
57. N. Robinson, *Jesus Christ Saves Men*, 82.

impressed with Anselm's argument that divine justice needed satisfying, but he reworked it in terms of criminal law.[58]

During the Reformation, contemporary ideas of absolute monarchy and jurisprudence dominated theology.[59] God is conceived of as a king, lawgiver, and judge, and sin is a violation of his law. Atonement is a device for exempting sinners from the punishment they deserve (Rom 1:32) without interfering with justice. The means for atonement is substitution. Punishment for sin must be inflicted and therefore Christ offered himself as a substitute for sinners and suffered in their place.[60] The penal substitution theory contains no trace of the alternatives to punishment or satisfaction (payback) found in the satisfaction theory. Christ's work is no longer a matter of reparation or compensation to God's offended honor. The law simply demands punishment, and the work of Christ is an endurance of that which is due humankind.[61] Humankind, because of sin, is under the wrath and curse of God (Gal 3:13) and apart from Christ is doomed to eternal punishment and separation from God (Rom 6:23). Christ, however, takes the stroke of God's wrath, thus satisfying God's justice and appeasing his anger.[62] While the penal substitution theory, like the ransom theory, speaks of the release of sinners, it presents the ransom price as paid to God, not to the devil.[63]

The penal substitution theory holds that retributive justice is inherent in the divine nature and is the necessary foundation of moral order. If sin goes unpunished, that moral order is violated. Moral order cannot be denied because it is rooted in the very nature of God and is equated with his holiness. God must punish sin. He may forgive and be merciful only after his retributive justice is satisfied by the vicarious punishment of Christ. In other words, his grace can be exercised only after his punitive justice is satisfied.[64]

One difference between the penal substitution theory and the satisfaction theory is that in the latter satisfaction is thought to be made by Christ's death only. Whereas, in the penal substitution theory, not only

---

58. Fiddes, *Present Salvation*, 98.
59. Smith, *Atonement in Light of History*, 98.
60. Smith, *Atonement in Light of History*, 101.
61. Grensted, *Doctrine of Atonement*, 199.
62. Smith, *Atonement in Light of History*, 103.
63. Smith, *Atonement in Light of History*, 102.
64. N. Robinson, *Jesus Christ Saves Men*, 82–83.

must retributive justice be satisfied but the law as well. Thus there is a double necessity: Christ must by his obedient life fulfill God's law, and he must, by his death, pay the penalty which justice requires. This is both a development of the earlier doctrine and an addition to it.[65]

The Lutheran and Reformed branches of the Protestant tradition disagree concerning the extent of the Atonement. Lutherans maintain that Christ died for all, although only those who believe are saved. Reformed theologians insist on a limited atonement: Christ died only for the elect. For, they argue, if Christ took the penalty for all, then justice requires that all be forgiven.[66]

Statements of penal substitution are found in several classic documents of Protestantism. The Thirty-Nine Articles of the Church of England (1563, 1571) say: "The offering of Christ once made is that perfect redemption, propitiation, and satisfaction, for all the sins of the whole world, both original and actual; and there is none other satisfaction for sin, but that alone" (Article XXXI).[67] The Westminster Confession of Faith (1647) refers to Christ as the mediator who "by his perfect obedience and sacrifice of himself . . . once offered up unto God, hath fully satisfied the justice of his Father" (VIII:5).[68] As Protestant orthodoxy continued to develop, the classic ransom idea of the Atonement was completely ignored in the realm of theology.[69]

In summary, the penal substitution theory is an objective theory in which atonement is effected through a legal transaction between God the Father and God the Son. Christ's death is viewed as a propitiation of the wrath of the Father. It is a variation of the satisfaction theory in that a debt to divine justice is paid, not by a gift of honor, but by a transfer of penalty. Christ's death is penal in that he bears the punishment demanded by a holy God against sin. Christ's death is substitutionary in that he bears the punishment in place of humankind. The death of Christ satisfies God's justice and moral order, and the obedient life of Christ satisfies God's law. The concept of God underlying the theory is,

---

65. Aulén, *Christus Victor*, 129–30.
66. McDonald, *Atonement*, 191–92.
67. Burnet, *Thirty-Nine Articles*, 350.
68. Carruthers, *Westminster Confession*, 107.
69. Aulén, *Christus Victor*, 133.

above all, a justice that imposes its law and demands satisfaction; only within these limits is God's love allowed to operate by showing mercy and forgiving sin.[70]

THE EXEMPLARIST THEORY: CHRIST'S DEATH AS THE SUPREME EXAMPLE

A variation of the moral influence theory, also subjective in nature, was introduced by Faustus Socinus in the sixteenth century. Socinus was an Italian theologian who settled in Poland and attracted a wide following.[71] His *De Jesu Christo Servatore* was a vigorous protest against the forensic and punitive view of the Atonement found in the penal substitution theory.[72] It is the classic work against the doctrine of satisfaction.[73]

In his critical rejection of penal substitution, Socinus puts forward several propositions that he believes prove the penal doctrine of the Atonement untenable. His basic understanding is that the idea of satisfaction excludes the idea of mercy. He presents the dilemma: if sin is punished, it is not forgiven; if sin is forgiven, it is not punished. These two actions—forgiveness and punishment—are, he states, clearly contradictory.[74] If the justice of God is satisfied by the infliction of judicial punishment, then the exercise of mercy is unnecessary.[75]

Socinus insists that sin is a personal matter and cannot be set to the account of another. The one who sins is the one who is guilty and therefore the only one who can be justly punished.[76] Retributive justice is not viewed as part of the divine nature but as an act of the will that can be executed or forgone.[77] Since both God's justice and mercy are subject to his will, he has the right to punish or pardon as he chooses.[78]

Socinus argues that the fact of the resurrection proves that Christ was not a substitute bearing the penalty for sin. This is evident because

---

70. Aulén, *Christus Victor*, 130.
71. Grudem, *Systematic Theology*, 582.
72. McDonald, *Atonement*, 197.
73. Gomes, "Satisfaction of Christ," 210–11.
74. Godbey, "Socinus," 138–39.
75. Godbey, "Socinus," 104–10.
76. Godbey, "Socinus," 99, 134.
77. Godbey, "Socinus," 4.
78. Godbey, "Socinus," 61.

the law demands eternal punishment or everlasting debt, and Christ did not endure such sufferings, for God raised him from the dead.[79] Because defenders of the penal substitution theory found it difficult to answer Socinus' logical arguments, they responded by stating that the Atonement is a mystery beyond reason and belongs to the realm of revelation.[80]

Socinus taught a theory of the Atonement proposing that the real purpose of the death of Jesus is as a beautiful example of the kind of dedication to God that humankind is to practice. It is an exaltation of Christ to his divine place at the right hand of God and a manifestation of God's love and power.[81] The Socinian proof verse is 1 Peter 2:21: "To this you were called, because Christ suffered for you, leaving you an example, that you should follow in his steps." There are many verses in Scripture that point out the need to follow the example of Christ, and in this verse Christ's example is directly linked with his death.[82] The view of Socinus is commonly referred to as the exemplarist theory of the Atonement.

The death of Jesus, from the exemplarist perspective, addresses primarily the need of humankind. Foremost, humans need an example of the total love of God that is necessary for salvation. Jesus loved God so completely that he was willing to die for the principles of his kingdom. His death motivates persons to follow a life of total commitment, and his life proves that such a life is attainable. What Christ did, humans can do also, although an individual may not be called to suffer or die in the same manner as Christ.[83]

It is essential to recognize that one's doctrines of sin, humanity, God, and Christ will color one's understanding of the Atonement. Unlike the objective theories, the understanding of humankind that lies behind the Socinian view is that persons are spiritually and morally capable of doing the will of God. Also, God is not viewed as a God who must have retributive justice. Therefore he does not demand some form of satisfaction from, or on behalf of, those who sin against him. Socinus saw no contradiction between the justice and mercy of God. Both are expressions of his will, and as such he may exercise either whenever he pleases.[84] According

---

79. Godbey, "Socinus," 160–61.
80. McDonald, *Atonement*, 198.
81. Grensted, *Doctrine of Atonement*, 289.
82. Erickson, *Christian Theology*, 784.
83. Erickson, *Christian Theology*, 783–84.
84. Grensted, *Doctrine of Atonement*, 282.

to Socinus, Jesus does not simply tell humans that the first and greatest commandment is to "love the Lord your God with all your heart and with all your soul and with all your mind" (Matthew 22:37). He also gives an example of what that love involves, as well as proves that a human being can be obedient even unto death. The death of Christ is viewed as an extension and manifestation of his teachings.[85]

From the exemplarist point of view, then, all that is really needed for humans and God to be reconciled is for humans to have faith in and love for God. For God to require something more would be to go against his nature of love. God and humans are restored to their proper relationship as people adopt the teachings of Jesus and seek to live according to the example set by his life and death.[86]

In summary, the exemplarist theory of Socinus presents Christ as Savior in that he demonstrates to humankind the way of eternal life. He expiates (wipes out) sin by assuring humans of their pardon following repentance. His death draws humankind to accept divine mercy, and his life is the supreme example of the way of salvation. The Socinian theory of the Atonement is significant for its deliberate rejection of the thesis that Christ's work satisfied God's divine justice. Socinus' criticism of Calvin's concept of divine justice caused some to modify their understanding of the Atonement and thereby gave rise to the views of Arminius and Grotius.[87]

THE GOVERNMENTAL THEORY: CHRIST'S DEATH AS THE GUARDIAN OF THE LAW

Hugo Grotius (1583–1645), a Dutch theologian and jurist, defended the orthodox doctrine against the view set forth by Socinus in his book *A Defense of the Catholic Faith concerning the Satisfaction of Christ*.[88] Socinianism had set out to refute the teaching of the Catholic Church concerning the Atonement, which insisted on the necessity of satisfaction to the justice of God by means of substitutionary punishment borne by Christ. God, according to Catholicism, is bound to punish sin. God, according to Socinus, is free to pardon sin if he so wills. Socinus argues that

---

85. Erickson, *Christian Theology*, 784.
86. Erickson, *Christian Theology*, 783–85.
87. Erickson, *Christian Theology*, 196–97.
88. Smith, *Atonement in Light of History*, 116.

the doctrine of substitution involves a double injustice: the guilty escape punishment and the innocent one is punished. Socinus also refuses to accept that punishment inflicted upon a substitute could be characteristic of true justice.[89]

Although Grotius purports to defend the forensic doctrine of the Atonement against the objections of Socinus, he actually modifies the theory in order to accommodate those objections. His theory, originally espoused in defense of penal substitution, came to be called the governmental theory. Socinus would eliminate justice and law entirely from an understanding of the Atonement, whereas penal substitution relates the Atonement to justice as an attribute of God. The governmental theory, however, relates the reason for Christ's death to the law of God rather than to his justice.[90] This idea followed the teaching of Jacobus Arminius.

Two ideas fundamental to the governmental theory are latent in the teachings of Arminius. The first is that the sufferings of Christ are demanded by justice, "that regard should be paid to her."[91] Second is the view that the death of Christ, as an expiatory sacrifice, is not an equivalence for the punishment due to sin. The sacrifice is neither the payment of a debt nor an exact satisfaction for sin. Christ did not bear the penalty due humankind for sin. Instead, his suffering and death is a "substitute for a penalty," which God accepts in lieu.[92] Christ did not endure the full penalty for sin because he did not endure eternal death. Had he borne the full penalty, the remission of sin would not involve the grace and compassion of God, but would be only just.[93]

Although Grotius intends to defend the penal substitution theory, he departs considerably from the views of his predecessors in the way he perceives the penalty for sin being paid and in how he understands justice being satisfied through the death of Christ.[94] Grotius accepts with Socinus that retribution is not a necessity based on the inherent justice of God. "It is not something internal in God or the very will of God, but a certain effect [choice] of his will."[95] The law is given by God, who is supe-

---

89. N. Robinson, *Jesus Christ Saves Men*, 83–84.
90. McDonald, *Atonement*, 199.
91. Arminius, *Works of James Arminius*, 349–50.
92. Arminius, *Works of James Arminius*, 349–50.
93. McDonald, *Atonement*, 200–201.
94. McDonald, *Atonement*, 203.
95. Grotius, *Satisfaction of Christ*, 83.

rior to it, for the purpose of expressing justice and for the good order of society.[96] Grotius conceives of God primarily as ruler rather than judge.[97] This gubernatorial relationship of God to humankind is the reason that this theory is commonly called the governmental theory.[98]

God, as the ruler of this world, may punish or pardon according to his will.[99] If God is conceived of as judge, his responsibility is to administer the law. He cannot free the guilty from punishment without hurting the law[100] and "doing harm to the moral order of the universe."[101] If God is conceived of as ruler, he still may not simply overlook or ignore the rules according to his own personal desires without doing a disservice to the system of law. Forgiveness, if too freely given, undermines the authority of the law and its effectiveness. Grounds for forgiveness, however, can be provided through the Atonement of Christ without harming the structure of the moral law of God,[102] because in Christ's death God "asserts the principle that sin deserves punishment."[103] God asserts his moral law "not by inflicting suffering on the sinner, but by enduring suffering Himself.... The mysterious unity of the Father and the Son rendered it possible for God at once to endure and to inflict penal suffering."[104] Christ becomes a penal example demonstrating God's hatred of sin.[105]

The governmental theory contains both subjective and objective elements. The subjective element is that humans are influenced by the sacrifice and penal suffering of Christ and are deterred from doing evil.[106] Grotius believes that the suffering of Christ has a far greater power to turn humans from sin than that of law or punishment.[107] The objective element is that God is able to deal mercifully with humans because the death of Christ is a real offering made to God (i.e., affecting God).[108]

96. Grotius, *Satisfaction of Christ*, 80.
97. Grotius, *Satisfaction of Christ*, 57.
98. McDonald, *Atonement*, 203–4.
99. Grotius, *Satisfaction of Christ*, 58.
100. Grotius, *Satisfaction of Christ*, 61.
101. Dale, *Atonement*, 359.
102. Erickson, *Christian Theology*, 790.
103. Dale, *Atonement*, 451.
104. Dale, *Atonement*, 452–53.
105. Fiddes, *Present Salvation*, 104.
106. Erickson, *Christian Theology*, 791.
107. N. Robinson, *Jesus Christ Saves Men*, 84.
108. Grensted, *Doctrine of Atonement*, 297.

Although the Atonement had an effect on God, its chief impact is on humankind, so the governmental theory is a more subjective theory. Christ did not die in order to satisfy the expectations of the just nature of God and enable him to do what he otherwise could not have done, that is, forgive sins. Rather, the sufferings of Christ serve as a deterrent to sin by impressing upon humankind the love of God as well as the gravity of sin. When humans repent, forgiveness is theirs.[109] According to the governmental theory the effect of the death of Christ is twofold: humans know themselves forgiven, while sin is shown to be exceedingly serious.[110]

In Grotius' view the death of Christ was necessary only in the sense that God saw it as the most prudent way to uphold his moral government.[111] Punishment in the government of God is used to promote the common good by preventing the corruption of human morals. God chooses to punish Christ for several reasons: because of his goodness, which is his foremost characteristic; because of his wrath against sin; and because of his wisdom. The means of atonement represent a decision freely made by God for strictly prudential reasons, and not a necessary outflow of his nature. God could have chosen otherwise, but he chose the best and wisest way to make reconciliation possible.[112]

In summary, the governmental theory of the Atonement starts from the position that God acts not as a judge or as a creditor, but as a ruler. A judge enforces the law and a creditor exacts precise payment of his due, but it is possible for a ruler to show mercy by modification of his law. The concern of a ruler is both the welfare of his people and the maintenance of civil order. Remitting the penalty for sin fails both concerns. It violates the governmental order of the world and is harmful to humans in that it emboldens them to persist in sin. Therefore, God, in his wisdom, devises a better way. Christ endures punishment so that humans might escape it and be deterred from further sin.[113] In this way God demonstrates his justice and offers his mercy.[114]

---

109. Erickson, *Christian Theology*, 791.
110. N. Robinson, *Jesus Christ Saves Men*, 84.
111. Letham, *Work of Christ*, 126.
112. Letham, *Work of Christ*, 168.
113. Smith, *Atonement in Light of History*, 117–18.
114. Hicks, "What Did Christ Accomplish," 157.

2

Logical, Moral, and Theological Objections to the Penal Substitution Theory

IF AN ORTHODOX THEORY of the Atonement could be said to exist within the Protestant church, it would be the penal substitution theory. Often, people are not even aware that it is a theory and is itself not found in Scripture. The merit of the theory is that it emphasizes two truths essential to any adequate understanding of Christ's death. One is that humankind has been alienated from God by sin, and the other is the substitutionary nature of the death of Christ. He provided for the salvation of humans by bearing their sin and suffering in their place. But the theory itself is still open to serious objections.[1] These objections can be categorized as logical, moral, and theological.

LOGICAL OBJECTIONS TO PENAL SUBSTITUTION

An idea in the penal substitution theory is that the suffering and death of Christ buys or obtains from God a salvation which, without such payment, he must withhold. This idea is different from a gospel of grace. Salvation cannot be by both grace and works (Rom 11:6). This contradiction presents a primary objection to the penal substitution theory. If the penalty is borne or the price paid for wrongdoing, it does not need

1. Smith, *Atonement in Light of History*, 105.

to be forgiven by grace. This is a simple contradiction.[2] Debt cannot be both forgiven and paid back at the same time.[3] If it is paid back it does not need to be forgiven; if it is forgiven it does not need to be paid back.[4] And if a debt is paid back there is certainly no need to commend the creditor as generous. Why would God be considered gracious if he would only forgive after being paid back?[5] Or, if the death of Christ is considered to be punishment inflicted by God, then sin was punished by him, making forgiveness unnecessary.[6]

Another logical objection to Christ's death as a substitutionary exchange demanded by God's justice is that Christ did not bear the true punishment for sin: eternal separation from God. If Christ suffered the punishment for sin, why did he not suffer it eternally?[7] This lack of equivalence has been a problem for the penal substitution theory since its beginning. It has sometimes been argued that the payment for sin is not a matter of quantity but of quality, the death of Jesus being of infinite value since he is the Son of God.[8] But would it not be considered an injustice that a lesser penalty be inflicted on a more important person?[9] And, if Christ's infinite value means a lesser punishment could be exacted, why did he need to suffer such severe torture and such a horrible death?[10]

MORAL OBJECTIONS TO PENAL SUBSTITUTION

In the history of the church the most sustained moral objection to any of its teachings is against the penal substitution theory. The objection is not to God bringing about reconciliation between himself and humankind, but to the explanation of *how* his actions achieved that end. The theory poses several ethical dilemmas. Why would God require a ransom to be paid to himself? What sort of God demands propitiation (appeasement)

---

2. Smith, *Atonement in Light of History*, 215.
3. Gomes, "Satisfaction of Christ," 227.
4. Gomes, "Satisfaction of Christ," 226.
5. Godbey, "Socinus," 99–100.
6. McDonald, *Atonement*, 197.
7. Godbey, "Socinus," 339; Gomes, "Satisfaction of Christ," 227; McDonald, *Atonement*, 197.
8. Hicks, "What Did Christ Accomplish," 156.
9. Godbey, "Socinus," 163.
10. Godbey, "Socinus," 167, 176.

by death? How can the death of one expiate (wipe out) the sins of another? What sort of judge can impose death on an innocent, or even on himself, as a substitutionary punishment, enabling the guilty to go free? Can anything restrain the forgiveness of God where there is true repentance and faith?[11]

This book does not deny the substitutionary nature of the death of Christ or that he died taking the penalty for the sin of humankind. Rather, it disagrees with the penal substitution theory's explanation as to *why* Jesus became a substitute and *why* he bore the penalty. The theory maintains that God, unable to forgive humankind without proper punishment, designed Christ's suffering and death to satisfy his just nature, his holiness, his abhorrence of sin. In contrast, this book asserts that substitution and penalty should be understood within the ransom, or classic, theory of the Atonement, and that when understood in this context they pose no moral problem.

To say that God punishes the innocent in place of the guilty in order that justice might be done is to wrong God's character. In the book of Ezekiel, God speaks of his judgment: "The one who sins is the one who will die. . . . The righteousness of the righteous will be credited to them, and the wickedness of the wicked will be charged against them" (Ezek 18:20). Each is responsible for their own actions and will be treated by God accordingly.[12] Sin is a personal matter and therefore cannot be set to another's account.[13] The same principle of justice is plainly written in the Mosaic law ("each will die for their own sin"; Deut 24:16) and applied in 2 Kings 14:6.[14] According to what God has revealed about his own justice it would be legally indefensible to transfer to Christ the punishment that belonged to sinners.[15] Many times Scripture condemns those who "shed innocent blood" (e.g., Jer 22:3). James issues a strong warning to those who "have condemned and murdered the innocent one" (Jas 5:6). How then can the penal substitution theory attribute to God what he has declared unjust? Ironically, the theory interprets the Atonement in terms of jurisprudence while being based upon a flagrant illegality.[16]

---

11. Hebblethwaite, "Doctrine of the Atonement," 64.
12. Gomes, "Satisfaction of Christ," 229.
13. McDonald, *Atonement*, 197.
14. Godbey, "Socinus," 135.
15. Smith, *Atonement in Light of History*, 108.
16. Smith, *Atonement in Light of History*, 110.

An analysis of this contradiction must distinguish between civil law and criminal law. The payment of debt comes under the purview of civil law, whereas sin falls under the jurisdiction of criminal law. Monetary penalties related to defaulting on a debt can be voluntarily paid by one person for another, because one person's money is just as good as another's. However, death and corporal punishment, being criminal penalties, are a very different matter. Justice is never served by their being vicariously endured. The acceptability of substitution in a civil matter is not analogous to substitution in the criminal matter of sin. Defenders of penal substitution blur this distinction as well as justify their position by pointing out that the sacrifice of Christ is voluntary.[17] Admittedly, Christ died voluntarily, but this does not diminish the problem related to the nature of justice. Justice is abandoned when the innocent suffer in place of the guilty, even if that suffering is voluntary.

Defenders also rebut the charge of injustice in the penal substitution theory by pointing out that it is not just any third party that suffers vicariously.[18] The penalty for sin is endured by God himself in Christ. That fact, however, simply does not remove the charge of injustice. Injustice remains injustice even if the one who suffers it is God himself. Regardless of how willing Christ might have been, God would have wronged him to require such suffering as punishment.[19]

Those who believe in penal substitution argue that in the Atonement God wanted to exercise his attributes of both justice and mercy and demonstrate them to humankind. On the one hand, he is said to be merciful in that he does not exact punishment for human transgressions. On the other hand, he is said to be just because he nevertheless punishes sins. Actually, the theory destroys both mercy and justice. God cannot be said to act justly in punishing the innocent, nor can he be said to act mercifully in forgoing payment after payment has already been made.[20]

Advocates of the penal substitution theory believe their view alone satisfies the requirements of the moral order, which is rooted in the divine nature. Divine justice or holiness, they say, has inexorable claims that must be satisfied or the pillars of moral order will collapse. They bring to the interpretation of the work of Christ a preformed view of

17. Erickson, *Christian Theology*, 817; Gomes, "Satisfaction of Christ," 229–30; Letham, *Work of Christ*, 137.
18. Erickson, *Christian Theology*, 817.
19. Godbey, "Socinus," 249.
20. Godbey, "Socinus," 137, 139.

morality that they take for granted as axiomatic.[21] This moral framework is a system of retributive justice that operates through rewards and penalties and demands that sin must be expiated (wiped out) by due suffering. Any view that does not fit into this ironclad system is charged with failing to "take sin seriously."[22] Emil Brunner takes this view in *The Mediator*:

> The divine law—the world order—requires that sin should receive its corresponding penalty from God. . . . Forgiveness . . . would mean the contravention of the logical result of the world law. . . . The law of penalty is the expression of the personal Will of God, of the Divine Holiness itself. Forgiveness, therefore, would be the declaration of the non-validity of the unconditioned order of righteousness which requires penalty. . . . Whenever anyone thinks he has the right to lay down the law about divine forgiveness he does not take the question of human guilt seriously. For whoever takes it seriously knows that he can only expect from God the penalty which he deserves. . . . For punishment is the expression of the divine law and order, of the inviolability of the divine order of the world. It is obvious that every man receives his deserts. This is the logic of the legal view of the world.[23]

Another example is found in Leon Morris' *Apostolic Preaching of the Cross*:

> Modern man may have largely lost sight of it, but the Bible insists that sin is followed by punishment. . . . [God] could not abolish the punishment bound up with [sin]. Nothing in the compass of the divine nature could enable Him to abolish a moral law, the law of holiness. That would be tampering with His own soul. It had to be dealt with. . . . What was done on Calvary concerned the inflexible law which is the very basis of the being of God.[24]

Like the elder brother of the prodigal son, advocates of penal substitution cannot accept the father's gracious welcome of the wayward brother (Luke 15:29). What sort of justice is this? If there must be punishment before there can be forgiveness, then the elder brother is right: the father's welcome of the prodigal is indeed a flouting of the moral order.[25] God

---

21. Erickson, *Christian Theology*, 816.
22. N. Robinson, *Jesus Christ Saves Men*, 107–9.
23. Brunner, *Mediator*, 446–49.
24. Morris, *Apostolic*, 270–71.
25. N. Robinson, *Jesus Christ Saves Men*, 107–9.

the Father, however, stands able and eager to forgive all who repent and come to him. The foundation of the parable is that when the father sees his returning son there is no anger in his heart against him but only an overflowing tenderness. He did not need to be appeased. It was enough that his son had repented and returned, so he took him to his breast and would not listen to his premeditated confession.[26] Punishment as a prerequisite for forgiveness defeats the purpose of forgiving.

THEOLOGICAL OBJECTIONS TO PENAL SUBSTITUTION

The Concept of Justice

The penal substitution theory of the Atonement relies upon a concept of God's justice that presents not only a moral issue but also a theological one. According to the theory, to say that God is just is to say that he must not allow sin to go unpunished. Justice means that sin must be punished, and since justice is an innate attribute of God, he has no alternative but to punish sin. This conclusion, however, is based on a deficient understanding of God's justice as well as his character.

That God is just or righteous is a truth clearly and repeatedly revealed in Scripture. That God judges sin is also a truth found throughout the Bible. But that God *has to judge sin* in order to be just or righteous is nowhere to be found. Indeed, the opposite is true. God is longsuffering with his people, calling them to turn away from their sin and return to him so that he might forgive and bless them (Exod 34:6; Ps 86:5; 2 Pet 3:9). God desires to bless his people and does so for all who come to repentance. As long as he sees a chance for repentance, he delays judgment. Judgment is not what God desires (Ezek 18:23, 32), and that is why God is said to be "slow to anger" (anger being a metonym for executing judgment; Exod 34:6; Num 14:18; Neh 9:17; Ps 86:15; 103:8; 145:8; Joel 2:13; Jonah 4:2; Nah 1:3). Only when people refuse to heed his commands and refuse to repent will he judge them (Exod 34:7; Num 14:18; Ezek 18:30).

The purpose of God's judgment is not always retributive but is often disciplinary (Heb 12:5–11). It serves for instruction and is frequently the means to continue the call to repent and be reconciled with God (book of Judges). God may exercise his judgment as he wills; it is his prerogative as the God of this universe. It is not within his prerogative, however, to

---

26. Smith, *Atonement in Light of History*, 153.

be unfair or unjust (Ezek 18:25–29). Therefore, retributive judgment will indeed be exercised in the absence of repentance (Exod 34:7; Num 14:18; Ezek 18:30–32).

Because God is just, humans are capable of recognizing justice, and the idea of justice is deeply embedded in us.[27] In order to establish what justice is, it is helpful to establish what it is not. The concept of justice cannot be confined to the administration of law. Even if the law is thoroughly and faithfully administered, it does not necessarily follow that justice is done. If someone is permanently disabled as a result of a crime committed against them, the wrong cannot be made right even though the wrongdoer is punished. Punishment may be beneficial for the one who has done the wrong, but punishment is not the same thing as justice. Neither does punishing the wrongdoer necessarily bring about reconciliation. Only repentance and forgiveness reconciles. Yet even when reconciliation occurs, the offended party may not receive justice. To say therefore that justice means punishing sin and mercy means letting sin go unpunished is an incomplete and inadequate view of justice.[28]

What is divine justice, the sort of justice that God gives? If true justice is merely the punishing of sin, then an unjust judge can, by punishing every wrongdoer, be called just. But the justice of God is much more. God gives every man, woman, and child fair play—he simply does nothing unfair. Punishment of the guilty may be a part of the justice of God, but it is not the whole of it.[29]

Justice is more than retribution. There can still be justice if retribution is forgone. The guilty party is surely not deprived of their rights or oppressed by injustice if the wronged party forgives. If they were, then wrongs could never be forgiven justly.[30] Perhaps rulers and judges can commit injustice when they acquit the guilty because, in doing so, they undermine the law's authority. But God, as the source of all authority, is not himself subject to a law that demands retribution.[31] For God to forgive sins without receiving literal satisfaction (payback) is simply to

---

27. MacDonald, *Character of God*, 245.
28. MacDonald, *Character of God*, 246–47.
29. MacDonald, *Character of God*, 249.
30. Godbey, "Socinus," 73.
31. Godbey, "Socinus," 74–75.

forgo his own right to punish.³² Everyone in his or her personal relations may do likewise.

The penal substitution theory, however, claims a law of retribution that has ultimate authority; even when the law is said to be God's own law, the theory still confines God to legal restraints. Law becomes a supreme principle preventing God from forgoing retribution even when people repent and return to him.³³ But God is the sovereign Lord of the universe whose will is exercised in accord with his own righteous nature.³⁴ God is always just or fair, but that is not to say that he always insists on retribution.

God Is Free to Remit Sins and Forgives Based on Repentance

The penal substitution theory does not insist that God apply the law of retribution in an exact manner. Law demands that the offender himself be punished, but in allowing a substitute to take his place, the theory violates the strict logic of the law. Why then should God not be free to dispense with punishment altogether?³⁵ In fact, he is and he does, as Scripture indicates time and again (Lev 4:20, 26, 31, 35; 5:10, 13, 16, 18; 6:7; 19:22; Num 15:25–28; 1 John 1:9). God forgives freely—that is, apart from satisfaction (payback)—and he is free to dispense with satisfaction altogether.³⁶

What, then, is the determining factor in God's choice between mercy and wrath? The state of the sinner's heart, which God sees and knows, is the deciding factor. Justice demands not payment but repentance; it is "satisfied" not by any penalty but by a change of heart that leads to a changed life. How beautiful is the revelation of God's heart: "Say to them, 'As surely as I live, declares the Sovereign Lord, I take no pleasure in the death of the wicked, but rather that they turn from their ways and live. Turn! Turn from your evil ways! Why will you die, people of Israel?'" (Ezek 33:11). The father wants nothing more than the return of his children to him.³⁷ God is ever ready to forgive when one repents

---

32. Godbey, "Socinus," 61.
33. Fiddes, *Present Salvation*, 101.
34. Gomes, "Satisfaction of Christ," 215–16.
35. Fiddes, *Present Salvation*, 102.
36. Gomes, "Satisfaction of Christ," 222.
37. Godbey, "Socinus," 104–5.

(Ezek 18:21–22; Deut 4:30–31; 30:2–3; 2 Chron 7:14; 1 John 1:9). This is the message of John the Baptist as the forerunner of Christ. He prepares the Lord's path by preaching "a baptism of repentance for the forgiveness of sins" (Mark 1:4; Luke 3:3). This is the message of the Law and the Prophets: God is merciful and faithful to forgive those who repent. Peter restates the OT truth that God delays judgment because he desires to forgive the repentant: "The Lord is not slow in keeping his promise, as some understand slowness. Instead he is patient with you, not wanting anyone to perish, but everyone to come to repentance" (2 Pet 3:9). God is not required by justice to forgive even the penitent. He does so because it is his desire, and having decreed that he will show mercy to the penitent, it is only right that he do so.[38] As Scripture declares time and again, salvation from sin is the gift of God's grace and is won for his people by Jesus.

One may object by asking whether free forgiveness undermines morality.[39] Although God forgives freely, he requires true repentance, which always involves emendation of life by those whom God has pardoned (Ezek 33:15). Righteousness in God's sight entails a change in conduct as well as a change of heart (Matt 3:8).[40] Paul preaches that people should "repent and turn to God and demonstrate their repentance by their deeds" (Acts 26:20). Peter also gives the same message: "Repent, then, and turn to God, so that your sins may be wiped out" (Acts 3:19).

An Inner-Divine Conflict

Another theological difficulty presented by the penal substitution theory is that it gives the appearance of a division within the Godhead.[41] A fundamental tenet of the Christian faith is that Christ is one with God. There is no division in character, purpose, or disposition toward humankind. The theory presents God as the judge who insists on punishment and Christ as the volunteer who endures God's wrath.[42] Jesus' cry of abandonment (Matt 27:46; Mark 15:34) is interpreted to mean that God's wrath fell on him.[43] That Christ endured the punishment due

---

38. Godbey, "Socinus," 76.
39. N. Robinson, *Jesus Christ Saves Men*, 178.
40. Gomes, "Satisfaction of Christ," 223.
41. McClendon, *Doctrine*, 208.
42. Smith, *Atonement in Light of History*, 106.
43. N. Robinson, *Jesus Christ Saves Men*, 117.

humankind is not a theological problem, but to say that he endured God's wrath is unacceptable. It is unimaginable that God should have said, "I will withdraw my wrath from guilty sinners and instead be angry with my innocent Son."[44]

Christ and the Father are so truly one that Jesus could say, "Anyone who has seen me has seen the Father" (John 14:9). Whatever Christ is the Father is also; whatever Christ does the Father does also through him. Is one to see in the death of Jesus a merciful savior appeasing an angry God? This cannot be the case if Christ and God are one. For if they are one, nothing is true of either that is not also true of the other.[45] In the penal substitution theory God and Christ are not one: God is propitiated (appeased), Christ propitiates (appeases); God inflicts punishment, Christ endures it; God exacts payment for the debt, Christ pays it. Any view of the Atonement that sets the work of the Father against that of the Son is theologically flawed. Jesus said, "My Father is always at his work to this very day, and I too am working" (John 5:17). The Father and Son are entirely one in the work of saving sinful people, for "God was reconciling the world to himself in Christ" (2 Cor 5:19).

Reconciliation

There is a fourth theological fault in the penal substitution theory. The theory focuses on God's need to be reconciled to sinners, which is a reversal of the NT doctrine. The NT does not speak of God being reconciled *to humankind* but of humans being reconciled *to God*, and of God as the reconciler.[46] Consider Paul's use of the term *reconciliation*. With a persistence and precision that show conscious and deliberate intention, he affirms that Christ reconciled the world to God and never that he reconciled God to the world.[47] Note the following examples (emphases added):

- For if, while we were God's enemies, *we were reconciled to him* through the death of his Son, how much more, *having been reconciled*, shall we be saved through his life! (Rom 5:10)

---

44. Smith, *Atonement in Light of History*, 106–7.
45. Smith, *Atonement in Light of History*, 168–69.
46. Baillie, *God Was in Christ*, 187.
47. Smith, *Atonement in Light of History*, 111.

- All this is from God, *who reconciled us to himself* through Christ and gave us the ministry of reconciliation: that *God was reconciling the world to himself* in Christ, not counting people's sins against them. And he has committed to us the message of reconciliation. . . . We implore you on Christ's behalf: *Be reconciled to God*. (2 Cor 5:18–20)
- His purpose was to create in himself one new humanity out of the two, thus making peace, and in one body to *reconcile both of them to God* . . . (Eph 2:15–16)
- For God was pleased to have all his fullness dwell in [the Son], and through him to *reconcile to himself all things* . . . through his blood, shed on the cross. Once you were alienated from God and were enemies in your minds because of your evil behavior. But now *he has reconciled you* by Christ's physical body through death . . . (Col 1:19–21)

These verses speak of an objective aspect of the Atonement—that which is accomplished apart from any response by humankind. This means subjective views of the Atonement emphasizing the human response to what God has done (moral influence and exemplarist theories) are insufficient. There is a sense in which reconciliation was accomplished by Christ independent of humankind and apart from any response by humans. This atonement is a historical event and is complete before the Gospel is preached.[48]

This objective aspect of atonement accomplished by Christ's death could be related to either the penal substitution theory or the ransom theory. Which view is held depends upon what one perceives to be the situation that needs addressing.[49] Those who hold to the penal substitution theory would say that it is God's wrath that needs to be propitiated (appeased). Those who hold to the ransom theory would say that it is Satan's hold on humankind that must be addressed—that a new relationship between God and the world resulted from the defeat of God's enemy who held humankind in bondage to sin and death.

However, even when Scripture refers to this historical, objective aspect of the Atonement as "reconciliation," it never speaks of God needing to be reconciled, for that would give the impression of a barrier to reconciliation within God himself. This fact presents a significant weakness to

---

48. Morris, *Apostolic*, 198, 201.
49. Morris, *Apostolic*, 219.

the penal substitution theory's contention that God's justice needed to be satisfied (paid off).

The Central Idea of the Atonement Is God's Love

Although proponents of the penal substitution theory would certainly insist that God's action in sending his Son stems from his love, it cannot be denied that the theory's main concern is the justice of God.[50] But in Scripture the central idea is not God's requirement but rather God's gift of love.[51] Jesus *gave* his life "as a ransom for many" and God so loved the world that he *gave* his only Son. Scripture expressly traces Christ's death to its source, the love of God; and this love is sacrificial love (Rom 5:8; 8:32, 35–39). As Forsyth says, "The Atonement did not procure grace; it flowed from grace. Procured grace is a contradiction in terms."[52]

Throughout the NT there is no trace of any conflict between the justice of God and his love. God's love for and mercy toward sinners is never regarded as the result of Christ's death, but always as its cause and source.[53] As G. W. H. Lampe says, "It is high time to discard the vestiges of a theory of atonement that was geared to a conception of punishment which found nothing shocking in the idea that God should crucify sinners or the substitute who took their place."[54]

SUMMARY

The penal substitution theory's argument that the work of Christ appeased God's wrath and satisfied his justice poses logical, moral, and theological dilemmas. First, if God freely forgives sins as an act of grace, can he first demand punishment for those sins? This conundrum exists regardless of who bears the punishment and even if it is borne voluntarily. Second, if Jesus paid the price for the sins of humankind, to whom was the payment made? Can the price have been paid to God? Can the grace of God be bought? Third, even if God had required a price and Jesus had died to pay it, could the penalty borne by one suffice for the sins of all? And

---

50. Letham, *Work of Christ*, 138–39.
51. Kehm, "Defilement," 51.
52. Forsyth, *Cruciality of the Cross*, 41.
53. Baillie, *God Was in Christ*, 106.
54. Lampe, "Atonement," 189.

finally, how could Jesus have borne the full penalty for sin when he did not become eternally separated from God?

These questions indicate that the penal substitution theory is logically problematic, but its moral shortcomings present an even weightier problem. Can a moral God, calling it justice, punish the innocent in place of the guilty and do so in violation of his own word?[55] Is it really conceivable that the sovereignty and grace of God are limited by an inviolable demand for retribution?

The penal substitution theory also poses theological difficulties. Can it be said theologically that retribution necessarily equals justice or redresses the wrong done? Does punishment bring about reconciliation or dispense with the problem of sin? Could there have been an inner-divine conflict such that the Son had to appease the Father in order for the Father to be reconciled to humankind? Was it not humans who needed to be reconciled to God as Scripture says? Does not Scripture also say that the driving force behind the Atonement was the love of God rather than a concept of God's justice that insists on retribution?

All these questions identify the serious objections to the penal substitution theory that have been raised in the centuries since its formulation. If the theory, at least for some, defies reason, morality, and sound theology, why has it been so widely held and why is it so often presented as scriptural fact when it is really a theory? In order to answer these questions the following chapter will examine the Scriptures that are commonly used to teach the penal substitution theory.

---

55. This objection also applies to the governmental theory, for "it leaves in place one difficulty which is quite enough to ruin the theory. A Governor who inflicts suffering on the innocent . . . is an unjust Governor." Franks, *Atonement*, 91.

3

Exegetical Objections to the Penal Substitution Theory

In addition to logical, moral, and theological difficulties with penal substitution, there is also inadequate scriptural support for the theory. This is not to say that there is inadequate support for regarding Christ's death as both substitutionary and penal. If one considers Christ's death substitutionary (he became our substitute) and penal (he took our penalty), it does not follow that he became a substitute or bore a penalty because God had to inflict punishment on someone in order to be just. That is theory and is not found in Scripture.

THE WRATH OF GOD

Proponents of the penal substitution theory argue that expiation (removal of sin) is no substitute for propitiation (appeasement for sin), that expiation is not sufficient for reconciliation. The reality of God's wrath is offered as proof that propitiation is the only viable option to achieve atonement. But does the wrath of God require propitiation or satisfaction (payback) as the penal substitution theory claims? What Scripture describes as "the wrath of God" is his personal reaction to sin, a holy displeasure that results in estrangement and immutability of judgment.[1]

---

1. Crawford, "Penal Theory," 271.

But care should be taken with such a concept. God's wrath is closely related to his love. It is his anger at all that harms his beloved—his beloved people and his beloved world. Many times in the OT, God, because of his love, withholds judgment as he awaits repentance (Exod 34:6; Num 14:18; Nah 1:3; Isa 48:9; Ps 103:8). By individual judgments he warns his people and exhorts them to repent before he proceeds to more severe judgments (Amos 4:6–10; Isa 9:12–17).

The people of Israel are denied the propitiatory means of averting God's judgment known and practiced by their neighbors. Instead, their prayers of intercession are directed to God's mercy. Thus Moses prays for the people (Exod 32:11–13; Num 11:2–3; 14:11–19; Deut 9:19; Ps 106:23) or for guilty individuals (Num 12:13; Deut 9:20); Amos prays for Israel (7:2, 5); Jeremiah prays for Judah (14:7–9; 18:20); and Job prays for his friends (42:7–10). God accepts the intercession, and the effects of the judgment are reduced (Num 11; 14; Deut 9). But the OT warns that a time may come when God no longer responds to intercession (Amos 7:8; 8:2; Ezek 14:14) and even forbids its offering (Jer 7:16).[2] Before this time the prophets announced that God's wrath could be averted by repentance (Jer 4:4, 8; 36:7; Dan 9:16).[3]

The NT also declares the wrath of God as well as his grace and mercy (Rom 1:18; John 3:36; Rev 14:10). But God does not become angry without cause; wrath is not a trait of the divine nature.[4] The phrase "the wrath of God" is used most often in the NT as a metonym for God's judgment. It is in this sense that John the Baptist says to the Pharisees, "Who warned you to flee from the coming wrath?" (Matt 3:7; see also Luke 21:23; Rom 1:18; 2:5; 4:15; 5:9; 13:4; Eph 5:6; Col 3:6; 1 Thess 1:10; 2:16; Rev 6:17; 11:18). God being "slow to anger" (Neh 9:17; Ps 103:8; 145:8; Joel 2:13; Jonah 4:2; Nah 1:3) means that he is slow to execute judgment. Romans 2:4–5 says, "Or do you show contempt for the riches of his kindness, forbearance, and patience, not realizing that God's kindness is intended to lead you to repentance? But because of your stubbornness and your unrepentant heart, you are storing up wrath against yourself for the day of God's wrath, when his righteous judgment will be revealed."

These verses show that God is patient with the sinner and gives ample time to come to repentance and thereby avoid judgment. Like the

---

2. Kleinknecht, *Wrath*, 50.
3. Kleinknecht, *Wrath*, 47.
4. Kleinknecht, *Wrath*, 116.

Exegetical Objections to the Penal Substitution Theory

OT, the NT speaks of God's forbearance (Rom 2:4; Rev 2:21; 2 Pet 3:9) as giving the sinner time for repentance and therefore as an aid to salvation (2 Pet 3:15; 1 Tim 1:16).[5] The question of how to be spared God's wrath is asked and answered at the beginning of the ministry of John the Baptist: "Repent for the kingdom of heaven is near" and "produce fruit in keeping with repentance" (Matt 3:2, 8).[6]

For those who refuse to repent, however, God's wrath will not be compromised; it will result in judgment (Rom 2:5, 8). Humankind will one day be divided into those who are exempt from God's wrath because they have chosen to be rescued by Christ, and those who remain under wrath because they have refused God's compassion.[7] "Whoever believes in the Son has eternal life, but whoever rejects the Son will not see life, for God's wrath remains on him" (John 3:36).

The idea of "drinking the cup" in both the OT and NT is often equated with experiencing the wrath of God. Indeed, the image is used in the OT to refer to those under the judgment of God—those who are forced to drink the cup of God's wrath (Job 21:20; Ps 60:3; 75:8; Isa 51:22; Jer 25:15; Ezek 23:31–34; Hab 2:16). The term *cup* is also used by Jesus in the NT to refer to the new covenant in his blood (Matt 26:27–28; Luke 22:20), yet this is a cup of blessing and grace, not of wrath.

When Jesus refers to his upcoming death in Jerusalem he again uses the term *cup* (Matt 20:20–23; Mark 10:37–39). His disciples James and John have come to seek a promise from him of places of honor in his kingdom. Jesus says that they have no concept of what they are asking. He asks them whether they can drink the cup he will drink. It is certain that this is not the "cup of God's wrath" but rather a cup of suffering, for Jesus goes on to say that they will indeed drink this cup. He did not say that he would drink the cup for them. They, too, will experience suffering.

Jesus, at Gethsemane, asks his Father whether it is possible for "this cup" to be removed (Luke 22:42). These words might be interpreted as the cup of God's wrath since this is how the term is so often used in the OT. However, because Jesus is clearly referring to his upcoming suffering and death when he uses the term *cup* in the earlier scene with James and John, Jesus himself defines the cup as an experience his disciples will also have. No one would argue that James and John would experience the cup

---

5. Kleinknecht, *Wrath*, 89.
6. Kleinknecht, *Wrath*, 129.
7. Kleinknecht, *Wrath*, 88.

of God's wrath as punishment while bearing the sin of the world (as the penal substitution theory claims for Jesus). Therefore, the symbol of the cup must only be a reference to the suffering itself. This understanding is why proponents of the penal substitution theory rarely use this reference in Gethsemane as evidence for the theory.

Proponents of the penal substitution theory sometimes claim that those who reject their theory reject the whole idea of the wrath of God. However, to reject propitiation is not the same thing as rejecting the concept of the wrath of God. To say that God hates sin and judges the guilty is not a proper defense of propitiation or the penal substitution theory. The wrath of God against sin is a truth revealed throughout the Bible; it is not an idea exclusive to the penal substitution theory. It does not prove that God cannot pardon the penitent without being propitiated (appeased) or without satisfaction (payback) being made.[8]

To deny penal substitution is not necessarily to take lightly the concept of the wrath of God. Sin lies under the wrath of God, causing estrangement between God and his creatures. If the sinner is to be reconciled to God, then God's wrath must be removed. However, this is accomplished not by propitiation (appeasement) or satisfaction (payback), but by the expiation (wiping out) of sin. God's wrath cannot be removed by a propitiatory gift or sacrifice as in pagan religions. When repentance and God's gracious pardon eliminate the source of human alienation, rebellion, and sin, humans can be reconciled to God. Verses 2 and 3 of Psalm 85 indicate this connection between forgiveness and the removal of wrath: "You forgave the iniquity of your people and covered all their sins. You set aside all your wrath and turned from your fierce anger." In no way does this removal of divine wrath through repentance and pardon deny the reality of the wrath of God or compromise God's hostility toward everything that is evil. The fact of the wrath of God simply cannot be used, as is commonly done, as proof of penal substitution. No NT text states that the sacrifice of Christ was intended to appease God's wrath or that Christ was himself the object of that wrath in the place of sinners.

---

8. An example of this kind of defense of propitiation is a statement by Erickson: "The numerous passages that speak of the wrath of God against sin are evidence that Christ's death was necessarily propitiatory." *Christian Theology*, 811.

HILASMOS IN THE NT: EXPIATION, NOT PROPITIATION

The Greek noun *hilasmos* (derived from the verb *hilaskomai*, "propitiate/expiate") is variously rendered "expiation," an equivalent term or phrase, or "propitiation." Expiation signifies the removal of sin, whereas propitiation signifies "the removal of wrath by the offering of a gift."[9] To propitiate is to placate or appease. The concepts of propitiation and expiation are distinguishable by the object of the action. Human sin is the object of expiation, whereas God himself is the object of propitiation. Sin is expiated, but God is propitiated. Many biblical scholars have declined to use the word propitiation in relation to God, preferring instead the term expiation.[10] To use the word expiate is to interpret the death of Christ as dealing with the sin of humankind. To use the word propitiate is to interpret his death as satisfying God's need for retributive justice.[11]

In the biblical sense, to expiate is to perform an act whereby guilt or defilement is removed. In the OT, if a person violated a taboo (such as contact with a dead body), the person or thing involved becomes defiled, or "unclean." The condition of defilement can be removed by performing the appropriate act: washing with water, sprinkling with blood, or offering a sacrifice. Such ritual cleansings were thought to serve, so to speak, as disinfectant. However, when God does the expiating (i.e., when God is the subject of the verb "to expiate"), the meaning is simply "to forgive."[12] Forgiveness means the sin is wiped out.

The significance of the concept of expiation is made clear in the sacrificial event on the Day of Atonement, in which the live goat is led away into the desert never to return. The goat symbolically carries away the sins of Israel to a place from which they could not return (Lev 16:20–22). Thus the psalmist can reflect on the magnitude of the forgiveness of Yahweh: "As far as the east is from the west, so far has he removed our transgressions from us" (Ps 103:12; see also Isa 44:22–23; Mic 7:19).[13]

Terms derived from the Greek verb *hilaskomai* are used only a few times in the NT. In Hebrews 2:17 the word is the infinitive *hilaskesthai* ("to propitiate/expiate," NIV "make atonement for"); in 1 John 2:2 and 4:10 it is the noun *hilasmos* (NIV "atoning sacrifice"); and in Romans

---

9. Morris, "Propitiation," 986.
10. Connell, "Atonement," 28.
11. Connell, "Atonement," 38.
12. Dodd, *Romans*, 54–55.
13. Letham, *Work of Christ*, 139.

3:25 *hilasterion* is variously taken as a noun ("propitiation/expiation," "mercy seat," or NIV "sacrifice of atonement") or as an adjective meaning "propitiatory."[14]

The usual meaning of the verb in classical Greek literature is not in doubt. It signifies "to propitiate" or "to appease," especially in the sense of appeasing the anger of a god by a sacrificial offering. Appeasing angry gods is a pagan concept; therefore, the connotation of *hilaskesthai* differs greatly when used in a scriptural context. Not once does Scripture use the phrase "to placate the anger of God" with this verb, and never is the verb found in the active voice with God as the object, as it is in Greek literature. The term is used in the Septuagint (the Greek translation of the OT, designated LXX) to render two Hebrew words, *kipper* ("make atonement")[15] and *salach* ("pardon" or "forgive").[16]

Theologically, *kipper* is an important term. In common usage it means "cover," hence its biblical meaning is "to cover sin," meaning to make atonement for sin. But cover is actually its derivative sense, the root idea of the verb being "wipe" or "smear." This is the meaning that occurs, for instance, in the command to Noah that he should "coat the ark with pitch" (Gen 6:14). From this root meaning come the various uses of the verb in the OT. Thus when a covenant is "smeared over" or "wiped away," it is said to be annulled (Isa 28:18). So also is sin "smeared over" or "wiped away" when it is pardoned or forgiven (Ps 65:3). *Kipper*, then, is a picturesque synonym for *salach*, "forgive" or "be merciful."[17] It signifies the removal of sin brought about by repentance and forgiveness, which results in the removal of wrath and in atonement; that is, in reconciliation. (It should be remembered that the English word *atonement* has moved away from its biblical meaning of "reconciliation.")[18]

When the Septuagint translators addressed the Hebrew Scriptures, they found themselves confronted by a great difficulty. The Greek

---

14. Smith, *Atonement in Light of History*, 156.

15. Lyonnet and Sabourin, *Sin, Redemption, and Sacrifice*, 126. There are three exceptions in which the Greek verb *hilaskesthai*, used in the active voice, is not the translation of *kipper* (Zech 7:2; 8:22; Mal 1:9). But since all other examples of *hilaskesthai* consistently translate *kipper*, especially when in the active voice, one can conclude that the meaning of the Greek verb can be revealed by the meaning of the Hebrew word *kipper*.

16. Smith, *Atonement in Light of History*, 156.

17. Smith, *Atonement in Light of History*, 157.

18. Baillie, *God Was in Christ*, 187.

language lacked soteriological terms that were common in Hebrew thought, and such terms as they had possessed a pagan color. *Hilaskesthai* was the closest approximation to the Hebrew idea of forgiveness, but it was not a true substitute. It carried the pagan notion of appeasing an angry god, a notion not part of the Hebrew religion. Nevertheless, the word was the best available and the translators were constrained to use it. But they employed it definitively, carefully eliminating its pagan implications. This is impressively clear from the fact that, whereas in classical literature *hilaskesthai* takes the deity propitiated as its direct object, it is never so constructed in the Septuagint. Its object there is not *God* but *sin*.[19] And since "propitiating sin" is an impossible idea, it is evident that the translators are giving it a different meaning. They are stripping it of its sense of appeasement and investing it with a sense of its conventional Hebrew equivalent, *kipper*, to wipe or purge away.[20]

USEAGE OF *HILASKESTHAI* IN THE NT: CONTEXT AND MEANING

The NT writers also used *hilaskesthai* following the LXX example and meaning. In none of the occurrences does the immediate context speak of the wrath of God (and certainly not of placating wrath). Instead, the context speaks either of God's act of disposal of sin (Rom 3:25; Heb 2:17; 8:12; 1 John 4:10) or of the guarantee of God's grace and mercy to the sinner in need (Luke 18:13; 1 John 2:2). *Hilaskesthai* should therefore be translated by words signifying expiation rather than propitiation.[21] However, even when expiation is used it must be enriched to include the concept of atonement (reconciliation; Hebrew *kipper*), the idea that the canceling of sin also introduces the believer into a new relationship with God.[22] When the sinner comes to God in faith and repentance, their sin is expiated and God forgives. God's wrath against sin is averted, but not through a propitiation in which the penalty for sin is inflicted on Christ by God. It is averted because the sinner repents and believes.

---

19. Except in a single instance, Zech 7:2. This is correctly rendered in the RSV "to entreat the favor of the Lord"; literally "to smooth the face of the Lord."
20. Smith, *Atonement in Light of History*, 158–59.
21. Baillie, *God Was in Christ*, 175–76.
22. N. Young, "Critics," 78.

Hebrews 2:17

In the NT the verb *hilaskesthai* occurs only once: "For this reason he had to be made like them, fully human in every way, in order that he might become a merciful and faithful high priest in service to God, and that he might make atonement for [NASB 'make propitiation for'] the sins of the people" (Heb 2:17). Here propitiation corresponds to the scriptural idea of "to make atonement for" or "to purge away" the sins of the people. The object of propitiation is not God but sins—"the sins of the people."[23] Because propitiating people's sins makes no sense, all translations modify the phrase in some way.[24]

The context of Hebrews 2:17 (beginning at 2:9) is a discussion of why Christ became human, and it is in this context that Jesus' ministry as high priest is mentioned (other references to Jesus' priesthood can be found in 2:14, 5:1, 9:28, and 13:12). The fact that he became a human being especially qualifies him to become high priest. Having suffered and been tempted himself, Jesus is merciful to those who sin and comforts those who are tempted. Jesus' ministry as high priest reminds the reader of the Day of Atonement, in which the sins of the people are expiated. References to the high priest, the sins of the people, and expiation make this clear. It is *sin removal* that is the background for the statement concerning Christ's purpose in Hebrews 2:17.[25]

Moreover, the initiative is Christ's (or God's); the purpose is to destroy the enemy (verse 14), to deliver (verse 15), and to help (verse 16); and the basis is his mercy and faithfulness (verse 17). The immediate context of Hebrews 2:17 does not involve the wrath of God.[26] The dramatic emphasis of the chapter is the destruction of the devil (verses 14–15)[27] and not the dispelling of God's wrath.

Which interpretation or translation of *hilaskesthai* gives the correct meaning in the context of Hebrews 2:17? First, it is as high priest that Jesus is said to *hilaskesthai* (propitiate/expiate) "the sins of the people." When did Jesus' high priesthood begin, and does the answer to this question affect the interpretation of *hilaskesthai*? In the OT the priestly function only began with the handling of the blood, not with the killing of the

---

23. Smith, *Atonement in Light of History*, 159–60.
24. N. Young, "Hilaskesthai," 171–72.
25. N. Young, "Hilaskesthai," 172.
26. N. Young, "Hilaskesthai," 172.
27. Jewett, *Letter to Pilgrims*, 46.

animal. Leviticus 4:22–35 states that the person who brings the offering for sin is to slay the animal (verses 24, 29, and 33). After the animal is killed, the priest handles the blood (verses 25, 30, and 34). Just as the work of the priest began after the sacrifice had already been slain, the same is true for the ministry of Jesus. According to the writer of Hebrews, Jesus' ministry as high priest is a heavenly one (9:11–12) and does not directly refer to his sacrificial death. A propitiatory meaning is prohibited since his work as high priest begins only after his death.[28]

A lack of propitiatory meaning is even more apparent when comparing Hebrews 1:3 with 2:17. Hebrews 1:3 does refer to the death of Jesus but does not use the word *hilaskesthai*. Instead the author chooses to speak of "purification" (*katharismos*) for sins. Hebrews 1:3 refers to what Jesus did before reentering heaven: "After he had provided purification for sins, he sat down at the right hand of the Majesty in heaven." The choice of a different word than *hilaskesthai* as well as a different tense indicates that the writer wishes to convey a different meaning in 1:3 than in 2:17. The Greek aorist tense used in 1:3 to describe Jesus' death signifies action that occurs at a particular point in history. The Greek present tense, however, which is used in 2:17 to describe Jesus' ministry in heaven as high priest, involves a continuing action directed toward "the sins of the people."[29] Those who argue for a propitiatory meaning attempt to get around the fact that the action is ongoing by claiming a continuous present application of the completed work of Christ. However, verse 18, which speaks of the comfort that Jesus also continuously gives to his people, makes it clear that the reference is not to his death. The term *propitiate*, then, is inappropriate in 2:17 because the verse refers not to Christ's sacrificial death but to his ministry in heaven as high priest. The idea of Christ continuously propitiating (appeasing) God, as a description of his heavenly ministry, is clearly incorrect and unacceptable.[30]

The second important point demonstrating that a meaning of "propitiate" is incorrect is that the action of the verb *hilaskesthai* is directed toward "the sins of the people" and not toward God. Propitiation focuses the action on the wrath of God rather than upon sins.[31] Hebrews 2:17

---

28. Lunceford, "*Ilaskomai* Cognates," 35, 53.
29. Ellingworth, *Hebrews*, 188.
30. Lunceford, "*Ilaskomai* Cognates," 53–56.
31. Lunceford, "*Ilaskomai* Cognates," 53–56.

reveals that Jesus, as high priest, is continuously expiating (wiping out) the sins of the people who repent.

A careful reading of Hebrews 2:17–18 reveals the passage is not referring to the death of Christ. Christ is declared to be a faithful and merciful high priest based on his being "made like them, fully human in every way" (verse 17) and on his suffering temptation (verse 18). A reference to the death of Christ does occur in verse 14, but nothing is said of propitiation. The purpose of Christ's death is "that by his death he might break the power of him who holds the power of death—that is, the devil" (2:14).

To summarize, one cannot assign a propitiatory significance to *hilaskesthai* in Hebrews 2:17. The context (Jesus' priestly ministry, not his death), the verb tense (the continuing present, not a finished work), and the stated object of the action (sins, not God's wrath) all prove that expiation rather than propitiation is the correct meaning. Notably, the NIV translation of "make atonement for the sins of the people" has an expiatory meaning.[32] Atonement means reconciliation, which is brought about by the expiation of sin. We are constantly being put back into proper relationship with God by the forgiveness of our sins.

Hebrews 8:12

Hebrews 8:12 says, "For I will forgive [*hileōs*; KJV 'be merciful to'] their wickedness and will remember their sins no more." The background for Hebrews 8:8–12 is the new covenant promise of Jeremiah 31:31–34, and these verses are quoted extensively. The author's particular concern seems to be the divine promise of forgiveness. Hebrews 10:17 picks up this concern again, "Their sins and lawless acts I will remember no more," and verse 18 continues the promise, "And where these have been forgiven, sacrifice for sin is no longer necessary." The immediate context is again directly related to sin and the forgiveness of sin through the divine initiative and mercy in the death of Christ.[33]

---

32. Joining the NIV in translating "make atonement for" are the Lexham English Bible, the New English Translation, and the New Testament for Everyone, among others. The NRSV similarly translates "make a sacrifice of atonement for," while the New American Bible (Revised Edition) and the New Catholic Bible translate "expiate the sins of the people." Intriguingly, the KJV's "make reconciliation for" is changed to "make propitiation for" in the NKJV.

33. N. Young, "Hilaskesthai," 172.

1 John 2:2 and 4:10

As a noun, *hilasmos* is used in John's designation of Jesus as the "atoning sacrifice [KJV 'propitiation'/ RSV 'expiation'] for our sins" (1 John 2:2; 4:10). In Hebrew the cognate noun of the verb *kipper* is *kippurim*, translated "atonement." The Septuagint, not having an equivalent word for "an atonement," therefore uses *hilasmos* to represent the Hebrew *kippurim*. Thus Christ is the *hilasmos* (propitiation/expiation) for our sins. In 2:2 the context is Christ's advocacy with the Father (see verse 1). As advocate, Christ defends his people against the satanic charges of sin. Christ deprives Satan of the right to accuse Christians, as they are "cleansed" from sins (1 John 1:7, 9). His death as a sacrifice for sin constitutes his advocacy as demonstrated by the parallel structure in 1 John 1:6—2:1. The repeated refrains in verses 6, 8, and 10 indicate that they parallel each other, as do verses 7, 9, and 2:1. Having an advocate with the Father (2:1) parallels the blood of Jesus cleansing us from all sin (1:7) and his faithfulness to clean us from all unrighteousness (1:9).[34] Advocacy, then, refers to forgiving and cleansing of sin. The language is reminiscent of the Day of Atonement (as in Rom 3:25 and Heb 2:17). Leviticus 16:16, 30, and 34 relate thoughts parallel to 1 John 1:7, 9, and 2:1-2: "On this day atonement will be made for you, to cleanse you. Then, before the Lord, you will be clean from all your sins" (Lev 16:30). Once again the initiative belongs to God, for "this is love: not that we loved God, but that he loved us and sent his Son as an atoning sacrifice [*hilasmos*] for our sins" (1 John 4:10).[35] Christ is the sin offering, the sacrifice for sins. The context is not the wrath of God but the love of God.[36]

Luke 18:13

Luke 18:13 describes a tax collector going to the temple to pray: "He would not even look up to heaven, but beat his breast and said, 'God, have mercy [*hilasthēti*, "be propitious"] on me, a sinner.'" These words appear to be drawn from the penitential opening address of Psalm 51:1. The need is for God, from his grace, to be merciful and forgive. The tax collector has no illusions about his need for divine pardon and his

---

34. Lyonnet and Sabourin, *Sin, Redemption, and Sacrifice*, 149–53.
35. N. Young, "Hilaskesthai," 173–74.
36. Baillie, *God Was in Christ*, 187.

lack of any merits that he might plead as grounds for divine favor. The physical posture and position he assumes clearly indicate his feelings of unworthiness and total reliance upon God. He describes himself as a sinner and desires forgiveness and acceptance. Jesus declares to those "who were confident of their own righteousness" (verse 9) that the tax collector "went home justified before God" (verse 14). There is no hint of the prayer propitiating God, or of God propitiating himself. It is solely a matter of repentance, forgiveness, and pardon for mercy's sake.[37]

Romans 3:25

Romans 3:25 says that God presented Christ as the *hilasterion*, variously translated "mercy seat," "propitiation," "expiation," or "sacrifice of atonement." Virtually every word in this verse has been debated. (Appendix A examines the context and terminology of Romans 3:21–26 and offers a fuller exegesis of the passage.) Briefly, Paul is asserting that God presents Christ as a type of the mercy seat (*kapōret*, the gold cover of the ark of the covenant; see Exod 25:17–22). Universal human sin is the immediate context in which the divine activity operates, whether it be the sin of the Jew or Gentile (verse 23), past (verse 25) or present (verse 26).[38] Paul's argument is that God meant Christ's death to expiate sin, not only of the covenant people but of all humankind.[39] God's initiative is stressed (verse 25), and the object of the action is not God himself but human sin.[40] In this passage it is God who puts forward the means, Christ, whereby the guilt of sin can be removed.[41] The action is a result of God's grace and mercy (verse 24) and is not connected with the wrath of God unless one argues that 3:25 refers back to 1:18, which seems too far away for comfort.[42]

Although the immediate context of Romans 3:25 does not include the wrath of God, the broad context (chapters 1–3) does reference God's wrath. Romans 3:25 is the only verse in the NT in which one of the *hilaskesthai* cognates appears within a broad context containing the phrase

---

37. N. Young, "Hilaskesthai," 169–70.
38. N. Young, "Hilaskesthai," 170–71.
39. Price, "Righteousness," 276.
40. N. Young, "Hilaskesthai," 170–71.
41. Dodd, *Romans*, 55.
42. Ziesler, "Salvation," 358.

Exegetical Objections to the Penal Substitution Theory

"the wrath of God." Therefore, if a form of *hilaskesthai* were to take on a propitiatory significance anywhere in the NT it would be here. However, this passage is set in contrast with the discussion of the wrath of God in Romans 1:18–20 by the disjunctive "but now" in 3:21. Also, Paul follows the discussion of Romans 3 with the example of Abraham, who became righteous in God's sight through faith, totally apart from any kind of sacrifice or mention of the wrath of God (Rom 4:1–3).[43]

How should *hilasterion* be translated in Romans 3:25? The first issue is determining the grammatical form of the word. It has been taken as an adjective by some translators, with the meaning "that which serves to propitiate/expiate/atone" (depending on one's understanding of the verb *hilaskesthai*). If *hilasterion* is accepted as an adjective the problem of its meaning is not solved, for advocates of the adjective form disagree as to whether the word means expiatory or propitiatory. In addition, a noun for the adjective to modify must be added to the text because none is found in the Greek. Most scholars add "sacrifice."[44] An argument against such an addition is that in the 26 occurrences of the word in the LXX it always refers to a place and never to an offering.[45]

Although some modern translations, including the NIV, have chosen to use this adjective form ("sacrifice of atonement"), many translations have opted for the noun form. If taken as a neuter noun, *hilasterion* would be a typological reference to the mercy seat (Lev 16). What does this location represent? First, it is the place where God dwells (1 Sam 4:4; 2 Sam 6:2; Ps 80:1). Here God reveals himself to his people and speaks to Moses (Exod 25:22; Lev 16:2; Num 7:89). The mercy seat also designates the place where once a year on the Day of Atonement the blood of the sacrifice is sprinkled to make atonement for the sins of the people (Lev 16:14–15). Therefore, a translation of "mercy seat" in Romans 3:25 gives a typological interpretation of Jesus as the *hilasterion*, which is clear and appropriate.[46]

A second argument in favor of a translation of "mercy seat" is the context of Romans 3:25. Paul has described the sinfulness of the world and the sacrifice (blood) of Christ as the means of atonement. Paul contrasts the new salvation to the sinner's position under God's law and wrath

---

43. Lunceford, "*Ilaskomai* Cognates," 103–4.
44. Lunceford, "*Ilaskomai* Cognates," 99–101.
45. Barton, "Romans," 91.
46. Fryer, "Romans," 106.

(3:21) as well as under his forbearance (3:25b–26). This redemption was the fulfillment of what was prophesied by the Law and Prophets.[47] The context also speaks of the justification of the sinner (3:24; 5:1, 9) and the resulting reconciliation (5:10–11) and peace with God (5:1), which was the purpose of the Day of Atonement. Christ is then revealed as the new covenant mercy seat, the context fully supporting both the analogy and translation.[48] Additionally, "mercy seat" is the customary translation of *hilasterion* and the way it is translated in its only other use in the NT (Heb 9:5; NIV "atonement cover"). There is no reason to depart from this usage. Such a translation prevents the presuppositions and theological bias of the translators from becoming an issue in the translation process or outcome. Paul boldly represents Christ as the new mercy seat effective for atonement by his own blood and "presented" (3:25) for all to see.[49] By using the word *hilasterion* in Romans 3:25, Paul is saying that Christ has been "presented" by God as being to all people what the mercy seat was to Israel. The mercy seat was the place where God dwelt, the place from which he spoke, and the place where he forgave sins. Jesus brings forgiveness following not just a year, as on the Day of Atonement, but an entire age of sin that passed under God's forbearance.[50]

Conclusion: Propitiation or Expiation?

The aim of this section has been to determine the correct interpretation and translation of *hilaskesthai* in the NT. In classical usage, *hilaskesthai* and related words describe the appeasement, conciliation, or pacification of the wrath of a god or person who has been offended. By definition the term *propitiation* involves an action that moves *from* a person *to* a god or, occasionally, an offended person.

In NT usage, however, the action moves from God to humankind. This is made clear by the fact that in not a single case is God or any person the object of a form of *hilaskesthai*. Never does the NT say that God is propitiated. In the two cases where the verb is used (Heb 2:17 and Luke 18:13), Jesus or God is the subject. In addition, a distinctive NT usage is certainly indicated in 1 John, where *hilasmos* is directly associated with

---

47. Goppelt, *Typos*, 148.
48. Fryer, "Romans," 106–7.
49. Davies, *Romans*, 239.
50. Bailey, "Mercy Seat," 222.

Exegetical Objections to the Penal Substitution Theory

the love of God rather than the wrath of God. Also, in only one occurrence of a *hilaskesthai* cognate in the NT is the wrath of God discussed anywhere near the immediate context (Rom 3:25). In the case of Romans 3:25, Jesus as the *hilasterion* (mercy seat) is set in contrast with the wrath of God resting on all humankind (Rom 2). Just as the OT sacrificial ritual, which culminated in the action before the mercy seat on the Day of Atonement, was designed and given by God for the removal of sin, so Christ, as the NT mercy seat, is given by God (John 3:16) for the removal of sin and guilt. What was true of OT sacrifice is also true of NT sacrifice: it originates with God and is God's gift for the purpose of reconciling humans to himself.

The distinctive NT usage of *hilaskesthai* and its cognates denies any interpretation that refers to a process for propitiating God's wrath. The *hilaskesthai* cognates are used with reference to offenses against God, but these offenses are forgiven to restore fellowship between persons and God, which is radically different from the classical idea of propitiation. In the classical meaning, the offended god would do harm to the offender in a fit of rage unless the offender offered the appropriate gift or somehow appeased his anger. In the NT, the God of love offers the means of overcoming sin as a free gift to be received by faith so that a relationship of fellowship may be established between God and the repentant sinner. This idea is utterly foreign to the classical idea of propitiation.[51]

What do the *hilaskesthai* cognates in the NT denote if not propitiation? In Hebrews 2:17 the verb *hilaskesthai* is used with Jesus as subject and "the sins of the people" as direct object. Because Jesus' high priesthood begins after his resurrection, *hilaskesthai* describes what Jesus is doing to "the sins of the people," not what he did through his death and resurrection. In the only other passage in which this verb occurs (Luke 18:13), God is the subject and the sinner is the indirect object. The context does not involve any form of sacrifice. Both verbs, therefore, point to what God does to sin—expiate it—for the sinner.

The noun form, *hilasterion*, in Hebrews 9:5 is clearly a reference to the mercy seat, the place where God shows his mercy by forgiving and thereby expiating sin. This book argues for a translation of "mercy seat" also in the only other occurrence of *hilasterion* in the NT, Romans 3:25. Paul represents Christ as the new mercy seat effective for atonement put forward by God for all to see. In 1 John 2:2 Jesus is said to be the *hilasmos*

---

51. Lunceford, "*Ilaskomai* Cognates," 143–45.

"for our sins." The action is directed toward the barrier to fellowship with God—our sins. Johannine usage is consistent with biblical usage in general. God is not the object of Christ's work; rather, his work is directed toward human sin and defilement, leading to reconciliation. The sense is of expiation, because the reference is not to placating the wrath of God but to annulling the guilt of sin.

In 1 John 4:10 the action again is directly from God who "sent his Son to be the *hilasmos* for our sins." Once more the object of the action is sins, and the reason for the action is God's love, not his wrath. The translation "propitiation" is therefore as unsuitable here as it is elsewhere. Nowhere in the NT is God said to be propitiated.[52]

After examining the four NT usages of *hilaskesthai* and its cognates, it is apparent that no single English word fully captures the extent of its meaning. "Expiation" at least directs the action toward sin and is consistent with the biblical view that salvation originates with God, not with humans. However, expiation makes no reference to the restoration of relationship that results from the sinner repenting and receiving forgiveness. The correct connotation of *hilaskesthai* in the NT, then, is best understood by the word *atonement*. The concept of atonement involves God's action in overcoming sin and the sinner's response of repentance and faith. The result is the expiation of sin and the restoration of a relationship of fellowship. This meaning is consistent with the OT concept of atonement (*kipper*, translated *hilaskesthai* in the LXX) and with the events of the Day of Atonement.

The consistent revelation of Scripture is that God is gracious. The very meaning of propitiate, however, is to make one gracious. Therefore it simply cannot be true that God must be propitiated, that something must be done by his Son to make God what he already is—gracious. To say that Christ causes a gracious God to be gracious is contradictory. To say that God, who is gracious, gives to himself a propitiatory sacrifice so that he may be gracious is even more contradictory. Add to this that the action in Scripture is directed toward sin, not God, and is based on the love of God, not the wrath of God, and it is apparent that "propitiation" is an incorrect interpretation/translation. Some may call it a paradox, but contradictory statements cannot be dismissed simply by calling them paradoxical.[53] The contradictions come from faulty interpretation and translation.

---

52. Lunceford, "*Ilaskomai* Cognates," 146–47.
53. Morris, *Apostolic*, 179.

Christ in Scripture is revealed as the "Lamb of God, who takes away the sin of the world," not the Lamb of God who takes away the wrath of God.

JESUS AS MEDIATOR

Just as neither the word *hilaskesthai* nor the concept of God's wrath can authenticate the penal substitution theory, neither can the image of Jesus as the mediator of the new covenant be used to imply that he placated the wrath of God or made satisfaction to it. Hebrews 9:15 states that "for this reason Christ is the mediator of a new covenant, that those who are called may receive the promised eternal inheritance—now that he has died as a ransom to set them free from the sins committed under the first covenant." Hebrews 8:6 and 12:24 further clarify that this new covenant mediated by Jesus is superior to the old. The term *mediator* refers to someone whom God employs to interpret and confirm his covenant. God confirmed the old covenant through Moses (Gal 3:19). As the mediator of the first covenant, Moses stood between the people and God and proclaimed to them the word of God (Deut 5:1–5). It is in this same traditional sense that the word mediator is used in Hebrews. To be the mediator of a covenant is to be the messenger of that covenant, thereby procuring its implementation.[54]

One verse in the NT speaks of Jesus as mediator without specific reference to the covenant. First Timothy 2:5 calls Jesus the "one mediator between God and mankind." This verse portrays Jesus as the mediator in the sense of being the one who effects atonement or reconciliation between God and humanity. There is, however, no indication that Christ in any way propitiates God or satisfies his demand for justice. Neither does he mediate in the sense of coming to God on our behalf to convince God to be gracious. Jesus told his disciples, "In that day you will ask in my name. I am not saying that I will ask the Father on your behalf. No, the Father himself loves you because you have loved me and have believed that I came from God" (John 16:26–27).

THE WAGES OF SIN

A verse commonly put forward by proponents of the penal substitution theory is Romans 6:23: "For the wages of sin is death, but the gift of God

---

54. Godbey, "Socinus," 67–76.

is eternal life in Christ Jesus our Lord." This verse makes no statement concerning the reason for the death of Jesus. Eternal life, as God's gift, is contrasted with eternal death, which is the "wage" of sin (also in verses 16 and 21). It is God's judgment upon sin (Gen 2:17) that results in alienation from him and brings about eternal death ("those things result in death"; Rom 6:21). But nowhere does this verse insinuate that God is unable to forgive sin without satisfaction first being made to his justice.

Humankind outside of Christ is described as being dead in sin, without God, and without hope (Eph 2:1, 11–12), destined for the judgment of God (Heb 9:27) and condemnation (Rom 5:12–21).[55] This is the "wages of sin"—the situation to which God responds when he sends his beloved Son into the world. However, none of these passages make any statement indicating that God could not forgive sins apart from satisfaction of his justice.

THE MEANING OF CHRIST DYING "FOR US" OR "FOR OUR SINS"

Advocates of penal substitution maintain that Christ dying "for" humankind or "for our sins" is to say that he made satisfaction to divine justice for the sins of humanity. However, no verse in which such a phrase is found mentions divine justice. Ideas that are not stated in these verses, or in all of Scripture for that matter, are added to a simple phrase in order to come up with this interpretation.

To die for sins simply means to die "because of" sins. It is because of the situation caused by sin that it was necessary for Christ to come and die. One does not die "in place of" sins but "because of" sins. Christ dies to provide humankind freedom from sin, its guilt, its punishment, and its power. Christ "gave himself for us to redeem us from all wickedness and to purify for himself a people that are his very own, eager to do what is good" (Titus 2:14).

Many verses speak of Christ dying "for" humankind (Rom 4:25; 5:6, 8; 8:32; 14:15; 1 Cor 15:3; 2 Cor 5:14–15; Gal 1:4; 2:20; 1 Thess 5:10). Various texts portray Jesus at the Last Supper establishing the sacrament of Communion and defining it as "the new covenant in my blood, which is poured out for you" (Luke 22:20; "poured out for many" Matt 26:28; Mark 14:24). Jesus talked of giving his flesh for the life of the world (John

---

55. Letham, *Work of Christ*, 125.

Exegetical Objections to the Penal Substitution Theory

6:51). John records how the high priest Caiaphas unwittingly prophesied that Jesus was to die on behalf of the nation and the whole children of God (John 11:51–52). In 1 John 3:16, John writes of Christ that he "laid down his life for us." Paul points to the Father delivering him up "for" us all (Rom 8:32), to God's love displayed in Christ dying "for" us (Rom 5:8), to his having died "a ransom for all people" (1 Tim 2:6), to one having died "for" all (2 Cor 5:14), and to his having delivered himself up "for" the church (Eph 5:25) and "for us" (Eph 5:2). Jesus himself spoke of his role as a servant, to culminate when he would "give his life as a ransom for many" (Matt 20:28; Mark 10:45).[56] None of these verses, however, mention Jesus satisfying a demand from God for justice. To say that Jesus dies "for" humankind is surely to say that he dies for our sake or for our benefit. A similar meaning is seen in 1 John 3:16 and Colossians 1:24.[57]

SUMMARY OF EXEGETICAL OBJECTIONS

Exegetical objections to penal substitution are made based on a lack of scriptural support for the theory. As stated previously, this is not to say that there is a lack of scriptural support for the substitutionary death of Christ. Neither is there a lack of scriptural support for the penal suffering of Christ. All that Jesus underwent was because the world, since the time of the fall, had been under judgment, or the divine penalty of sin. (These two aspects of the Atonement will be examined in part 3.) However, these two factors do not in themselves amount to a theory of penal substitution in which atonement is achieved through a transfer of penalty in order to satisfy God's wrath or justice. Such a theory requires an Anselmian view of debt repayment (debt must be paid or satisfaction of some kind made) and a Roman view of criminal justice (retribution is required by justice). Advocates of penal substitution equate the idea of paying a debt to divine justice with a sacrificial ritual "propitiating" God. The effect is to portray atonement as a transaction, or legal settlement, between God the Father and God the Son. Although the idea of penal substitution references biblical texts, it nevertheless remains an interpretation of scriptural elements and therefore is only a theory of the Atonement.[58]

---

56. Letham, *Work of Christ*, 135.
57. Godbey, "Socinus," 111.
58. Fiddes, *Present Salvation*, 98–99.

This chapter considers the concepts of propitiation and expiation, concluding that expiation is the accurate scriptural view. To accept expiation instead of propitiation is not to abandon the wrath or judgment of God. Other scriptural concepts (Christ as mediator, the wages of sin, and Christ dying "for sins") commonly used in support of penal substitution also do not require acceptance of the penal substitution theory. Scriptures related to these concepts can be interpreted to support penal substitution, but they may also be legitimately interpreted in other ways.

CONCLUSION TO PART I—PENAL SUBSTITUTION NEED NOT BE THE DEFAULT

Part 1 of this book contends that the penal substitution theory of the Atonement will not bear the light of reason, conscience, or Scripture.[59] Without scriptural support, the theory can be rejected on the grounds of its affront to logic, morality, and theology.[60]

J. I. Packer, in his lengthy defense of the penal substitution theory, makes the following statement:

> Rationalistic criticism since Socinus has persistently called in question . . . the need for penal-satisfaction as a basis for forgiveness. This, however, is naturalistic criticism, which assumes that what man could not do or would not require God will not do or require either. Such criticism is profoundly perverse, for it shrinks God the Creator into the image of man the creature and loses sight of the paradoxical quality of the gospel of which the NT is so clearly aware. . . . The way to stand against naturalistic theology is to keep in view the reductionist method which makes man the standard . . . to stress that according to Scripture the Creator and his work are of necessity mysterious to us, . . . and to remember that what is *above* reason is not necessarily *against* it.[61]

This statement is tantamount to admitting that the penal substitution theory stands in opposition to humankind's reason and moral understanding. That God's ways are mysterious and above human reason is a common reaction of those with no answer for logical, moral, or

---

59. Forsyth, *Cruciality of the Cross*, 40.
60. Macquarrie, *Principles of Christian Theology*, 315.
61. Packer, "Cross," 35–36.

theological objections to the penal substitution theory. They argue that God is not human, or that God's ways are not our ways, or that God is a great mystery. These observations, though true, do not help provide an understanding as to how God has reconciled humanity to himself in and through the death of Christ. It is a worthy thing to seek such understanding. It is not, however, a worthy thing, in the face of unanswerable criticism, to rely on "it's a mystery" as an argument. That is tantamount to saying, "It's my theory and I'm sticking to it." Actually, one might find it acceptable if all advocates of penal substitution would argue that "it's my *theory*," rather than declare it as scriptural truth.

PART II

A Defense of the Ransom Theory

PART 2 DEFENDS THE ransom, or classic, theory of the Atonement through a thorough examination of its history and scriptural basis. The defense is largely based on the work of Swedish theologian Gustaf Aulén in his classic treatise *Christus Victor*, published in English in 1931. The NT foundation of the ransom theory is given to demonstrate the theory's compatability with Scripture and to provide background for how changing interpretations of scriptural concepts influenced the ransom theory's acceptance and rejection at various points in history. Finally, several objections to the ransom theory are presented and answered, and the theory is placed within the broader context of atonement theory.

4

Ransom Theory

Early Development and New Testament Support

THE "CLASSIC" IDEA OF THE ATONEMENT

THE RANSOM THEORY OF the Atonement is called by Gustaf Aulén the "classic" theory because it was the dominant concept of atonement throughout the early church period and for the first thousand years of church history. It would be difficult to overstate its long and honorable history in Christian doctrine. The history of the theory and the thought of those who espoused it is important because often the theory is presented as a set of crude and misguided ideas of long ago. Yet it did not suddenly spring into being in the early church, for this "dramatic" view of atonement, with its central theme of conflict and victory, is the dominant idea in the NT and is not derived from any other source.[1]

In the classic view, God in Christ triumphs over the powers of evil, which are hostile to his will. This dramatic idea of the Atonement differs significantly from other views. It does not set forth a change taking place in humans (as do subjective theories) or a change taking place in God (as in the penal substitution theory); it declares a complete change in the situation. Atonement is seen from the perspective of the story of the world's salvation.[2]

---

1. Aulén, *Christus Victor*, 6.
2. Aulén, *Christus Victor*, 4–6.

This chapter summarizes the work of Gustaf Aulén in his *Christus Victor* (1931). This work forms the classic, and singular, written defense of the ransom theory of the Atonement.

REASONS FOR THE NEGLECT OF THE CLASSIC VIEW

Prior to examining the classic view itself, an important question should be asked: Why has a view of atonement that held such a significant place in doctrinal history received negligible consideration from modern theologians? Several reasons may be suggested. The first is the controversial atmosphere of theology during the eighteenth and nineteenth centuries. At that time, historians of dogma were engaged in either attacking or defending the Protestant orthodoxy of the seventeenth century. The theologians of the Enlightenment attacked the orthodox penal substitution theory with vigor, and the controversy between "objective" and "subjective" views has continued ever since. The atmosphere was bitter, and the disputants had little attention to spare for other theories that lay outside their viewpoints.[3]

A second reason that the classic view has not been given much attention is that it is considered to have had only a temporary significance. Because it is an objective theory (the essential element being God's action rather than humanity's response), nineteenth-century theologians often treated it as the crude beginnings of the satisfaction theory. Neither the conservative theologians who defended the orthodox satisfaction view nor the liberals who attacked it gave serious consideration to the classic view. The conservatives disregarded the classic view because they believed it had never set forth a clearly formulated theory. They regarded it as representing a lower level of thought and as being able to contribute only images and symbolic expressions, not a precisely worked-out theological proposal. They believed that Anselm's proposal was far superior as a rationally expressed theory.[4]

The theologians of the liberal school criticized the forms in which the patristic teaching had expressed itself, especially the imagery of the deception of the devil and the victory of Christ over him. They considered the whole dramatic view "mythological." Examples of rejection of the ransom theory by both liberals and conservatives abound, with the

---

3. Aulén, *Christus Victor*, 7–8.
4. Aulén, *Christus Victor*, 8–9.

words "crude" and "grotesque" often being used to describe the theory. Many reject the concept of God "doing a deal" with Satan. Today's systematic theology books generally express the same attitude.[5] Unfortunately, their analysis goes no deeper than the surface layer of the theory, with no serious attempt being made to penetrate its shell and evaluate the underlying idea.[6]

The most important reason, however, that modern theologians have rejected the ransom theory is the unpopularity of dualism among liberal Protestant theologians of the eighteenth and nineteenth centuries.[7] The classic idea depicts the Atonement as a drama taking place in a dualistic world. If one does not believe in the existence of powers hostile to God, dualism is eliminated and there is no basis for the classic view. Of course, it is impossible for any theologian to deny the presence of a dualistic element in the NT. However, many have followed the Enlightenment, which branded dualism as demonological mythology and explained its occurrence as an accommodation on the part of Jesus and his disciples to then-contemporary thinking.[8]

THE THOUGHT OF THE CLASSIC THEORY AS IT DEVELOPED HISTORICALLY

Irenaeus and the Fathers

Every interpretation of the Atonement claims NT authority and seeks to base itself upon the text. It is difficult today to read the texts that have been cited in defense of a certain theory without associating them with

---

5. For example, Grudem allocates only a short paragraph to the theory in his *Systematic Theology*. He states that the ransom theory was "held by Origen . . . and after him by some others in the early history of the church." He also states that "this theory has no direct confirmation in Scripture and has few supporters in the history of the church." "This view," he says, "fails to deal with the texts that speak of Christ's death as a propitiation offered to God the Father for our sins, or with the fact that God the Father represented the Trinity in accepting the payment for sins from Christ" (581). Not one Scripture verse is referenced in the very brief discussion of the theory.

6. Aulén, *Christus Victor*, 9–11.

7. Aulén, *Christus Victor*, 4–5. Dualism is used only in the sense of the opposition between God and that which resists his will in his own created world, an idea which constantly occurs in Scripture. This is not to be confused with any other kind of dualism.

8. Aulén, *Christus Victor*, 11–12.

that theory. The teaching of the Fathers is significant because they had the obvious advantage of not having preconceived notions of the Atonement as they read the Scriptures and because of their proximity to the apostolic age. Irenaeus is the earliest patristic writer to treat the subject of the Atonement comprehensively. His view will be examined because it is thoroughly representative of the early church fathers. Having lived only a hundred years after the apostolic age, his writing is also significant because it is bound to throw light on the teaching of the apostles.[9]

According to Irenaeus the work of Christ is first and foremost a victory over the forces that hold humankind in bondage: sin, death, and the devil. The victory of Christ creates a new situation in which the rule of these forces has ended and humanity is free from their dominion. Irenaeus emphasizes three points: God himself, in Christ, overcomes sin, death, and the devil; God's victory through Christ is the central idea in restoring creation; and this restoration does not end with Christ's victory but continues through the work of the Holy Spirit in the church.[10] It will culminate with Christ's return.

What, according to Irenaeus, is the relationship between the forces of sin and death that are conquered in Christ? Sin is an objective power holding humans in a bondage that they cannot break. Sin is also something voluntary that alienates humans from God. There is an enmity between God and humanity expressed on God's side in punishment—the corruption that entered the world. Irenaeus views sin and death as inseparable because disobedience to God brings separation from him, and that separation is death.[11]

Irenaeus also emphasizes salvation as the conferral of life. Life means for him partaking of the life of God in fellowship with him, resulting in a liberation from sin. Sin is much more than wrong deeds; it is a state of alienation from God. Salvation is much more than freedom from sin's punishment; it is life in fellowship with God, or at-one-ment.[12]

To Irenaeus, Satan is the lord of sin and death. Men have followed him and may even be called his sons since they do his works. The victory of Christ is a victory over Satan, who leads humans into sin and has the power of death. Jesus, as a man, overcame him and made him subject to

---

9. Aulén, *Christus Victor*, 16.
10. Irenaeus, *Against Heresies*, 67, 152–60, 363; *Apostolic Preaching*, 64.
11. Irenaeus, *Ante-Nicene Fathers*, 47, 50–51, 93, 129.
12. Irenaeus, *Ante-Nicene Fathers*, 129.

humanity. Irenaeus also incorporates justice in his view of atonement. Although God is almighty he deals in a just way even with Satan. Humankind, after all, is guilty and has sold itself to the devil. God redeems that which was his own, not by violence, but by Christ giving himself as a ransom in exchange for humanity's deliverance.[13]

How, according to Irenaeus, is the actual work of atonement accomplished? Irenaeus does not emphasize just Christ's death. The obedience of Christ throughout his life also carries great weight. The disobedience of one man, which inaugurated the reign of sin and death, is answered by the obedience of another who brings life. It is Christ's obedience that is his triumph. The earthly life of Christ is regarded as a continuous process of conflict and victory and his death as the final, decisive battle. Atonement is the result of a new relation between God and the world, for God has delivered humankind from the powers of evil. Resurrection is the expression of that victory and deliverance. Following Christ's resurrection the Spirit continues the work of God in the earth through his people and within the souls of humankind.[14]

The ransom theory presents a clear and simple answer to the question, Why did God become human? God himself, in becoming a man, entered the world of sin and death to battle the powers of evil and achieve the decisive victory. This victory establishes a new relationship between God and the world; atonement has been made. God, in his great compassion, delivers humanity from the doom it faces. The work of redemption is accomplished by Christ as a man, but atonement does not depend on an offering made to God by Christ from humanity's side, as in penal substitution. From the beginning to the end God brings about redemption.[15]

The essential features of the classic view, as expressed in the teaching of Irenaeus, may be summarized as follows: This view of the Atonement has a dualistic framework accepting as reality forces of evil that are hostile to God. The work of atonement is depicted in dramatic terms as conflict with, and triumph over, the powers of evil. The work of atonement is carried out by God himself, not merely in the sense that he authorizes or initiates the plan of salvation, but that he is actually the one who brings it to pass. It is God himself who enters into the world to overcome the enemies that hold humanity in bondage. It is God's love that creates a

---

13. Irenaeus, *Ante-Nicene Fathers*, 51, 56, 121.
14. Irenaeus, *Against Heresies*, 358, 361.
15. Irenaeus, *Against Heresies*, 342; *Ante-Nicene Fathers*, 121.

new relationship between humanity and himself, a relationship that does not involve any sort of justification by legal righteousness.[16]

The Fathers in the East and the West

The same ideas found in Irenaeus recur like a theme in the later Fathers, with some interesting variations.[17] The classic idea of the Atonement was so widely held during this period that it may be said to dominate the whole of Greek patristic theology. Augustine's acceptance of the classic idea is especially significant because of his theological importance. In spite of philosophical differences among the Fathers, there is a basic agreement in their interpretation of Christ's work.[18]

A prominent characteristic of the teaching about redemption in the later Fathers involves the connection between the Incarnation and atonement. The central thought, like that of Irenaeus, is that God himself enters the world of sin and death for the deliverance of humanity, to take up the conflict with the powers of evil and bring about atonement between himself and the world. Gregory of Nazianzus sums up the purpose of the Incarnation in this way: "That God, by overcoming the tyrant, might set us free and reconcile us with Himself through His Son."[19]

Incarnation is central in the thinking of Athanasius as well. He argues that sin has subjected humanity to death's power, and therefore death has legal rights over the human race. But God does not abandon his purpose because his love for the fallen race endures in spite of his judgment upon them. He therefore becomes human that he might restore the life that was lost; the life of God enters the world and conquers death. The work of Christ is the overcoming of death and sin.[20] In one passage Athanasius asks whether God could have chosen some way other than that of the Incarnation. He answers that repentance might have sufficed for the gaining of salvation had sin been the only problem, and not corruption and death as a consequence of sin. The work of Christ relates not just to sin but also to the repercussions of sin in the world.[21] Athanasius

---

16. Irenaeus, *Ante-Nicene Fathers*, 113.
17. Aulén, *Christus Victor*, 35.
18. Aulén, *Christus Victor*, 37–39.
19. Aulén, *Christus Victor*, 42.
20. Athanasius, *Against the Arians*, 68, 163.
21. Athanasius, *On the Incarnation*, 56–57.

says that Christ came "that he might set all free from sin and the curse of sin, and that all might evermore live in truth, free from death, and be clothed in incorruption and immortality."[22] Death is overcome because sin is first overcome. Where there is no sin death has no power. Christ's victory over death, according to the Fathers, is the starting point for his present work in the world in which, through the Spirit, he continually breaks down sin's power.[23] In a similar way Gregory of Nyssa compares Christ's life, which overcomes death, to light that drives away darkness.[24]

The Greek Fathers frequently discuss whether God could not have saved humankind simply by choosing to use his power to overthrow the tyrants and restore the fallen. Although various answers are given, a frequent response is that God's righteousness would not have been manifested if he had used only his power. Some writers imply that the devil has certain rights over humankind that God respects. The argument that the devil has rights over humans, however, is never intended as a rational argument for the necessity of the Incarnation. Unlike Anselm the Fathers exhibit no preoccupation with rational demonstration.[25]

No other aspect of the teaching of the Fathers on the subject of redemption has provoked such criticism as their speculation concerning the dealings of Christ with the devil. It is mainly on this ground that their teaching has been generally regarded as unworthy of serious consideration. The judgment that Anselm marks a great advance in the early church doctrine rests primarily on his elimination of the idea of a transaction with the devil, along with the notion of a deception of the devil.[26]

The Fathers are by no means in agreement on the subject of Christ's handling of the devil, and on some points they differ sharply from one another. Their speculations, sometimes couched in mythological language, may be rejected without rejecting the underlying view of redemption. All agree that the devil was rightly and reasonably overcome, that humankind was created by God to belong to God, that the devil's dominion over humanity is a perversion of the right order, and that God is both creator and redeemer. The most common view is that ever since the fall the devil possesses a right over fallen humanity, and therefore a

---

22. Athanasius, Against the *Arians*, 69, 163.
23. Athanasius, Against the *Arians*, 69, 163.
24. Gregory of Nyssa, *Catechetical Oration*, 76–79.
25. Aulén, *Christus Victor*, 44–45.
26. Aulén, *Christus Victor*, 47.

settlement is necessary. Sometimes, however, the devil is regarded as a usurper without any rights. Both views may regard the devil as having been deceived by God or Christ.[27]

Gregory of Nyssa, for example, was anxious to show God's justice in our deliverance from the devil's power; he claimed that the way of salvation demonstrates not only God's love but also his wisdom and righteousness. God does not bring about his desire by force. Gregory uses redemption as the analogy: if a slave is set free by an act of violence, then they are not rightfully set free. He says, "In the same way, once we had sold ourselves freely, the one who was out of his goodness to lead us back again into freedom must think up a method of recall which was not tyrannical but just, and therefore must be one which allowed the captor to select any ransom he might choose in return for his captive."[28] This view, in the teaching of the Fathers, is considered to be the natural suggestion of the ransom image: the life of Christ paid as a ransom for humankind. Some, however, challenged this understanding of the ransom price. Gregory of Nazianzus, for instance, denied that the devil had any rights over humankind.[29]

In spite of some criticism, the idea of a transaction with the devil was firmly established in the early church and frequently recurs in the Fathers. It is often speculated that the devil exceeded his rights in his treatment of Christ and was therefore deprived of his rights and lost his kingdom. Thus Chrysostom, commenting on John 12:31 ("Now is the time for judgment on this world; now the prince of this world will be driven out"), writes:

> It is as if Christ said, "Now shall a trial be held, and a judgment be pronounced. . . . [The devil] smote the first man because he found him guilty of sin; for it was through sin that death entered in. But he did not find any sin in Me; wherefore then did he fall on Me and give Me up to the power of death? . . . How is the world now judged in Me? It is as if it were said to the devil at a seat of judgment: 'Thou didst smite them all because thou didst find them guilty of sin; wherefore then didst thou smite Christ? Is it not evident that thou didst this wrongfully? Therefore the whole world shall become righteous through Him.'"[30]

27. Aulén, *Christus Victor*, 48.
28. Gregory of Nyssa, *Catechetical Oration*, 73.
29. Aulén, *Christus Victor*, 49.
30. Aulén, *Christus Victor*, 50.

The same idea occurs in Augustine and in Luther, who quotes Chrysostom.[31] The idea of the deception of the devil brings about the use of much imagery in the writing of the Fathers. There are several variations on the theme that Christ's appearance (at the Incarnation) was incognito, his divine nature being hidden under his human nature. Origen quotes 1 Corinthians 2:7–8: "We declare God's wisdom.... None of the rulers of this age understood it, for if they had, they would not have crucified the Lord of glory." Gregory of Nyssa compares Christ to prey that Satan goes after like a fish goes after bait.[32] Augustine uses the simile of a mousetrap, with Christ again as the bait. However inappropriate the images may seem, the idea is still that God overcomes the devil by a sacrifice of himself. Evil is overcome not by an external use of force but by an internal self-offering. The idea behind the concept of a deal with the devil is not that Satan has power and is a force to be reckoned with; rather, it is a moral issue intended to express that God's dealings with the devil have the character of fair play. It asserts the responsibility of humans for their sin and maintains that the resulting judgment is righteous judgment. The power of evil, however, ultimately overreaches itself, and in doing so loses the battle.[33]

The following section will examine in greater detail the teaching of the NT that forms the basis of the dramatic view and ransom theory held by the church Fathers.

THE NEW TESTAMENT TEACHING

To most interpreters of the Atonement it is entirely self-evident that their doctrine is the scriptural doctrine. Protestant orthodoxy has taken it for granted that the theory of the satisfaction of God's justice is to be found everywhere in the NT as well as the OT. The assumption is that the satisfaction concept found in the penal substitution theory underlies Romans 3:25–26 and every other reference to wrath, redemption, sacrifice, the blood of Christ, Christ dying for sins, and Christ suffering for humanity's sake or in its stead.[34] This assumption was challenged in chapter 3.

---

31. Aulén, *Christus Victor*, 50–51.
32. Gregory of Nyssa, *Catechetical Oration*, 78.
33. Aulén, *Christus Victor*, 51–55.
34. Aulén, *Christus Victor*, 62.

This chapter will attempt to show that the classic interpretation of the victory of Christ is the dominant theme in Scripture underlying the meaning of the Atonement. It should be remembered, however, that the ransom idea, like all theories of the Atonement, is a *theory* based on this theme. But unlike the penal substitution theory, it is logical, moral, theologically sound, and based on a solid scriptural foundation.[35]

What is meant by a "solid scriptural foundation"? It is one which encompasses NT teachings on redemption, the bondage of humanity to sin and death, the nature of Satan's dominion in the world, the narrative of conflict, the crucifixion as the final battle, the resurrection as the declaration of Christ's triumph, the deliverance of humankind, freedom from the curse of the Law, and the nature of the Atonement that is effected through the work of Christ.

Redemption

The atoning work of Christ in the NT is expressed by the term *redemption*, a notion derived from the OT, and by the concept of "buying back," an idea used by Greek writers referring to the emancipation of slaves and expressed by the Greek verb *agorazō*, which refers to the marketplace (*agora*).[36] Paul uses this word twice in 1 Corinthians: "You are not your own, you were bought at a price" (1 Cor 6:19–20), and "You were bought at a price; do not become slaves of human beings" (1 Cor 7:23). He also speaks of redemption in Galatians, saying, "Christ redeemed us from the curse of the law" (Gal 3:13) and "God sent his Son . . . to redeem those under the law, that we might receive adoption to sonship" (Gal 4:4–5). Peter also mentions the Lord's purchase of humankind in reference to the lying teachers "even denying the sovereign Lord who bought them" (2 Pet 2:1). The book of Revelation speaks of the sacrifice of Christ: "You were slain, and with your blood you purchased for God persons from every tribe and language and people and nation" (Rev 5:9). Revelation 14:3 refers to those who "sang a new song before the throne," which nobody could sing except those 144,000 "who had been redeemed from the earth."

Because Scripture portrays humanity as being held in bondage, redemption is a theme that runs throughout the Old and New Testaments.

---

35. Aulén, *Christus Victor*, 61.
36. Lyonnet and Sabourin, *Sin, Redemption, and Sacrifice*, 104.

Verses that express this theme of redemption abound: "In him we have redemption through his blood (Eph 1:7); "[Christ Jesus] gave himself as a ransom for all people" (1 Tim 2:6); "He entered the Most Holy Place once for all by his own blood, thus obtaining eternal redemption" (Heb 9:12); "It was not with perishable things such as silver or gold that you were redeemed . . . but with the precious blood of Christ" (1 Pet 1:18); "To him who loves us and has freed us from our sins by his blood . . ." (Rev 1:5); and, "[Christ Jesus] has destroyed death and has brought life and immortality to light" (2 Tim 1:10). The express reason stated in Scripture for Christ's coming is to deliver humankind from the evil powers of sin, death, and the devil, which hold it in bondage. "The reason the Son of God appeared was to destroy the devil's work" (1 John 3:8b).[37]

The blood of Christ (Rev 5:9) shed in becoming a curse "for us" (Gal 3:13) is the price of the acquisition of which 1 Corinthians 6:20 and 7:23 speak. The work of redemption is understood according to the laws of buying and selling inasmuch as Christ paid the price to someone. According to the NT, the master under whose rule the sinner lived was the devil. Although it is nowhere explicitly stated in the NT (and thus remains theory), one can logically conclude that the contract of purchase, so to speak, was made with the devil and that to him the price was paid.[38]

The price was paid to free the slave from bondage, and the NT emphasizes this new freedom: "If the Son sets you free, you will be free indeed" (John 8:36). However, this new freedom creates a paradox. The Christian is no longer their own (1 Cor 6:20) but is a slave of Christ (1 Cor 7:23). One is redeemed in love (John 3:16) that they might belong to God.[39]

This notion of acquisition, found throughout the OT, reveals God's unchanging purpose, the purchase of a people for himself. This purchase includes liberation from Egyptian slavery. God calls Israel his "treasured possession . . . a kingdom of priests and a holy nation" (Exod 19:5–6; see 1 Pet 2:9; Rev 5:10); "You are his people, his treasured possession" (Deut 26:18; see Deut 7:6; 14:2); and "the nation you purchased long ago, the people of your inheritance, whom you redeemed" (Ps 74:2; also 135:4). Concerning the future acquisition *in the messianic times* God says, "On the day when I act, . . . they will be my treasured possession. I will spare

---

37. Aulén, *Christus Victor*, 65–66.
38. Lyonnet and Sabourin, *Sin, Redemption, and Sacrifice*, 105.
39. Lyonnet and Sabourin, *Sin, Redemption, and Sacrifice*, 109.

them, just as a father has compassion and spares his son who serves him" (Mal 3:17).

The ideas of purchase or acquisition and liberation seem to be virtually identical. The liberation from Egyptian slavery corrected the negative situation, while the acquisition, effected by the Sinaitic covenant, formed the positive aspect of Israel's redemption. In Jeremiah 31:31–32 (quoted in Heb 8:8–9) the prophet makes the Sinaitic covenant coincide with the very day of Passover: "'The days are coming,' declares the Lord, 'when I will make a new covenant with the people of Israel and with the people of Judah. It will not be like the covenant I made with their ancestors [the Sinaitic covenant] when [at the Passover] I took them by the hand to lead them out of Egypt.'" It is clear from these verses that the idea of redemption in the OT forms the background and context for the concept of redemption in the NT.[40]

The NT speaks explicitly not only of liberation but also of God purchasing a people for himself. First Peter 2:9 uses the very words of Exodus 19:5, "You are a chosen people, a royal priesthood, a holy nation, God's special possession." Titus 2:14 joins the ideas of purchase and liberation or redemption: "[Christ] gave himself for us to redeem us from all wickedness and to purify for himself a people that are his very own [redeemed], eager to do what is good." In Acts 15:14 James relates "how God first intervened to choose a people for his name from the Gentiles." In Acts 20:28 Paul says, "Be shepherds of the church of God, which he bought with his own blood." It is evident that the blood is not offered to God. What God does receive is a people whose sins had separated them from their Father. They become his precious possession that he had "lost" but now has "found" again.[41] In other words, a purchase effected by God in Christ liberates humankind, the emancipation being essentially an acquisition or reunion of humanity with God.[42]

The Greek term *agorazō* (buy or purchase) is used in the NT according to the Greek social condition of slaves, freedmen, and a contract of purchase, but it has been infused with the OT idea of acquisition. It can only be understood by remembering that God not only freed humankind but also purchased a people for himself. The phrase used in Ephesians 1:14, "The redemption [Greek: *apolytrōsis*] of those who are God's

---

40. Lyonnet and Sabourin, *Sin, Redemption, and Sacrifice*, 110–12.
41. Lyonnet and Sabourin, *Sin, Redemption, and Sacrifice*, 112–15.
42. Lyonnet and Sabourin, *Sin, Redemption, and Sacrifice*, 115–19.

possession," confirms that Paul understood the idea of purchasing as an aspect of redemption. Here the idea of purchase or acquisition explains or even defines the idea of redemption. Understood in this way, the term *redemption* is closely related to *atonement* according to its etymology, at-one-ment.

Bondage to Sin

The redemption theme appears in the words of Jesus concerning his mission: "The Son of Man did not come to be served, but to serve, and to give his life as a ransom for many" (Mark 10:45). He states that humans are in bondage to sin and that his purpose is to set them free.

> To the Jews who had believed him, Jesus said, "If you hold to my teaching, you are really my disciples. Then you will know the truth, and the truth will set you free." They answered him, "We are Abraham's descendants and have never been slaves of anyone. How can you say that we shall be set free?" Jesus replied, "Very truly I tell you, everyone who sins is a slave to sin. Now a slave has no permanent place in the family, but a son belongs to it forever. So if the Son sets you free, you will be free indeed." (John 8:31–36)

To understand what Jesus came to accomplish, in what way he came to set humankind free, the nature of sin itself must be examined. What is this sin that binds, and how does Christ bring freedom? Sin is a force that holds humans in bondage, a reality deeper than the external deeds that manifest its presence. John also speaks of sin as *anomia* ("lawlessness," or "iniquity" KJV) in 1 John 3:4.[43] The context, 1 John 3:3–10, contrasts the sinner and the Christian by comparing their moral behavior and by indicating what inward reality motivates or inspires their actions. John describes the

---

43. Lyonnet and Sabourin, *Sin, Redemption, and Sacrifice*, 42–43. Most commentators believe that *anomia* means what its etymology suggests, *anomos*, "lawlessness," disobedience to the law. According to this view John was commanding the keeping of the law against liberties who maintained that sin lies outside the realm of morality. In that case, however, would not John have written, "Any transgression of the law is sin," just as he wrote in 5:17, "All wrongdoing (*adikia*) is sin"? Also, law is not mentioned in the context of 3:4. In addition, nowhere in the NT is *anomia* related to *nomos*, "law." In the LXX, *anomia* had become practically a synonym for *hamartia*, just as in the Jewish apocryphal literature. At Qumran *anomia* was the Greek equivalent of *awel*, "iniquity." A similar meaning is found in Matthew, the long ending of Mark, and also in the writings of Paul.

sinner's inward spiritual state. To commit sin is not only to make a wrong choice, it is "iniquity," revealing the sinner's inner condition. Again, the problem of sin runs deeper than straying from God's way.[44]

This view of sin is also indicated by Christ's words to the Pharisees: "You brood of vipers, how can you who are evil say anything good? For the mouth speaks what the heart is full of" (Matt 12:34). His words on what defiles teach the same view of sin, that it lies in the very heart of humans (Matt 15:10–20; Mark 7:14–23). "For it is from within, out of a person's heart, that evil thoughts come—sexual immorality, theft, murder, adultery, greed, malice, deceit, lewdness, envy, slander, arrogance and folly. All these evils come from inside and defile a person" (Mark 7:21–23). This concept of sin makes it obvious that forgiveness without a change of heart (repentance) would be ineffective. Thus when Christ called people to himself he said, "The kingdom of God has come near. Repent and believe the good news!" (Mark 1:15).[45]

Although the Synoptics speak of "the remission of sins" (always in the plural), in John's gospel Christ "takes away the sin of the world" (in the singular; 1:29). Although John occasionally also uses the plural (20:23; 1 John 2:12), a state or a power is suggested by his use of the singular. In what way did Christ "take away the sin of the world"? When Christ communicates the Holy Spirit to humans (John 1:33) he gives them the means to avoid sin and therefore be rescued from its dominion.[46] Paul speaks of Christians as "led by the Spirit" (Rom 8:14) and exhorts them to "walk by the Spirit" that they "not gratify the desires of the flesh" (Gal 5:16). Christ "takes away sin" because, in the words of John's First Epistle, "In him is no sin. No one who lives in him keeps on sinning" (3:5–6). Again, "No one who is born of God will continue to sin, because God's seed remains in them; they cannot go on sinning, because they have been born of God" (3:9). The opposition between God and sin is such that communion with him destroys sin. The Christian's resistance to sin is measured by the extent of their depending on God's life within them. It corresponds to the degree to which God's word, taught by the Spirit, becomes their inward standard of conduct.[47] It is in this sense, then, that Christ came to take away the sin of the world.

---

44. Lyonnet and Sabourin, *Sin, Redemption, and Sacrifice*, 42–43.
45. Lyonnet and Sabourin, *Sin, Redemption, and Sacrifice*, 34–35.
46. Lyonnet and Sabourin, *Sin, Redemption, and Sacrifice*, 38–41.
47. Lyonnet and Sabourin, *Sin, Redemption, and Sacrifice*, 41–42.

Romans 3:9 and Galatians 3:22 declare that all humankind is under the dominion of sin. From Romans 5:12 to 8:10 the term *sin* in the singular occurs forty times. In these chapters of Romans (5–8), sin is depicted as a power which, having entered into the world through Adam's transgression, has infiltrated all of humanity (5:12–21) and affects even the material world (8:19–22). This power dwells within humans and operates through their flesh (7:18, 25b; 8:3–13) or their mortal bodies (6:12; 8:13). This power is not Satan—a hostile power outside humanity—but since Satan acts through sin, Paul can say in Romans 7:11 that sin seduces humans just as the serpent seduced Eve (Gen 3:13). In Romans 8:3 he declares that God sent his Son, who "condemned sin," just as John sees that "the prince of this world now stands condemned" (John 16:11). Satan is "driven out" when Jesus is "lifted up" to be crucified (John 12:31–32).[48]

In Romans 7:7–24 Paul speaks of the slavery of humanity as being "sold as a slave to sin" (verse 14). How can humankind be liberated from this bondage to sin? Because sin dwells in the innermost part of humans, in the free will itself, it follows that freedom from sin requires more than just a pardon. It requires a response of one's self-determination. When a person responds to God in repentance and faith, they become a new creation (2 Cor 5:17) and have the opportunity to live a new life (Rom 6:4, 6) in which the governing power is the Spirit: "Through Christ Jesus the law of the Spirit who gives life has set you free from the law of sin and death" (Rom 8:2). Sin is a "law," a power resulting in death, but the Spirit of God gives life. Humans are thereby liberated from slavery to sin and its resultant death.[49] In this view, the power of sin is broken, humanity has been freed, and a change occurs in humankind itself through redemption. This represents a much broader concept of redemption than a juridical or forensic event in which the removal of the penalty of sin constitutes salvation.[50]

Sin Leads to Death

Sin occupies the central place among the powers that hold humans in bondage; others stand in direct relation to it. Death, personified as "the last enemy to be destroyed" (1 Cor 15:26), is always closely connected

---

48. Lyonnet and Sabourin, *Sin, Redemption, and Sacrifice*, 55.
49. Lyonnet and Sabourin, *Sin, Redemption, and Sacrifice*, 56–57.
50. Lyonnet and Sabourin, *Sin, Redemption, and Sacrifice*, 294.

with sin. If sin reigns, death reigns also. To be freed from sin's rule through Christ is also to be delivered from death's dominion: "Just as sin reigned in death, so also grace might reign through righteousness to bring eternal life through Jesus Christ our Lord" (Rom 5:21).[51] Sin separates humankind from God and leads to death, the definitive separation from God.[52] From death, too, Christ came to set humanity free, "that by his death he might break the power of him who holds the power of death—that is, the devil—and free those who all their lives were held in slavery by their fear of death" (Heb 2:14–15).

Romans 5–8 asserts the link between sin and death not less than 15 times. Even here on earth sinners receive "the wages of sin" (i.e., death) and are now perishing (Rom 6:23; 2 Cor 2:15–16) just as the righteous enjoy even now the firstfruits of the Spirit and are now being saved (Rom 8:14–17, 23; 2 Cor 2:15–16). Death is not just the punishment of sin; it is its result, for "those things result in death" (Rom 6:21). Death, as the wages of sin, includes both "temporal" and "eternal" death (Rev 2:11; 20:6, 14).[53]

Just as sin is much more than transgressions that need to be forgiven, so is death more than physical death. It is a state of separation from God, which is a result of sin. In delivering humans from death, Jesus is effecting at-one-ment, eliminating our alienation from God.

Sin Means Domination by Satan and the Powers of Evil

According to the NT the source of the spiritual reality of *anomia*, "iniquity," is the devil: "The one who does what is sinful is of the devil" (1 John 3:8), belongs "to the evil one" (3:12), is "from the world" (2:16; 4:5) and a "[child] of the devil" (3:10; John 8:44). Just as Christians live under the influence of God within them, so do sinners live under the influence of the devil.[54]

This influence is pervasive, for "the whole world is under the control of the evil one" (1 John 5:19). For Jesus, Satan was the "strong man," and the world was "the strong man's house" (Matt 12:29). Just as Jesus proclaimed the coming of God's kingdom, he acknowledged the present reign of Satan.[55]

---

51. Aulén, *Christus Victor*, 67.
52. Lyonnet and Sabourin, *Sin, Redemption, and Sacrifice*, 43.
53. Lyonnet and Sabourin, *Sin, Redemption, and Sacrifice*, 55.
54. Lyonnet and Sabourin, *Sin, Redemption, and Sacrifice*, 44.
55. Aulén, *Christus Victor*, 76.

The NT likewise speaks of an array of other forces hostile to God: "principalities," "powers," "thrones," and "dominions" (Rom 8:38; Eph 1:21; 6:12; Col 1:16; 2:15) that rule "the present evil age" (Gal 1:4). God has permitted them to have dominion temporarily. Satan is undoubtedly the leader of these demonic forces (1 John 5:19; Rev 20:2), and it is into this world that Christ comes to defeat the evil power and dethrone the devil: "Now is the time for judgment on this world; now the prince of this world will be driven out" (John 12:31). The broad purpose of Christ's coming is stated in 1 John 3:8: "The reason the Son of God appeared was to destroy the devil's work." In Jesus "the prince of this world now stands condemned" (John 16:11).[56]

Christ's mission is inaugurated by facing Satan himself in a conflict Luke explicitly links with the final clash of the passion (Luke 4:1–13; 22:3, 53).[57] In this first confrontation Satan says to Christ, "I will give you all their [the kingdoms of the world] authority and splendor; it has been given to me, and I can give it to anyone I want to" (Luke 4:6).[58] This initial confrontation becomes a lifelong conflict. Peter speaks of the life of Jesus, in which he "went around doing good and healing all who were under the power of the devil" (Acts 10:38). The disciples also joined themselves in the battle (Mark 3:15; 6:7). Upon returning from a mission, the seventy-two celebrated: "Lord, even the demons submit to us in your name" (Luke 10:17). Paul's mission to the pagan nations is to "turn them from darkness to light, and from the power of Satan to God" (Acts 26:18).[59] Paul declares to the Gentiles that they no longer have to live in darkness or remain in the kingdom of Satan. They are free.

The triumph over hostile powers is essential to Paul's thought. They are not as yet entirely destroyed, however. Rather, Paul looks to the "end" when all power shall be taken from Christ's "enemies." Christ shall at last deliver up the kingdom of the Father, "after he has destroyed all dominion, authority and power" and "put all his enemies under his feet" (1 Cor 15:24–25), with the ultimate triumph "that at the name of Jesus every knee should bow, in heaven and on earth and under the earth" (Phil 2:10).[60]

---

56. Lyonnet and Sabourin, *Sin, Redemption, and Sacrifice*, 35–36.
57. Lyonnet and Sabourin, *Sin, Redemption, and Sacrifice*, 35–36.
58. Helm, "Doctrine of the Atonement," 260.
59. Lyonnet and Sabourin, *Sin, Redemption, and Sacrifice*, 35–36.
60. Aulén, *Christus Victor*, 70.

The Battle

The synoptic narrative tells us that on three different occasions Satan tried to deceive and weaken the will of the Son of God: once at the beginning, a second time at the turning point, and the third time at the very end of his life. In the wilderness temptation, Satan himself answers the baptismal proclamation with a strong counterattack (Mark 1:12–13). In Matthew 16:23 he speaks through the mouth of Peter, the trusted disciple of Christ. In Gethsemane the demonic attack on the Son's will takes its most severe form (Mark 14:33–34). Jesus cries out to his Father with his desire to be delivered from death and asks if there is any other way to accomplish God's will (Mark 14:35–36). Throughout Christ's life the attacks of the adversary are repelled; he never succumbs to the seductions of the serpent. Shortly before his death, Christ declared, "The prince of this world is coming. He has no hold over me" (John 14:30). Jesus' exercise of his free will in obedience to God in his earthly life and in his death provides salvation for "whoever will" and alters the course of history.[61]

The life of Jesus as a battle, however, was not just one of defense against the assaults of Satan and the demons; he went on the attack.[62] Jesus enters the earthly battlefield as the all-powerful opponent (Matt 12:29; Luke 11:17–22; recall also 1 John 3:8; Mark 4:39). He knows the powers that are hostile to creation and he subdues them. He knows the demons that work mischief in the hearts of humans and he overcomes them. He restores to health all who have become ill at the hand of Satan (Acts 10:38). The demons know who is before them, and fear grips them (Mark 1:24). Yet they make a legal protest—their time has not yet come: "Have you come here to torture us before the appointed time?" (Matt 8:29). Jesus does not taunt them, neither does he carry out final sentence upon them. But whenever he confronts them he drives them out, for God is with him (Mark 5:12–13; Acts 10:38). Hence Jesus' teaching concerning the kingdom has a polemical quality: "But if I drive out demons by the finger of God, then the kingdom of God has come upon you" (Luke 11:20). The kingdom of God exists where the dominion of the adversary is overthrown.[63]

---

61. Stauffer, *New Testament Theology*, 124.
62. Stauffer, *New Testament Theology*, 124.
63. Stauffer, *New Testament Theology*, 124.

The Victory: Crucifixion and Resurrection

According to Scripture, the crucifixion and death of Jesus wins the decisive, if not the final, victory over Satan. That Satan was plotting the crucifixion is clear from his direct "entering" of Judas, leading him to betray Jesus (Luke 22:3). If "the rulers of this age" are interpreted to be the "principalities and powers," then it is revealed that these rulers did not know what would be the results of their crucifying Jesus, for had they known, they would not have done so (1 Cor 2:8). Christ's victory over the forces of evil through his death is expressed in Colossians 2:15: "Having disarmed the powers and authorities, he made a public spectacle of them, triumphing over them by the cross."[64]

The victory of Christ is seen not just in his death, but also in his life. He allows nothing to turn him from his purpose of living in perfect obedience to God, which constitutes his victory (Phil 2:8; Rom 5:19). The crucial moments in the path to victory are the temptation, the decision to go steadfastly toward Jerusalem, the anguish in the garden, and, finally, his suffering and death. As he approached his death, Jesus said to his disciples, "I will not say much more to you, for the prince of this world is coming. He has no hold over me" (John 14:30). The victory of obedience was finished when he cried out, "Father, into your hands I commit my spirit" (Luke 23:46).[65] The resurrection and exaltation of Jesus is the sign and seal of that victory. All the powers of evil, including death itself, could not hold the sinless Christ, whom "God raised . . . from the dead, freeing him from the agony of death, because it was impossible for death to keep its hold on him" (Acts 2:24). The classic theory interprets this to mean that the demonic world had no power to hold him because it had no right to punish him.[66]

The book of Revelation depicts Christ as the Lamb *and* the Lion, images that each reflect conflict and victory. "Worthy is the Lamb, who was slain, to receive power . . ." (5:12); "The Lion of the tribe of Judah . . . has triumphed" (5:5).[67] The NT quotes Psalm 110:1 in speaking of the victory of Christ over all enemies: "The Lord said to my Lord: Sit at my right hand until I make your enemies a footstool for your feet" (Acts 2:34; Heb 1:13). The NT also speaks of the end of the age as the final victory of

---

64. Aulén, *Christus Victor*, 65–66.

65. Gerrish, "Atonement and 'Saving Faith,'" 189–90.

66. Stauffer, *New Testament Theology*, 133.

67. Stauffer, *New Testament Theology*, 74.

Christ over all enemies: "Then the end will come, when he hands over the kingdom to God the Father after he has destroyed all dominion, authority and power. For he must reign until he has put all his enemies under his feet. The last enemy to be destroyed is death" (1 Cor 15:24–26). Clearly, Christ's death as a victory over Satan is plainly and repeatedly stated. Any atonement theory, therefore, that omits this aspect of the work of Christ contains a critical omission.[68]

The Purpose: Deliverance from Sin and the Law

The victory of Christ over Satan brings about a new situation for the world. Humankind, due to sin, had fallen into the power of the adversary, but the work of redemption changed that. Redemption is ransom (1 Tim 2:6; 2 Pet 2:1). *From* whose ownership was humanity ransomed? From the curse of the law is the answer that Paul gives in Galatians 3:13, explaining that this curse involves subjection to the elementary powers of this world (Gal 4:3–5; see also Col 2:20). *For* whom was humankind ransomed? That answer is given in Revelation 5:9: "And with your blood you purchased for God persons from every tribe and language and people and nation." Ransom is liberation from the power of darkness into the kingdom of God (Luke 1:71; Acts 26:18; Rom 6:18; 8:2; Gal 1:4; Col 1:13–14; 1 Pet 2:9). The classic theory interprets this to mean that God takes seriously his own world order resulting from his judgment on humanity. Therefore, he sacrifices his own Son to save the world in a way that does not dispense with this order.[69]

In Scripture, redemption is closely related to the forgiveness of sins, for in Jesus Christ there is "redemption through his blood, the forgiveness of sins" (Eph 1:7; see also Luke 1:68, 77; Rom 3:24; 1 Cor 1:30; Col 1:14; Heb 9:15). The classic theory interprets this to mean that Christ's victory makes settling the problem of sin possible.[70] Jesus "gave himself for us to redeem us from all wickedness" (Titus 2:14), and in doing so he also "destroyed death" (2 Tim 1:10). According to the classic theory this deliverance of humankind from the bondage of sin, death, and the devil is the end, or purpose, of the work of Christ.

---

68. Worrall, "Substitutionary Atonement," 356.
69. Stauffer, *New Testament Theology*, 136–37.
70. Stauffer, *New Testament Theology*, 136–37.

The triumph of Christ also provides deliverance from the law. The law, of course, is not an evil power, but it relates to sin in that it creates awareness of the standard (Rom 5:13; 7:7–13), causing failure to be manifested openly (Rom 5:20–21).[71] The law is "holy, righteous and good" (Rom 7:12), and yet "the sting of death is sin, and the power of sin is the law" (1 Cor 15:56). As a result, "all who rely on the works of the law are under a curse" (Gal 3:10). Deliverance from the law is needed because it cannot deliver from the power of sin. Paul says, "When the commandment came, sin sprang to life and I died" (Rom 7:9). Thus the law is an enemy from whose tyranny Christ came to save: "You also died to the law through the body of Christ, that you might belong to another, to him who was raised from the dead" (Rom 7:4); "Christ redeemed us from the curse of the law" (Gal 3:13) and has "canceled the charge of our legal indebtedness, which stood against us and condemned us; he has taken it away, nailing it to the cross" (Col 2:14). Humans no longer need strive to achieve righteousness in an impossible way, for "Christ is the culmination of the law so that there may be righteousness for everyone who believes" (Rom 10:4). The law is no longer the way in which humans relate to God.[72]

Atonement and Its Dual Drama

Because Christ brings the law to an end, righteousness that comes by law cannot reconcile God and the world. The triumph of Christ over the powers of evil whereby he delivers humanity is a work of salvation and atonement, for the two ideas cannot be separated. Salvation, in which Christ overcomes evil, makes possible atonement, or reconciliation between God and humans. God, through Christ, establishes a new relationship and provides a way of salvation for humankind from his own judgment and his own law.[73] "All this is from God, who reconciled us to himself through Christ and gave us the ministry of reconciliation: that God was reconciling the world to himself in Christ, not counting people's sins against them. And he has committed to us the message of reconciliation" (2 Cor 5:18–19).

---

71. Lyonnet and Sabourin, *Sin, Redemption, and Sacrifice*, 55.

72. Aulén, *Christus Victor*, 67–68.

73. Aulén, *Christus Victor*, 71.

Christ's deliverance of humanity can also be viewed in cosmic terms without much difficulty. If the NT word *Satan* is accepted as designating a reality and not a myth, then the history of salvation, including the atoning death of Christ, becomes one momentous struggle between two kingdoms. All world events press toward the goal expressed in Revelation 12:9–11:

> The great dragon was hurled down—that ancient serpent called the devil, or Satan, who leads the whole world astray. He was hurled to the earth, and his angels with him. Then I heard a loud voice in heaven say: "Now have come the salvation and the power and the kingdom of our God, and the authority of his Messiah. For the accuser of our brothers and sisters, who accuses them before our God day and night, has been hurled down. They triumphed over him by the blood of the Lamb and by the word of their testimony; they did not love their lives so much as to shrink from death. Therefore rejoice, you heavens and you who dwell in them!"

Viewing Satan and evil powers as realities results in a dualistic doctrine of the Atonement whose main theme is the struggle with Satan.[74]

This dramatic view of the Atonement includes two additional consequences of the struggle. The devil and death over which Christ triumphs are also, from another point of view, the executants of God's judgment on sinful humanity. Humanity is under the judgment of God and in bondage to Satan. Liberation from the powers of sin, death, and the devil is at the same time deliverance from God's judgment on sin. The law, like the tyrants holding humanity in bondage, is considered an enemy from which humankind needs to be delivered.[75]

Summary of the New Testament View

The teaching of the NT itself provides a solid foundation for the classic view of the Atonement. The teaching of the early church is clearly based on a view of the Atonement that permeates the NT and does not present logical, moral, or exegetical problems. In neither the NT nor the early

---

74. Helm, "Doctrine of the Atonement," 264–65.
75. Aulén, *Christus Victor*, 55–56.

church is there a rationally developed theological doctrine of the Atonement, but rather both express a motif repeatedly and in many ways.[76]

On the other hand, as has been demonstrated in chapter 3, the NT does not reflect the particular features of the satisfaction theories (of Anselm or penal substitution), as the idea of satisfaction grew up in Western Christendom and was based on the doctrine of penance. Aulén says that "many have attempted to find in the NT the Latin doctrine of the Atonement" primarily because the classic view "had dropped clean out of sight so that theologians had no conception of the possibility of any other idea of the Atonement than the so-called objective doctrine on the one hand [satisfaction] and the so-called subjective view [moral-influence] on the other."[77] We will see that the rise of the satisfaction theory, unlike the classic theory, did not originate in the teaching of the NT.

---

76. Aulén, *Christus Victor*, 78.

77. Aulén, *Christus Victor*, 78–80. William P. Loewe, although a critic of Aulén, credits Aulén with revealing the incompleteness of this objective-subjective representation. "*Christus Victor* Revisited," 1–2.

5

Luther's View and Common Objections to the Ransom Theory

To gain greater historical perspective on the adoption of penal substitution by much of Protestant orthodoxy, some discussion is needed regarding the rise of the idea of satisfaction, the position of Luther and his successors, and the outlook of the Enlightenment and subsequent centuries. Luther's view is considered because he has been commonly claimed by supporters of the satisfaction view, when in fact his view was classic.

SATISFACTION PRIOR TO THE REFORMATION

The satisfaction doctrine had its beginnings early in the Patristic Period in the Western church, although it was never the dominant view even in the West. Tertullian taught the basic concepts of satisfaction and merit, and upon these ideas Cyprian built a theory of the Atonement. Satisfaction is the compensation that a person may make for their fault. He writes:

> How absurd it is to leave the penance unperformed, and yet expect forgiveness of sins! What is it but to fail to pay the price, and, nevertheless, to stretch out the hand for the benefit? The Lord has ordained that forgiveness is to be granted for this price:

He wills that the remission of the penalty is to be purchased for the payment which penance makes.[1]

Thus penance is satisfaction, the receipt of temporal penalty to escape eternal loss.[2]

The idea of merit is related to the performance of that which is commanded, the observance of the law. Superfluous merit can be gained by going beyond what is required. The notion that superfluous merit can be transferred from one person to another was not found in Tertullian, but it arrived in Cyprian, and the way was prepared for the satisfaction theory. It was Cyprian who began to apply the principle of excess merit to the work of Christ and to interpret his work as satisfaction. It was on the basis of the penitential system, then, that the satisfaction idea grew up—a fact that reveals the true character and structure of the doctrine. Its root concept is that humans must make an offering or payment to satisfy God's justice.[3]

As previously discussed, the satisfaction theory was first fully developed in the *Cur Deus Homo?* of Anselm, which emphasizes payment of satisfaction as the safeguard of moral uprightness. Anselm meets every objection to the necessity of satisfaction with the reply, "You have not yet fully weighed the gravity of sin." Thomas Aquinas teaches that Christ's work of satisfaction includes the endurance of punishment (a difference not involving any real change of outlook),[4] which Calvin developed into the penal substitution theory. This theory became the dominant view of the Reformation and has remained the orthodox Protestant view ever since. The teaching of Luther on the Atonement, however, does not follow this pattern.

LUTHER

According to Aulén, no aspect of Luther's theology has been more grossly misinterpreted than his teaching on the Atonement.[5] It is a fundamental mistake to say that his understanding belongs to the Anselmian satisfaction

---

1. Tertullian, *Treatises on Penance*, 24.
2. Aulén, *Christus Victor*, 81.
3. Aulén, *Christus Victor*, 82–83.
4. Aulén, *Christus Victor*, 93.
5. Aulén, *Christus Victor*, 103–11.

type. Luther's view can only be rightly understood as a revival of the classic atonement motif taught by the Fathers, but treated in greater depth.[6]

Luther regularly uses the images and forms of expression found in the classic idea of the Atonement. He constantly refers to the deception of the devil, and it is clear that his idea of the devil is not as a myth. The war with the devil is fought in the human arena and is identical with the war against the other "tyrants."[7] But the decisive proof that his understanding is of the classic type is that in those places where it is altogether necessary for him to express himself with the greatest care and exactness (in the catechisms, for instance), he always speaks in accord with the dramatic idea. In his *Small Catechism*, the crucial words concerning the work of Christ are clear: "He has delivered, purchased, and won me, a lost and doomed man, from all sins, from death and the devil's power." Innumerable attempts have been made for centuries to twist these words into the satisfaction doctrine of the Atonement, but it is plain that they reflect the classic view. The three enemies are the familiar trio of sin, death, and the devil. Luther weighed every word in the *Small Catechism* with extraordinary care, but any remaining doubts are dispelled by the *Large Catechism*. Luther states that all of salvation depends on grasping that Christ is Lord. He says:

> What is it now to be a Lord? It is this, that He has redeemed me from sin, from the devil, from death, and all woe. For before, I had not yet had any Lord, nor King, but had been held captive under the devil's power, doomed to death, ensnared in sin and blindness . . . Now, therefore, those tyrants and gaolers are all crushed, and in their place is come Jesus Christ, a Lord of Life, righteousness, all good and holiness, and He has snatched us poor lost men from the jaws of hell, won us, made us free, and brought us back to the Father's goodness and grace.[8]

Another quote from his *Commentary on Galatians* (on Gal 3:13) is also significant:

> Therefore the article of Justification must, as I am continually saying, be exactly understood. For in this all the other articles of our faith are included, and if this remain whole then all the others remain whole. When therefore we teach that men are

---

6. Aulén, *Christus Victor*, 101–2.
7. Aulén, *Christus Victor*, 110.
8. Pelikan, *Luther's Sermons*, 164.

justified through Christ, and Christ is the conqueror of sin, death, and the everlasting curse, then at the same time we testify that He is in His nature God.

In Luther's view, that humans are justified through Christ is linked inseparably to the fact that Christ is the conqueror of sin and death.[9]

This double aspect of the classic view (the defeat of sin and death and humanity's justification) is also taught and expanded by Luther. The wrath of God is an enemy from which Christ brings deliverance. In the common medieval teaching the wrath of God was relegated to the judgment to come; in Luther it is active in the present. In Luther, the wrath of God takes the place of retributive justice, the personal term replacing the juridical term of medieval teaching. Luther maintains the dualistic outlook, and yet God's victory over Satan is also a victory over the curse, God's judgment against sin. Christ, in becoming human, bears the burden of the punishment that, on account of God's wrath, rests on the world. It is a vicarious redemption.[10]

Luther's understanding of the Atonement can also be seen in his words on satisfaction. He spoke very strongly against using the word in the context of divine justice: "We will not allow it in our schools or on the lips of our preachers, but would rather send it back to the judges, advocates, and hangmen, from whom the Pope stole it."[11] Nevertheless, Luther could use the word in relation to the work of Christ. He speaks of satisfaction but without any legal claims of divine justice. Rather, God himself prevails over the wrath and the curse, demonstrating the strength of divine love; satisfaction is made by God and not merely to God. Both *merit* and *satisfaction* are used by Luther in direct connection with Christ's conflict and victory over the "tyrants." These words are simply incorporated into his dualistic view of redemption. It would be incorrect to say that Luther's occasional usage of *satisfaction* defines his thinking on the Atonement.[12]

Misinterpreting Luther's teaching on the Atonement was possible for several reasons: (1) arguments were based on terms and not on the meanings actually given to those terms, (2) Luther's teaching on the Atonement was taken in isolation from the rest of his theology, (3) there has been little

---

9. Pelikan, *Lectures on Galatians*, 282–83.
10. Aulén, *Christus Victor*, 113–16.
11. Aulén, *Christus Victor*, 118.
12. Pelikan, *Luther's Sermons*, 92–93.

awareness of the classic theory, and (4) the only alternative to the satisfaction doctrine was thought to be the so-called subjective view. The fact that Luther's teaching on the Atonement was fully objective and contained the idea of vicarious suffering seemed sufficient proof that it was in line with Anselmian satisfaction. However, Luther stands out in the history of Christian doctrine as expressing the classic idea of the Atonement with greater clarity than any before him. From the sideline of the satisfaction idea he turns back to the mainline, making a direct connection with the NT and the Fathers. But in his time he was an isolated figure.[13]

SINCE THE REFORMATION

It appears that those of Luther's age were unable to grasp his meaning. Luther's view of the Atonement was not followed by either his contemporaries or his successors. They reverted to the satisfaction doctrine in spite of the fact that Luther expresses the classic teaching of the Atonement with power and authority and supreme clearness. It pervades all of his work and is not hidden away in his lesser-known writings.[14]

The man who stood closest to Luther himself in the Reformation is actually the one who guided atonement theology in another direction. Melanchthon, a fellow Reformer and collaborator of Luther, restated much of Luther's theology but in doing so compromised it. This compromise became clear by the deeper study of Luther that took place in Sweden and Germany in the twentieth century. Even as early as 1542, in the *Loci praecipui theological*, Melanchthon stated Luther's doctrine of the Atonement in terms of the satisfaction theory.[15]

How is it that the satisfaction doctrine so soon returned in full force? Part of the explanation, as already noted, is that Luther had used the terminology of the Latin doctrine to give the terms new meaning. But the new significance of the terms was missed, for they had a long history and carried associations from which it was not easy to free them. It is also important to remember that the doctrine of the Atonement was not considered one of the controversial issues of the Reformation. Because

---

13. Aulén, *Christus Victor*, 120–22.
14. Aulén, *Christus Victor*, 123–24.
15. Aulén, *Christus Victor*, 123–24.

it was less polemical than his teaching on justification or on the church, Luther's teaching on the Atonement attracted less attention.[16]

Melanchthon indeed upheld the central doctrine of the Reformation, humanity's acceptance by God's grace, but this teaching was preserved at the price of its incorporation into a rigid judicial scheme. The result is a legalistic view of humankind's relation to God that came to characterize Protestant orthodoxy. God's righteousness (as in Rom 3:21–26) as exclusively retributive and punitive came to be the accepted understanding; thus Luther's teaching on the meaning of God's righteousness disappeared.[17]

The law had come to be taken as the central basis of humanity's relationship to God. Luther's fundamental thought, that the law is tyrannical and an enemy from whose power Christ came to set humankind free, was abandoned. Instead, law provided the scheme by which everything was interpreted, including salvation. Perfect obedience to the law, perfect fulfillment of that law, was required for salvation. This understanding gave the context in which the work of Christ was interpreted. God is primarily a judge who punishes transgression, and Christ offers to God in humankind's place the obedience required by retributive justice.[18]

THE DOCTRINE OF THE ATONEMENT IN PROTESTANT ORTHODOXY

Therefore, before a theory of the Atonement could be clearly established during the period of the Reformation, the satisfaction view had regained control and dominated Protestant theology. The doctrine of Atonement in Lutheran orthodoxy is not identical with that of Anselm, but the differences are slight. Curiously, the medieval doctrine of the Atonement remained, in a slightly modified form, while the penitential system and the idea of penance, on which it had originally been conceived, completely disappeared.[19]

---

16. Aulén, *Christus Victor*, 124–25.

17. Hirsch states the matter thus: "The pre-Lutheran idea of the divine righteousness, admitted by preference into Anselmian-Melanchthonian scheme, perverted the original Protestant conception of God." *Die Theologie des Andreas Osiander*, 246.

18. Aulén, *Christus Victor*, 127.

19. Aulén, *Christus Victor*, 128.

The broad similarity of the nascent penal substitution theory to the view of Anselm is that it is dominated by the idea of satisfaction. Satisfaction is regarded as a rational necessity, the only possible method by which atonement can be effected. Protestant orthodoxy states the problem in the same juridical manner and repeats the contention that the payment of satisfaction is the only alternative to condoning moral laxity. The legal structure, however, is even more dominant than it was in Anselm. Not only does the retributive justice of God have to be satisfied by Christ's death, the law must also be satisfied. There can be no atonement unless a person obeys all God's commandments. Hence the penal substitution theory sets forth a double necessity: Christ must by his obedient life fulfill all God's law, and he must by his death pay the penalty that justice demands. The decision of God to justify humans is treated as an act of his mercy, as he is gracious enough to accept the satisfaction offered by another and as the Atonement is seen to have had its origin in his will.[20]

THE ARRIVAL OF THE SUBJECTIVE OR HUMANISTIC DOCTRINE OF THE ATONEMENT

The doctrine of the Atonement in Protestant orthodoxy is then indisputably a clear and logical expression of satisfaction. It came to be regarded as the palladium of Protestant orthodoxy as if it, and it alone, had been the understanding of orthodox Christians through all the centuries. Therefore, the assault of the Enlightenment on orthodox theology centered on the doctrine of the Atonement, subjecting it to fierce criticism. The criticism begun with Abelard (and never completely silenced) now dominated the theological debate. The thought of God needing to be propitiated through a satisfaction offered to him was intolerable. But among the critics there were various ways of regarding the Atonement: as a seal set upon Christ's teaching, as a vindication of the moral order of the universe, as a lofty example, or as a symbolic expression of God's readiness to be reconciled.[21]

The theologians of the Enlightenment regarded God's attitude as one of unalterable benevolence, meaning that from God's perspective the Atonement was not a necessity. If a person repents and amends their life, God responds, and they are reconciled. The result of this subjective view

20. Aulén, *Christus Victor*, 128–31.
21. Aulén, *Christus Victor*, 133–34.

is that it might appear that orthodox theologians may have been right after all. They had always claimed that the only alternative to the satisfaction of God's justice was an indulgent love, and now it appeared as if the rejection of orthodox doctrine involved weakening the idea of sin and toning down the radical opposition of God to evil.[22]

Beginning in the nineteenth century, the post-Enlightenment era is characterized by the continuous debate between the subjective and objective views of the Atonement, the latter having survived the assaults of the Enlightenment. What all failed to see is that there *is* an alternative idea of the Atonement besides that of orthodox Protestantism or the subjective view of the Enlightenment: the classic view.[23]

During the first part of the twentieth century, the classic view regained a degree of respect, if not acceptance, with the publication of Aulén's *Christus Victor*. Yet it is still often not taken seriously today by either liberal or conservative theologians, largely because of the objections to the idea that are discussed below.

OBJECTIONS AND REPLIES TO THE RANSOM THEORY

Both liberal and conservative theologians have expressed objections to the ransom theory. Six common objections are: (1) a ransom paid to Satan elevates him to the status of a rival god and results in an unacceptable dualism; (2) it is ethically repugnant to think of Satan having moral rights with respect to sinners; (3) it is unreasonable to suppose that Satan would accept Jesus as a ransom for captive humanity; (4) the ransom theory seems to deny human freedom; (5) even though the ransom theory may be logical, there must have been a less costly, less bloody way to save humanity; and (6) the ransom theory is committed to an intolerable supernaturalism. One objection that will not be considered is that the ransom theory is inconsistent with the NT portrayal and theology of the Atonement.[24] Sufficient biblical support to answer such an objection has been presented in chapters 2 and 3.

---

22. Aulén, *Christus Victor*, 135.
23. Aulén, *Christus Victor*, 135.
24. Taliaferro, "Atonement," 82.

Ransom Paid to Satan Results in Dualism

The first objection, that payment of a ransom implies a form of cosmic dualism with Satan as a rival god, seems the least potent of the six. To say that Christ gave his life as a ransom paid to Satan, and in so doing defeated this enemy of God and humanity, does not imply that Satan is a god or God's equal. In Scripture it is clear that Satan is no god and is no match for God. Beginning at Genesis 3:15, he is presented as the enemy of God and of humanity who will strike a serious blow but ultimately be totally defeated. The classic theory has always maintained the creaturely, non-divine nature of Satan.[25]

Satan Having Moral Rights Is Repugnant

The notion that Satan had just rights or lawful jurisdiction over humans is a more thought-provoking question. There are two ways in which ransom theorists have historically portrayed Satan's relationship to humanity. The first is that Satan had divinely sanctioned rights over humans, and the second is that his rule has been allowed by God but without specific divine sanction for his domination. Both possibilities are worth consideration.[26]

The first thesis, that Satan was a legitimate ruler of sinners, argues that through Adam's transgression Satan gained control of the world. Scriptural support can be found for Satan's authority, but it must be kept in perspective. God is still the all-powerful ruler of the universe, and Satan's dominion only represents a temporary and limited conquest. This view considers Satan's power as legitimate or "legal" because it was gained as a result of humanity's free will and God's judgment on humankind. Satan may be thought of as an evildoer carrying out just punishment.[27]

The second thesis is that Satan had no rightfully gained position because his rule was gained by force (deception). God has created a world in which people are freely able to harm one another. Of course, no act of cruelty is approved by God, but there is allowance within this system for some to dominate or rule others through power, not by right. This possibility also exists for Satan, the most powerful evildoer. Sinful choices

---

25. Taliaferro, "Atonement," 83.
26. Taliaferro, "Atonement," 84.
27. Taliaferro, "Atonement," 84–85.

place humans in discord with God and in harmony with the will of Satan. If Satan has gained preeminence (it is not necessary to be able to identify or understand the precise nature of what Scripture calls human bondage) and has some ability to inflict harm, then it is logical and coherent to say that he might accept a ransom in exchange for the relinquishment of that power to influence or inflict harm.[28]

Some question the first idea of Satan having "rights" because it appears to elevate him. For others, the notion of rights is essential because then the payment of a ransom, the sacrifice of the blood of Jesus, becomes a necessity. Atonement cannot be effected in any other way. The second view, however, poses problems for others. If Satan's position was gained by force, then God would be morally free to take it back by force. Payment of a ransom would no longer have been a necessity; it would simply be God's chosen method of salvation. Which approach is taken depends on one's view of the question of necessity, which will be addressed in a later objection.

Satan Accepting Jesus as Ransom Is Unreasonable

Why would Satan accept Jesus as a ransom, and why would he take on such a formidable foe? As for the second part of the question, ransomists have differed in their opinions. Some have argued that Satan was acting in partial ignorance of the nature of the God-man Jesus. Presumably he thought he could do battle with the man Jesus and be victorious. Others have theorized that he acted in full knowledge of Jesus' power and divine nature.[29] In this case he was either foolish enough to think he could win or evil enough to be willing to lose humankind for the opportunity to inflict so great a blow to Christ.

Historically, the theory that the devil acted in partial ignorance has been presented in two ways: that God deliberately deceived the devil or that Satan was simply not able to perceive the outcome of his actions. The notion of God knowingly deceiving Satan regarding the divine nature of Jesus, a position held by many of the Fathers, has often made the ransom theory objectionable, because it would have God engaging in falsehood to get his desired result. Therefore many have gone to great lengths to argue that God was not involved in any form of deception. They take the

28. Taliaferro, "Atonement," 85–86.
29. Taliaferro, "Atonement," 87.

alternate view that Satan, not being omniscient, simply did not know the true nature of his foe.[30] These positions, however, are speculations, and neither is an essential part of the classic theory.

The second question, concerning Satan's knowledge of his ultimate defeat, also involves speculation and is not an essential element of the classic theory. It is reasonable to assume that Satan did not know the result of his actions, that he miscalculated, and as a result he lost the battle and humankind as well. It is equally conceivable that, knowing he would lose the war, Satan would attempt to inflict as strong a blow as possible before his defeat. Either option involves *opinion* concerning a side issue and is nonessential to the ransom theory proper.

Ransom Theory Denies Free Will

A fourth objection to the ransom theory is that it seems to deny humans their free will, portraying them as subservient to higher powers. Nothing in this theory, however, should cause its adherents to view humans as controlled by supernatural powers. The ransom theory clearly includes the idea that Satan has some power over humans who have assented to his influence. To say that they cannot release themselves entirely from his realm is not to say that they have no freedom. The ransom theory seems realistic in its depiction of evil as involving a slavish side as well as free will. It does not view human evil as the only source of the world's evil, but this does not abrogate human responsibility for its part in creating evil.[31]

God Would Have Chosen a Different Way

Even if it is acknowledged that humankind needed to be redeemed from the power of Satan, some argue that there must have been a better way to provide salvation than one involving the horror of crucifixion. Ransom theorists would answer that the reason for the costliness of redemption is related to the free choice of fallen humans. They do not see God orchestrating the crucifixion to satisfy himself. It was not possible for God to redeem humanity in any other way because it would not have been appropriate for God to override human choice. This theoretical necessity is a strength of the classic view, for surely if there had been an alternative,

---

30. Taliaferro, "Atonement," 87–88.
31. Taliaferro, "Atonement," 89.

God would have chosen it. According to the ransom theory, then, Christ met with such a horrifying death because of human and satanic cruelty.[32]

Ransom Theory Requires That Satan Exists

The final objection is that the classic theory insists on an unacceptable supernaturalism. There is really no reply to this objection. Admittedly, if one rejects the possibility of the existence of Satan, they must also reject the ransom theory of the Atonement.[33] This objection indicates a fundamental difference in one's view of Scripture.

There are liberal theologians, however, who view Satan mythologically and still believe the classic view of the Atonement to be the prevalent idea in the NT.[34] They treat atonement as the "conflict between good and evil in the creation. . . . The intention and result of atonement are described as the ending of humanity's enslavement to false ideologies and uncontrollable psychological forces."[35]

THE THREE TYPES OF ATONEMENT THEORY

Chapter 1 discussed six theories of the Atonement in chronological order, thereby emphasizing the evolution of atonement theory over time. Alternatively, these six theories can be sorted into three types based on *what* atonement achieves and *how* it is achieved. The classic, or ransom, theory emerged with Christianity itself and dominated for a thousand years (classic type). The satisfaction theory of Anselm arose during the Middle Ages and became the dominant view of that period (satisfaction type). The subjective moral-influence view of Abelard was articulated in response as a strong objection (subjective type).[36] The penal substitution theory was developed during the Reformation but is in reality only a variation of Anselm's theory (satisfaction type). The exemplarist theory of Socinus is very similar to the earlier teaching of Abelard (subjective type). The potent criticisms of the penal substitution theory by Socinus resulted in its modification into the governmental theory of Grotius, but

---

32. Taliaferro, "Atonement," 90.
33. Taliaferro, "Atonement," 90–91.
34. Macquarrie, *Principles of Christian Theology*, 318.
35. F. Young, *Sacrifice*, 90.
36. Aulén, *Christus Victor*, 143.

it is still only a variation of the penal substitution theory (satisfaction type).[37] The three main types of atonement theory, then, are classic, satisfaction (Anselm, penal substitution, and governmental), and subjective (moral-influence and exemplarist).

There has been little direct controversy between the classic view and the other types, the classic theory often being considered only the crude beginnings of atonement theory. On the other hand, the controversy between the satisfaction and subjective views has been bitter from the start. The first full treatment of the satisfaction doctrine was followed immediately by the sharp criticisms of Abelard, and the criticisms were renewed in full force by the theologians of the Enlightenment. In the process of the unending debate, the two rival views have thoroughly exposed one another's weaknesses. Meanwhile, the classic theory dropped almost out of sight in the realm of theology, although it never completely disappeared.[38]

These three main types of atonement theory can be analyzed in terms of how they perceive the nature of the work of atonement and their concepts of sin, salvation, God, and the incarnate Christ.

The Nature of the Work of Atonement

In the classic type of atonement theory, the work of reconciliation has continuity in that it is carried out by God himself in Christ. There is a dualistic outlook in which the victory of Christ breaks the evil that holds humans in bondage. There is no satisfaction of God's justice, for humanity's relation to God is not viewed in terms of merit or justice, but in terms of grace.[39]

In the satisfaction theories any violation of God's justice is unacceptable. The payment of satisfaction abandons the continuity of divine action, for the satisfaction is offered by Christ, as a human, on behalf of sinners. The work of atonement, however, is still the work of God since he is thought to have planned it. The theories do not require that there be any change in God's attitude toward humanity, although that is often taught.[40]

37. Yung, "Theories of Atonement," 541.
38. Aulén, *Christus Victor*, 144–45.
39. Aulén, *Christus Victor*, 145–46.
40. Aulén, *Christus Victor*, 146.

Luther's View and Common Objections to the Ransom Theory

In the subjective type of theory, atonement is not considered to be carried out by God. Rather, reconciliation results from a change in the heart of a converted sinner.[41]

Each of these three perspectives relates the nature of Christ's work to its perception of the nature of the obstacle to reconciliation.[42] In the classic theory, Satan is the obstacle; in the subjective theories, human ignorance is the obstacle; and in the satisfaction theories, the necessity of punitive justice is the obstacle. Each atonement model arises out of a wider theological system.[43]

Sin

Each type of atonement theory also has a distinct perception of the nature of sin. In the classic view, sin is an opposing power in the universe and the Atonement is the triumph of God over that power. Christ's triumph over sin includes victory over the devil as its source and death as its consequence. Forgiveness plays a positive role as the entrance into life.[44]

The satisfaction view, however, has an understanding of sin based on merit and the penitential system. The justice of God can be satisfied by a compensation for sin or the endurance of the punishment for sin. Forgiveness is regarded negatively as the remission of punishment. God then transfers or imputes Christ's merit to humans.[45]

In the subjective theories the idea of sin is weakened. Sin is not a major obstacle overcome by Christ's work; it is simply a human infirmity. This view of sin results in a humanistic interpretation of atonement in which one is able to overcome sin.[46]

Salvation

In the classic view of the Atonement, salvation is based on Christ's final victory, and it is experienced by humans through the work of the Holy

---

41. Aulén, *Christus Victor*, 146
42. Packer, "Cross," 19.
43. Peters, "Final Scapegoat," 155.
44. Aulén, *Christus Victor*, 147–50.
45. Aulén, *Christus Victor*, 147–49.
46. Aulén, *Christus Victor*, 148.

Spirit. Justification and atonement are really the same thing. Justification is the initial, individual experience of atonement or reconciliation.[47]

Conversely, in the satisfaction theories the actual atonement consists of the offering of satisfaction by Christ and God's acceptance of it. Justification is a separate act in which God imputes to humans the merits of Christ. Sanctification is a process that follows.[48]

In the subjective theories, salvation primarily involves a change taking place in humans through the influence of Christ as the perfect example.[49]

Christ and the Incarnation

The answer to the question, Why did God become man? is entirely different in each of the three types of atonement theory. In the classic view, the Incarnation emphasizes that God becomes man in order to win the victory and reconcile the world to himself. In the satisfaction type, the Incarnation is essential because only God could live a perfect life and make a perfect offering on humanity's behalf. In the subjective type, the Incarnation emphasizes the human nature of Christ and that his purpose is to demonstrate the pattern of life.[50]

Concept of God

Each of the three types of atonement theory differs somewhat in its perception of God. In the classic view God moves onto the battlefield to contend with the forces of evil. The view is dualistic, yet God is still the all-powerful, sovereign ruler of the world. Although atonement is presented as the divine victory over the forces that hold humankind in bondage, those same powers are in some measure executants of God's own judgment against sin. God's victory over the evil powers therefore is also a victory over the curse. The redeeming work of Christ is seen as a divine sacrifice that costs God greatly.[51]

---

47. Aulén, *Christus Victor*, 150.
48. Aulén, *Christus Victor*, 150.
49. Aulén, *Christus Victor*, 151.
50. Aulén, *Christus Victor*, 151–53.
51. Aulén, *Christus Victor*, 153–54.

The satisfaction view of God emphasizes the concept of retributive justice. God's justice receives a compensation for human sin so that he is free to act in his mercy. Subjective atonement theories attempt to present a "purified" concept of God in which his chief characteristic is an unchanging love.[52]

The three types of atonement theory can also be contrasted by the extent of God's action. God moves toward humankind in the classic view and is fully and personally involved in the work of deliverance. In the satisfaction theories God is seen as standing more at a distance, for the satisfaction is said to be paid to God by humankind in the person of Christ. In the subjective view God seems to be still more distant, with the emphasis on humanity's need to move toward God.[53]

CONCLUSION TO PART II—A DEFENSE OF THE RANSOM THEORY

Chapters 4 and 5 defend the ransom, or classic, theory of the Atonement by explaining the reasons for the neglect of the classic view since the Reformation, answering the most common objections to the theory, and demonstrating its exegetical soundness from the NT. Any problems with the theory are not as weighty as those presented by the satisfaction theories, which are founded on the Roman Catholic idea of penance. The ransom theory is neither illogical nor does it set up any moral dilemmas.

Although the scriptural foundation for the ransom theory is its most important commendation, another approach to its defense is a discussion of its historical development following the NT church age, which reveals a long and honorable history with nearly universal support for a thousand years. The view of Luther is also examined, not because one man's theological and historical significance is reason for accepting any theory, but because he emphasizes the classic view.

Part 2 concludes with a summary of the three types of atonement theory and their differing views on the nature of atonement, sin, salvation, Christ and the Incarnation, and their concept of God.

---

52. Aulén, *Christus Victor*, 154.
53. Aulén, *Christus Victor*, 154.

PART III

The Victorious Substitution Theory of the Atonement

PARTS 1 AND 2 provide the necessary foundation for the victorious substitution theory of the Atonement, which is the focus of part 3. Chapter 1 examined the history of atonement theory and discussed six different theories, while chapters 2 and 3 refuted the penal substitution theory's assertion that Christ died to satisfy God's retributive justice by raising logical, moral, theological, and exegetical objections. Chapter 4 defended the ransom theory primarily through a presentation of the extensive NT evidence for this "dramatic" view of the Atonement. Chapter 5 answered objections to the ransom theory and placed it in historical and thematic context as it relates to other atonement theories.

This chapter presents a theory of the Atonement that combines the thought of the ransom theory with the substitutionary and penal aspects of Christ's work. The victorious substitution theory views the Atonement as a historical event, as an event in the life of a Christian, as the provision of victory to be applied in an ongoing process in the life of a Christian, and as the yet-to-be-complete restoration of "all things" in Christ.

Although the concept of substitution is soundly based on Scripture, the acceptance of substitution does not require the acceptance of satisfaction. In other words, one can reject the conclusions of the penal substitution theory without rejecting the substitutionary nature of Christ's death, which can be understood within the ransom framework as the necessary payment of the ransom price or the provision for a great exchange. Christ was the substitute for humankind, bearing the penalty for, or consequences of, its sin. God's justice, however, did not demand substitution or penalty. Rather, Christ's sacrificial submitting of himself to the power of the evil one was the ransom price that liberated humankind from his power. The substitutionary and penal aspects of the death of Christ are properly related, then, to the cosmic struggle between good and evil.

The key concepts of sacrifice (in the context of the OT sacrificial system), atonement, substitution, and penalty will be examined to show that Christ's substitutionary death was a necessity and was, in a sense, penal. Victorious substitution will be presented as a theory that is logical, moral, and theologically and exegetically sound. It incorporates both subjective and objective elements and does not compromise God's wrath or justice. However, it is still just a theory, and an effort will be made to distinguish between scriptural fact and theory (or speculation based on fact).

6

The Scriptural Foundations of Victorious Substitution
Sacrifice and Atonement

THE BIBLICAL CONTEXT OF SACRIFICE AND ATONEMENT

FROM NT TIMES ONWARD there has never been a time when the language of sacrifice has not been used in reference to the Atonement.[1] It is certainly true that Jesus thought of his own death in terms of sacrifice, for at the Last Supper he spoke of the new covenant in his blood. The apostles, too, make an analogy between the sacrifices of the law and the sacrifice of Christ, the former being types of the latter:[2] "For Christ, our Passover lamb, has been sacrificed" (1 Cor 5:7); ". . . the precious blood of Christ, a lamb without blemish or defect" (1 Pet 1:19); "But when this priest had offered for all time one sacrifice for sins, he sat down at the right hand of God . . . For by one sacrifice he has made perfect forever those who are being made holy" (Heb 10:12, 14).

Advocates of the penal substitution theory insist that the OT sacrificial ritual, which foreshadows the sacrifice of Christ, is proof that Christ's death satisfied the law and the justice of God by transferring sin and punishment to a substitute, although Scripture nowhere states it to

---

1. N. Robinson, *Jesus Christ Saves Men*, 131.
2. A. Hodge, *Atonement*, 147.

be such.³ They understand the offering as a compensation to God for a person's sins and as a means of propitiating the wrath of God. Sacrifice is assumed to imply substitution, satisfaction, and propitiation, and all sacrificial references are interpreted in this light.⁴ The laying on of hands, for instance, is said to be a "natural and expressive symbol of transfer [of sins] from the person" making the offering to the animal.⁵ The animal is thought to be experiencing the original sentence pronounced by God upon all sin—death (Gen 2:17; 3:3, 17, 19). The NT verses most often quoted are Romans 6:23 ("The wages of sin is death") and Hebrews 9:22 ("Without the shedding of blood there is no forgiveness"). According to advocates of penal substitution the effect of the sacrifice is "to expiate the guilt of the offender and to propitiate God."⁶ The slain animal is regarded as a substitute for the death-deserving sinner who offers it, and the death of Christ is considered the fulfillment of this transaction in that he died as a substitute for sinners.⁷

But does the OT bear out this explanation of sacrifice? Did Christ fulfill the law in this substitutionary sense? A careful examination of sacrifice in the OT reveals that substitution is only one of many ways to interpret the meaning of sacrifice.

THE MEANING OF SACRIFICE

What is the meaning of sacrifice, and what does it teach concerning atonement? Sacrifice is the expression of a person's desire for friendship with God, and it is the means of reconciliation appointed by God himself

---

3. Crawford, "Penal Theory," 257; Connell, "Atonement," 35. "Any attempt to understand the religious ideas underlying the sacrificial worship of Israel must always bear in mind two things. First the Old Testament nowhere gives us a direct exposition of the meaning of this worship; it is possible to arrive at various conclusions *a posteriori*, but never with more than a certain degree of probability. The certainty with which judgments are at times expressed on this point and on the subject of the whole pattern of development of the idea of sacrifice is usually in inverse proportion to what the available evidence will bear. Secondly, the gaps in the Old Testament tradition cannot simply be filled in from the comparative study of religion on the tacit assumption that everything must have happened in Israel exactly as it did everywhere else." Eichrodt, *Old Testament*, 141.

4. F. Young, *Sacrifice*, 87.

5. A. Hodge, *Atonement*, 134.

6. A. Hodge, *Atonement*, 136–37.

7. N. Robinson, *Jesus Christ Saves Men*, 23–24.

in his grace. An offering, usually in the form of blood, is brought to God. The blood symbolizes the life or soul of the offerer, which is presented to God. Sin is forgiven, the offerer is cleansed, and communion with God is restored. Yet there was no provision of sacrifice for defiant, unrepented sins that were punished by death or excommunication (Num 15:27–31). Sacrifice was closely connected with sin and its forgiveness in that it served the divine purpose of emphasizing the heinousness of all sin in the sight of a holy God. It provided the way of drawing near to God and was a promise and symbol of God's readiness to forgive and accept those who followed the appointed means of restoring their covenant relationship.[8]

The significance of the sacrificial ritual is apparent in each action that takes place. A person comes to make their offering and identifies with the animal by the laying on of hands. The animal is slain, symbolizing the surrender of the offerer's life to God. The priest takes the blood, which represents the life surrendered, into the holy place, signifying God's acceptance of it. The body of the animal is burned upon the altar, signifying the offerer's total giving of themselves to God. There follows a meal indicating that peace and fellowship with God are restored. God and the worshipper are reconciled. "Life is offered, completely surrendered, accepted by God, transformed, and shared."[9] This summary forms a composite of the elements of the sacrificial ritual that are not found together in any one type of sacrifice. Yet all these actions are a part of one type of sacrifice or another. No vicarious punishment is suggested by the actions taken in making sacrifice. The essential element is the surrender of life, not its destruction.[10]

Two facts about the sacrificial animal itself indicate that God's justice is not propitiated by punishing an animal as a substitute sinner. First, there was an alternative to using an animal for sin offerings; a cup of grain could also be offered by a poor person (Lev 5:11). The idea of a transferred penalty resulting in death would be absurd here, but the pouring out of the cereal, like the pouring out of blood, could be conceived as fresh life being offered to God. Second, the animal provided for a sin offering had to be without blemish. If sin was transferred to the animal then it would no longer be pure. There is certainly a transfer of sins envisioned in the ritual of the scapegoat in Leviticus 16, but the

---

8. N. Robinson, *Jesus Christ Saves Men*, 25–26.
9. N. Robinson, *Jesus Christ Saves Men*, 132.
10. N. Robinson, *Jesus Christ Saves Men*, 132.

scapegoat was not a sacrifice offered to God. It did not suffer death and cannot therefore be understood as the object of God's punishment.[11]

APPOINTED BY GOD

It should be stressed that "sacrifice is the result of God's grace and not its cause. It is given *by* God before it is given *to* Him" (emphasis in original).[12] Individuals may respond to the way appointed by God by bringing the offering, but God, in his mercy, takes the initiative in providing the means of reconciliation.[13] God is the one who expiates or covers sin.[14] Therefore when one brings a sacrifice it is not so much that they bring a gift to God as they come to appropriate God's gift—the institution of sacrifice itself.[15] The sacrificial ritual reveals God's heart; he does not desire the death of a sinner but their restoration. (The NT also stresses the activity of the Father in restoration: Romans 3:25; 5:8–9; Colossians 1:13, 20; Ephesians 1:6–7; 2:4–5). God does not save, however, against the will of the sinner; he does not override the freedom he has granted to human beings.[16] Any Israelite was free to choose whether or not to bring a sacrifice. Sacrifice, then, is not something humans do to God (propitiation) but something God does for humankind (expiation). Theories of propitiation miss this vital point: sacrifice is intended to heal broken lives here and now. It is an attack upon the defilement in human life and brings about expiation of sins.[17]

THE MEANING OF BLOOD

Advocates of the penal substitution theory, following Calvin,[18] trace the necessity of Christ's death to the divine curse upon sinners (Gal 3:10) and to the need of bringing blood to pacify God.[19] Hebrews 9:22 is cited

11. Fiddes, *Present Salvation*, 73.
12. Forsyth, *Cruciality of the Cross*, 89.
13. Baillie, *God Was in Christ*, 187.
14. N. Robinson, *Jesus Christ Saves Men*, 132.
15. Forsyth, *Cruciality of the Cross*, 90.
16. N. Robinson, *Jesus Christ Saves Men*, 140.
17. Fiddes, *Present Salvation*, 71.
18. Calvin, *Institutes*, 130–32, 185–91.
19. Kehm, "Defilement," 40. Calvin believed the ancient widespread use of blood

in support of the latter idea: "Without the shedding of blood there is no forgiveness." This verse indicates an inseparable connection between blood and forgiveness (expiation of sin), but it clearly does not say that the purpose of the blood is to pacify God or satisfy God's judgment. That conclusion is an interpretation, not stated in Scripture, of *why* blood was necessary.

Scripture does state, however, that the sacrifice of the animal expiates sin, or removes the guilt or uncleanness from the offerer. How does the blood accomplish this expiation? What is the meaning of the blood? This question is significant because the NT also refers to the blood (of Christ) as the redeeming or cleansing agent in a variety of ways, such as: "The new covenant in my blood" (Luke 22:20; 1 Cor 11:25); "He bought with his own blood" (Acts 20:28); "With your blood you purchased for God" (Rev 5:9); "Redemption through his blood" (Eph 1:7; see 1 Pet 1:19; Rev 1:5); "Through the shedding of his blood" (Rom 3:25); "Justified by his blood" (Rom 5:9); "Making peace through his blood" (Col 1:20); "Brought near by the blood of Christ" (Eph 2:13); "The blood of Jesus, his Son, purifies us from all sin" (1 John 1:7); "The blood of Christ . . . cleanse our consciences" (Heb 9:14); "Sprinkled with his blood" (1 Pet 1:2; see Heb 12:24); "Make the people holy through his own blood" (Heb 13:12); "By the blood of the Lamb" (Rev 12:11); "Without the shedding of blood there is no forgiveness" (Heb 9:22).

The NT emphasizes that the sacrificial blood of Christ is expiatory and foreshadowed by the sacrifices of the OT, which are fulfilled and annulled by Christ's superior and more effectual sacrifice. The NT gives no explanation as to *how* the blood expiates sin. The thought patterns underlying the NT are Hebrew, and it is only natural that, once cut from its Jewish roots, pagan ideas and explanations came to be used to interpret both OT and NT sacrificial language. Thus ideas of propitiation were introduced to explain *how* Christ's blood could expiate sin.[20]

If not by propitiating God, how does blood expiate sin and reconcile God and humans? Several passages in the OT reveal the significance and

---

sacrifice could be attributed to the fact that it was instituted by God with Adam and Eve. He thought that, in spite of the degenerate practices of ancient pagan sacrifices, they nevertheless contained some indication of the true meaning of sacrifice. However, it could just as easily be argued that the pagan practice of attempting to pacify angry gods was a perversion of God's original purpose.

20. F. Young, *Sacrifice*, 73.

value of blood. Once understood, they give a meaningful interpretation of how the offering of blood cleanses from sin and reconciles to God.

Leviticus 17:11 gives the clearest statement of the meaning of blood. It says, "For the life of a creature is in the blood, and I have given it to you to make atonement for yourselves on the altar; it is the blood that makes atonement for one's life." Genesis 9:4 and Deuteronomy 12:23 also indicate that the blood is the life. In addition, there is the prohibition of eating blood or flesh with the blood in it (Lev 3:17; 7:26–27; 17:10–14). Blood is never to be consumed for it is too sacred.[21] The relationship between blood and life extends to human life too, as God's covenant with Noah equates "lifeblood" with "life" and gives as its basis that humankind is made in the image of God (Gen 9:5–6). These verses "represent a formidable body of evidence and indicate that among the Hebrews there was a recognized close connection between life and blood."[22]

If blood symbolizes life, then the thing pleasing to God is not death but the humble offering of life. The blood is shed with the purpose of separating it from the body and presenting it to God.[23] The material sacrifice is the outward symbol of the inner sacrifice of the offerer: a life and will surrendered in repentance and self-sacrifice to God.[24] The will is what persons cling to and give up last; therefore, the blood as life means one's whole being is submitted to God in love. Scripture consistently states that God values the heart of obedience more than any outward act. Therefore, in the NT a widow's mite could be more precious than the wealth of many (Mark 12:41–44), and in the OT obedience was better than sacrifice (1 Sam 15:22).[25]

---

21. Forsyth, *Cruciality of the Cross*, 90.

22. Morris, *Apostolic*, 110. This statement is made by Morris even though he represents the penal substitution view of sacrifice. Against this "formidable body of evidence" he offers Numbers 35:33, "Bloodshed pollutes the land, and atonement cannot be made for the land on which blood has been shed, except by the blood of the one who shed it." He says, "Here we have explicit mention of atonement, but it is certainly the execution of the murderer that is spoken of and not any presentation of his life before God." Morris maintains that this verse should be considered a commentary on Lev 17:11, which he says is ambiguous (could be considered the presentation of life or the infliction of death), as are all the other references to "blood" and "life." *Apostolic*, 114.

23. Forsyth, *Cruciality of the Cross*, 89.

24. F. Young, *Sacrifice*, 55.

25. Forsyth, *Cruciality of the Cross*, 91–92.

As the performing of expiation purifies the human soul, the blood sacrifice purifies or consecrates such sacred places and persons as the altar, the sanctuary, the priest, or an Israelite. The blood is effective in either the establishment (in the covenant sacrifice) or restoration (in the sacrifice of expiation) of union between God and his people. When a person is separated from God by their sin they may seek to be restored by bringing their sacrifice, offering their life to God. They are forgiven by God, their sins are expiated, their guilt is removed, and their conscience is cleansed. The sin that separated them from God is removed, and they are reunited and at peace with God. Atonement has taken place.[26]

The immolation, which every sacrifice with blood necessarily presupposes, expresses a great truth: no reconciliation with God takes place unless one dies to their egotism or, to use the biblical term, to their flesh. They must surrender their life. The effectiveness of sacrifice, therefore, does not depend on any external ceremony but on the internal act of the worshipper.[27]

THE MESSAGE OF THE PROPHETS

The vanity of an outward sacrifice without a corresponding inward reality is emphasized by the prophets, who saw clearly that sacrifice was of no avail without amendment of life. They taught that sins were forgiven if a person turned to God in repentance (Isa 55:7; Ezek 18:21–22). They also proclaimed that it is the moral offenses (rather than ceremonial) that are important: injustice, dishonesty, bribery, perjury, oppression, violence, cruelty. So long as these sins go on, God cares not at all for offerings. In fact, he hates them, refuses to accept them, and will not look with favor on any who offer them.[28]

> "The multitude of your sacrifices—what are they to me?" says the Lord. . . ." Stop bringing meaningless offerings! Your incense is detestable to me. . . . Your New Moon feasts and your appointed festivals I hate with all my being. They have become a burden to me; I am weary of bearing them. When you spread out your hands in prayer, I hide my eyes from you; even when

---

26. Lyonette and Sabourin, *Sin, Redemption, and Sacrifice*, 180–81.
27. Lyonette and Sabourin, *Sin, Redemption, and Sacrifice*, 169.
28. Baillie, *God Was in Christ*, 176.

you offer many prayers, I am not listening. Your hands are full of blood!" (Isa 1:11–15)

The teaching of the prophets is beautifully expressed by Norman Robinson in his book *How Jesus Christ Saves Men*. He asks what the words of the great prophets contribute to the subject of the Atonement or to the reconciliation of sinful humanity to God. He says that in these prophets we recognize a very different emphasis from that of the law. He says:

> The prophets have a far profounder and more searching view of sin. Whereas, sacrifice dealt largely with sin as ritual transgression, the prophet's sole concern is with spiritual disobedience, with moral iniquity, with failure to "do justly, to love mercy and to walk humbly with God." Sin to them is rebellion against God, disobedience to his righteous will, unfaithfulness to the covenant-bond, and this is shown chiefly in social injustice and inhumanity. Upon such sin in the clearest and strongest terms the prophets pronounce God's sure judgment.
>
> Moral iniquity and God's inexorable judgment thereon, is that all the prophets have to declare? By no means. They have a Gospel too, for they believe in God's gracious covenant with his people, and they abound in declarations of God's long-suffering and readiness to forgive his people, if they will but truly repent and return to him. "Let the wicked forsake his way, and the unrighteous man his thoughts: and let him return unto the Lord, and he will have mercy upon him; and to our God, for he will abundantly pardon" (Isa 55:7). "Come now, and let us reason together, saith the Lord: though your sins be as scarlet, they shall be as white as snow; though they be red like crimson, they shall be as wool" (Isa 1:18). God will forgive and restore the penitent nation, yes, and the truly penitent individual too; such in brief is the prophetic Gospel. Who can forget the cry of God's longsuffering love in Hosea, "How shall I give thee up Ephraim?"... or the wealth of gracious promises of pardon and restoration in Isaiah, Jeremiah and other prophets?[29]

The sacrificial system taught the rudiments of relationship with a holy God, "the alphabet of sin and pardon," but the prophets deepened the revelation by speaking the words of judgment and mercy directly, thus preparing the way for him who was "the word made flesh" and "the

---

29. N. Robinson, *Jesus Christ Saves Men*, 26–27.

Lamb who takes away the sin of the world."[30] Although sacrifice had its part in the education of God's people and in preparation for the coming Christ, the time would come when one stone of the temple would not be left upon another and the blood of bulls and goats would give way to another offering. In the new covenant, Christ's blood—the sacrifice of a completely surrendered will—would provide the way of atonement. The OT sacrifices were all types of this pure and holy offering that was fulfilled in Christ. The prophets saw that the true meaning of animal sacrifice was a spiritual offering of love and obedience, the only real sacrifice pleasing to God.[31]

THE SCAPEGOAT

To support the penal substitution view of sacrifice, specifically that the blood of the animal is shed in place of the blood of the offerer, advocates refer to the ceremony of the scapegoat on the Day of Atonement (Lev 16:8–10, 20–22). The penal substitution interpretation *assumes* that in the regular sin offering the sins of the offerer are symbolically placed on the sacrificial animal by the laying on of hands in the same manner as with the scapegoat. But there are differences between the scapegoat and the sin offering. The scapegoat is not killed and its blood is not shed. It is sent into the desert. The sin offering, however, is pure and is offered to God. The scapegoat is impure, and anyone who touches it is also considered impure. Therefore, the priest who carried out the ceremony and the one appointed to release the scapegoat in the wilderness both had to purify themselves afterward (Lev 16:26). In addition, both hands of the priest are laid on the scapegoat whereas only one is placed on the sin offerings and the other sacrifices in which there is no thought of removing sin (such as the burnt offering and the peace offering). Most revealing is the fact that not once in the NT, when the authors speak of the sacrifice of Christ, is the ceremony of the scapegoat mentioned.[32]

The scapegoat, then, is not a type of Christ, for in the ceremonies of the Day of Atonement the two ideas of a sacrificial victim and sin-bearing are mutually exclusive. An animal could be sacrificed or offered to God only because it was thought *not* to be contaminated with the sins of the

---

30. N. Robinson, *Jesus Christ Saves Men*, 29–30.
31. N. Robinson, *Jesus Christ Saves Men*, 133.
32. Lyonnet and Sabourin, *Sin, Redemption, and Sacrifice*, 182–83.

people. This clearly presents a contradiction for juridical theories of the Atonement. The use of the blood signified the expiation or washing away of sin by a sinless life that had been offered to and accepted by God.[33] On the Day of Atonement one goat symbolized the *means* of atonement and the other the *effect* of atonement: bearing away the sins of the people to the land of forgetfulness.[34] The ritual contains no idea of punishment.

It was during the Reformation that the exegesis of the rite changed to reflect the newly developed penal substitution theory.[35] The scapegoat provided a ready illustration of a theory of the Atonement founded on the alleged imputation of sins to Christ.[36] However, there is no scriptural evidence for interpreting the scapegoat as a type of Christ. Attempts to create such comparisons are mere exercises in typology unfounded in Scripture. A change in the Christian understanding of redemption is what allowed the association of Christ with the scapegoat. As Lyonnet says, "The NT writers kept clear of these speculations by simply ignoring the scapegoat ritual. The best way to avoid exegetical and doctrinal deviations in that area is to follow their example."[37]

THE DOUBLE ASPECT OF SACRIFICE

God is represented in the NT as both making the sacrifice (John 3:16) and receiving it (Heb 9:14).[38] The OT merely hints that sacrifice was a costly matter for God. The words of God in Leviticus 17:11 link the statement that "the life of a creature is in the blood" with the words "and I have given it to you." Life belongs to God, and here is the seed of the idea that it is God himself who gives the life. The thought becomes apparent in the NT, which reveals that God gives his only Son as the Lamb to be slain.[39]

Unlike the OT, the NT does not so much depict God as receiving a sacrifice (although that is true) as making it. And the sacrifice of Christ is seen not so much as the agony of suffering (although that is true) as the agony of surrender. Gethsemane represents the epitome of the death

---

33. Quick, *New World*, 100–101.
34. A. Hodge, *Atonement*, 135.
35. Lyonnet and Sabourin, *Sin, Redemption, and Sacrifice*, 269.
36. Lyonnet and Sabourin, *Sin, Redemption, and Sacrifice*, 281.
37. Lyonnet and Sabourin, *Sin, Redemption, and Sacrifice*, 289.
38. Aulén, *Christus Victor*, 116.
39. Fiddes, *Present Salvation*, 75.

The Scriptural Foundations of Victorious Substitution

of self-will. The sweat that was "like drops of blood" (Luke 22:44), as well as the blood shed at Calvary, represents the total giving of himself. The saving work of Christ involved a struggle and surrender in the very core of his being.[40]

Not only did Jesus surrender his life in sacrifice, but the Father also made a sacrifice in the giving of his Son. The Father's sacrifice was as great as the sacrifice of the Son. Could the suffering of his Son have been less painful for him? Has it been comprehended how much it cost the Father to effect atonement? God's mercy for sinners is the source of the sacrifice of both Father and Son, not just the result of the process.[41]

Therefore sacrifice as an analogy that interprets the work of Christ has two sides. The sacrifice of Christ is connected to both God and the powers of evil.[42] On the one hand, Christ was a sacrifice to God in his perfect and complete offering of himself to do the work of atonement. On the other hand, it is God himself who makes the sacrifice of his Son for the redemption of humankind from bondage to the evil forces.

The picture of sacrifice with its two sides in no way depicts Christ's sacrifice as part of a legal scheme.[43] Just as Christ fulfilled the OT picture of sacrifice, Christians, too, are called to complete dedication of themselves to God. In the OT God appoints the ritual of sacrifice, symbolically asking for devotion of life. In the NT God plainly asks for the same: "Whoever finds their life will lose it, and whoever loses their life for my sake will find it" (Matt 10:39).

THE PURPOSE OF SACRIFICE

God's purpose in the way and place of sacrifice was to blot out sin. Recall that "wiping away" or "covering over" is the meaning of the Hebrew word *kipper* (atone). The fact that sacrifice was understood to expiate sin in the sense of wiping it away or covering it over is clear from the OT concept of sin itself. The OT often depicts sin as uncleanness, a patch of dirt and disease that needs to be cleansed away. Unless action is taken, it will spread with disastrous effect for the community. The sin offering is understood as disinfecting or wiping away the dangerous spot, and images

---

40. Forsyth, *Cruciality of the Cross*, 92.
41. Baillie, *God Was in Christ*, 188.
42. Aulén, *Christus Victor*, 31.
43. Aulén, *Christus Victor*, 77.

of sprinkling blood or washing are part of this view of sin as a destructive power that must be removed from the community. The ritual of the Day of Atonement pictures this removal of sin not only by the cleansing of sacrifice but also by symbolically banishing sin with the scapegoat. Some sin, however, premeditated and done in defiance of God, was so serious that it could only be removed from the community by the removal the sinner (Num 15:27–31). Whether by sacrifice, scapegoat, or in some cases capital punishment, sin had to be removed.[44]

The purpose of sacrifice is "to make atonement for sin" and "to reconcile," and the promise given to the one who brings sacrifice is always "and they will be forgiven" (Lev 4:20, 26, 31; 8:15; 16:10).[45] The expiation of sin brings about atonement because sin is removed from the believer's conscience and from the presence of God.[46] "Sacrifices are mimes of pardon intended to illicit faith and repentance" and to emphasize the importance of holy living.[47] In the OT a person was to come to God, giving themselves in repentance and faith in God's appointed means of reconciliation; that is, sacrifice. In the NT a person is to come to God, giving themselves in repentance and faith in God's appointed means of reconciliation; that is, Jesus. The life of Jesus demonstrates what a sacrifice really is, and believers, in dependence on him, are to "offer [their] bodies as *living* sacrifices" (Rom 12:1, emphasis added).[48]

---

44. Fiddes, *Present Salvation*, 72–73.
45. A. Hodge, *Atonement*, 138.
46. Crawford, "Penal Theory," 269.
47. Kehm, "Defilement," 47.
48. Gunton, *Actuality of Atonement*, 122–23.

7

The Scriptural Foundations of Victorious Substitution

Substitution and Penalty

REEVALUATING SUBSTITUTION AND PENALTY

THREE PATTERNS OF THOUGHT have led to misunderstanding the Atonement. (1) Those who reject the penal substitution theory in favor of more subjective theories usually feel constrained to reject substitution as a part of the work of Christ, in spite of scriptural evidence to the contrary. (2) Those who accept Christ's death as substitutionary usually feel constrained to accept the penal substitution theory in spite of its serious problems. (3) Those who hold to the ransom theory generally pay little, if any, attention to the concepts of substitution or penalty. Victorious substitution provides a solution that addresses each of these misunderstandings.

The "core of vital truth"[1] found in the penal substitution theory, that Christ's death is vicarious and penal, leads to its general acceptance among orthodox Protestants. However, many thinkers would reject the penal substitution theory if they could be convinced that they do not have to thereby reject substitution and penalty as vital parts of the Atonement. Both substitution and penalty are important scriptural aspects of the work of Christ that do not insist on Christ's death as the satisfaction of God's justice or the propitiation of his wrath. These concepts can be

---

1. Hodges, *Pattern of Atonement*, 46.

separated from the penal substitution theory and interpreted in the context of the ransom theory.

One can hold that Christ's death is substitutionary and yet differ from the penal substitution view on the nature of the action that Jesus performs in humanity's place. The nature of substitution and the reason for penalty must be carefully considered.[2] This chapter will present Christ's substitutionary death as the ransom price paid, not to God, but to the powers of evil, thereby aligning substitution with the classic theory of the Atonement. Substitutionary death in the context of the ransom theory eliminates the objectionable features of substitution as a means of atonement in the penal substitution theory.

The scriptural basis for considering Christ's death both substitutionary and penal will first be examined within the OT concepts of substitution and penalty found in Isaiah 53 and then in a variety of NT passages. (It will be helpful to the reader if they will keep in mind that the sole purpose of this section is to establish that Christ's work is vicarious. The *way* in which his work is vicarious will be considered later.) Having established a solid scriptural basis from the OT and the NT, this chapter will then relate the concepts of substitution and penalty to the ransom theory of the Atonement. Finally, it will be emphasized that relating substitution and penalty to the ransom concept does not compromise the reality of God's justice or his wrath against sin.

SUBSTITUTION AND PENALTY IN THE OLD TESTAMENT: THE SUFFERING SERVANT

The previous chapter examines the sacrificial ritual in the OT and concludes that sacrifice is not substitutionary in nature. The idea of substitution in the sense of one suffering for another does appear in the OT, however, but not within the context of the sacrificial ritual. Its most profound expression is in the passage concerning the Suffering Servant, Isaiah 52:13—53:12.[3]

The Lord introduces his servant (52:13) and announces first of all the servant's exaltation.[4] God then begins a description of the servant's

---

2. Packer, "Cross," 19.
3. N. Robinson, *Jesus Christ Saves Men*, 24–25.
4. E. Young, *Isaiah*, 335.

suffering and degradation.[5] The substitutionary nature of his suffering is emphasized by the use of the words "our" and "he" throughout the passage.[6] "Surely he took up our pain and bore our suffering . . . But he was pierced for our transgressions, he was crushed for our iniquities; the punishment that brought us peace was on him, and by his wounds we are healed" (Isa 53:4–6).

To say that he "took up our pain" is to say that he took it away. But the verb *nasa* means also a lifting up and carrying. The parallel between "took up" and "bore" in verse 4 indicates this meaning. The servant takes the sicknesses (consequences of sin) that belong to humans and lifts them upon himself and bears them away. Peter brings out this meaning when he alludes to Isaiah: "He himself bore our sins in his body on the tree" (1 Pet 2:24).[7] He suffers in his own body the punishment for sins. He bears sin's consequences. Ezekiel 18:20 likewise uses this idea of bearing the consequences: "The child will not share the guilt ['bear (*nasa*) the iniquity' KJV] of the parent, nor will the parent share the guilt of the child." Christ, as the servant of the Lord, not only carries sins away, he also bears the consequences of sin.[8]

Isaiah 53:5 brings out the reason for the servant's suffering: "He was pierced for our transgressions, he was crushed for our iniquities," meaning he bears the penalty that is rightfully due humankind.[9] This is not to say that humanity's sins are transferred to him. Emphasizing the substitutionary nature of his suffering, verse 5 also states that "the punishment that brought us peace was on him, and by his wounds we are healed." There is an exchange: he suffers, and humans are given peace. He is wounded; humans are healed.[10]

Isaiah 53:6 makes it clear that it is the will of the Lord that the servant bear the consequences, or penalty, for sin: "The Lord has laid on him the iniquity of us all." Iniquity is not something that can be literally "laid on" a person. The verse is saying that the servant is suffering the consequences of the iniquity of others.

5. E. Young, *Isaiah*, 337.
6. E. Young, *Isaiah*, 345.
7. E. Young, *Isaiah*, 345–46.
8. E. Young, *Isaiah*, 345.
9. E. Young, *Isaiah*, 348.
10. "Isaiah does not mean a true chastisement, for we learn from Psalm 73:14 that chastisement can, by metonymy, mean rebuke or affliction. The rebukes and afflictions were endured by Christ for the sake of our peace." Godbey, "Socinus," 106.

Isaiah 53:10 says, "Yet it was the Lord's will to crush him and cause him to suffer." The NIV brings out the understanding that the Lord's "pleasure" ("it pleased the Lord to bruise him" KJV) is in the accomplishment of his own will,[11] meaning that the death of Jesus functions for the divine purpose of redemption.[12] The Hebrew mind views the Lord as the ultimate cause of all things, and in this sense he causes the servant to suffer. Verse 10 also links sacrificial language with substitution: "The Lord makes his life an offering for sin."[13] The sacrifice of both the Father and Son is that Jesus becomes the substitute, bearing the penalty for sin. The substitutionary element does not mean that grace comes through a transfer of punishment but that the servant bears the consequences of the sins of others.[14] When Moses offered to bear the punishment for the Israelites' worship of the golden calf, God declined to punish him, simply stating, "Whoever has sinned against me I will blot out of my book" (Exod 32:33). This indicates God was unwilling to accept a subsitute, even if one were to volunteer.

In Isaiah 53, verses 10–12 repeat the statement of the Suffering Servant's exaltation that begins the passage (52:13), emphasizing his victory. As a result of his expiatory offering he will "see his offspring and prolong his days," "see the light of life and be satisfied," "justify many," and receive "a portion among the great"—words that bring to mind the exaltation of Revelation 5:12: "Worthy is the Lamb, who was slain, to receive power and wealth and wisdom and strength and honor and glory and praise!"

The doctrine of the vicarious suffering of the servant of Isaiah 53 is also found in the NT. However, none of these passages, or all of them together, amount to a doctrine of Christ propitiating God.[15]

SUBSTITUTION AND PENALTY IN THE NEW TESTAMENT

The substitutionary nature of the Suffering Servant's death connects with the words of Jesus when he states that he will "give his life as a ransom for many" (Mark 10:45; Matt 20:28). The "many" here alludes to the "many"

11. Godbey, "Socinus," 354.
12. Gunton, *Actuality of Atonement*, 159.
13. Quick, *New World*, 100.
14. Mather, "Atonement," 267.
15. Franks, *Atonement*, 91.

found in Isaiah 53:11.[16] The phrase to "give his life" is also reminiscent of the description of the Suffering Servant.[17] To say that Christ came to "give his life as a ransom for many" indicates substitution, and substitution is "the putting of one person or thing in place of another."[18] Christ gave his life "in place of," or in exchange for, humankind.

Some theologians refuse the word *substitution* because of its close connection with the penal substitution theory.[19] However, the concept of redemption or ransom requires a substitutionary payment. What is the price that Christ pays? What does Christ do in humanity's place? The price is his blood and he dies in humanity's place (Rom 3:24; Eph 1:7; Heb 9:12). He submits himself to the one who has the "power of death," suffering the consequences of sin.

NT support, then, for the substitutionary nature of the work of Christ is found in the use of *ransom* and *redemption*. The LXX use of the noun *lytron* is clear and consistent and involves a process of ransoming with a definite price for release (Exod 30:12). The use of the verb *lytroō* is, however, more complicated, for it sometimes occurs with no ransom price involved: "Without money you will be redeemed. . . . For the Lord has comforted his people, he has redeemed Jerusalem" (Isa 52:3, 9). Therefore, to fully understand the LXX meaning of redemption, its Hebrew roots must be examined. The two Hebrew roots *g'l* and *pdh* underlie almost all of its OT occurrences.[20]

The primary sense of the root *g'l* is to resume a claim or right that has lapsed, or to reclaim. It involves the concept of family law, meaning to do the part of a kinsman, and in all its shades of meaning it never quite loses this context. In many important passages God is the subject of *g'l*. God is viewed as the great Kinsman of his people to whom they might turn when their liberty is lost or threatened. Examples include the rescue from bondage in Egypt (Exod 6:6; 15:13; Ps 74:2; 77:15; 78:35; 106:10) and the later deliverance from Babylon (Ps 107:2; Isa 43:1; 44:22, 23; 48:20; 52:3, 9; 63:9; Jer 31:11; Hos 13:14; Mic 4:10) as well individual examples. Jacob refers to "the God who has been my shepherd all my life to this day, the Angel who has delivered [redeemed] me from all harm"

16. Mather, "Atonement," 267.
17. Mather, "Atonement," 267.
18. *Oxford English Dictionary*, s.v. "substitution," Sept. 2023, https://doi.org/10.1093/OED/3312074345.
19. Packer, "Cross," 17–18.
20. Morris, *Apostolic*, 9–12.

(Gen 48:15–16) and the psalmist to a God who "redeems your life from the pit" (Ps 103:4; see also Ps 69:18; 72:14; 119:154). It is sometimes argued that the verb has lost its original significance and means simply "to deliver." However, the fact that it is never so used with a human subject argues against this conclusion.[21]

The other Hebrew root that underlies the verb *redeem* is *pdh*. In this case, the meaning is undoubtedly "to ransom by the payment of a price," involving commercial transactions rather than family relations. There is no element of obligation or family duty. Its use with a human subject always involves a substitutionary payment (Exod 13:13; 21:8; Lev 19:20; Num 18:15–17). However, as in the case of *g'l*, when God is the subject there is often no payment involved (Deut 7:8; 9:26; 13:5; 15:15; 24:18; 2 Sam 4:9; 7:23; 1 Chron 17:21; Neh 1:10; Ps 25:22; 31:5; 69:18; 78:42; 119:134; 130:8; Isa 1:27; 35:10; 51:11; Jer 31:11; Hos 7:13; 13:14).[22] The primary thought is that of deliverance, yet the underlying sense of price is still present, as God acts on behalf of his people with a great effort.[23]

From these two Hebrew roots underlying "redeem," the basic idea is deliverance by the payment of a price. Both terms, however, can be used metaphorically when God is the subject.[24] Based on the usage of *g'l* and *pdh*, strong evidence is required before removing a substitutionary meaning from a passage containing either root.[25] Far from weakening a meaning of substitution, the NT reinforces it by the specific mention of the ransom price: Christ "gave himself for us" (Titus 2:14). In 1 Peter 1:18–19 the price is even more clear: "the precious blood of Christ," which is contrasted with "silver or gold."[26] The NT use of the words *ransom* and *redeem*, then, constitutes strong evidence for regarding the work of Christ as substitutionary.

Time and again scholars have emphasized that Scripture nowhere states to whom the ransom price is paid, although the price is represented as being paid by God (Christ).[27] According to the penal substitution theory the price is paid *by* God (Christ) *to* God (the Father). However,

---

21. Morris, *Apostolic*, 12–14.
22. Morris, *Apostolic*, 15–16.
23. Morris, *Apostolic*, 14, 16–17.
24. Morris, *Apostolic*, 22.
25. Morris, *Apostolic*, 29.
26. Morris, *Apostolic*, 35.
27. Ridderbos, *Paul*, 195.

according to the victorious substitution theory the price is paid *by* God rather than *to* God. The price is not something God exacted and Christ paid, but "it is the cost to God of his work for men."[28]

The few verses in the NT that are clearly substitutionary, other than references to ransom or redemption, indicate that Christ endures the penalty for sin. "For Christ also suffered once for sins, the righteous for the unrighteous, to bring you to God. He was put to death in the body but made alive in the Spirit" (1 Pet 3:18). "Christ redeemed us from the curse of the law by becoming a curse for us: for it is written: 'Cursed is everyone who is hung on a pole ["a tree" KJV]'" (Gal 3:13). The curse of the law is its penalty. The wrath, or curse, of God is his displeasure and judgment that rest on every infraction of the law.[29] Christ submits himself to the consequences of human sin inflicted upon him by Satan, but these consequences result from the original judgment of God on sin. (It is only because of God's judgment that Satan has any power or authority. All power and authority is derived from God.) Jesus' sacrifice is that he endures the death of a criminal, which is the penalty for sin.[30]

Second Corinthians 5:14–15 also expresses the substitutionary nature of Christ's work: "One died for all, and therefore all died. And he died for all, that those who live should no longer live for themselves but for him who died for them and was raised again." Clearly, in some sense Christ takes humanity's place.[31] Three times this passage uses the Greek preposition *hyper* (translated "for" in "one died *for* all . . . he died *for* all . . . him who died *for* them"), which normally means "on behalf of" rather than "instead of," but the meanings may well blend together. Linguistic grounds do not require the notion of substitution; however, the words "therefore all died" imply substitution. The death of Christ "for" all involves the death "of" all. Christ in some way dies humankind's death. As Worrall says, "If we all *died* in that Christ died *for* us there must be a sense in which that death of his is *ours*. . . . he is not simply a person doing us a service; he is a person doing us a service *by filling our place and dying our death*" (emphasis in original).[32]

---

28. Cave, *Work of Christ*, 300.
29. J. Murray, *Redemption*, 44.
30. Quick, *New World*, 101.
31. Lee, *Romans*, 80–81.
32. Worrall, "Substitutionary Atonement," 343.

The penal substitution theory is accurate in emphasizing substitution and penalty, and this emphasis has resulted in the theory's widespread acceptance. But it goes wrong in insisting that Christ, as our substitute, bears our penalty as a ransom payment to God's retributive justice. Before being taken captive, Christ says in reference to his coming suffering and death, "This is your hour—when darkness reigns" (Luke 22:53). As the Suffering Servant and the Lamb of God, he submits to all that the darkness (not God) would do to him that he might forever break its power.

Christ's death, then, according to the victorious substitution theory, is a substitutionary ransom payment to God's enemy. In being a substitute, bearing the penalty humanity deserves, Christ buys humankind's freedom and simultaneously, by being without sin, wins an eternal victory over Satan and the aforementioned powers of darkness. Christ's death becomes a necessity because of the situation created by God's judgment against human sin following the fall. That is not to say, however, that Christ's death is a necessity in order to *satisfy* God's retributive justice. No contradiction exists in affirming that Christ dies as a substitute while denying that his death satisfies the demands of God's retributive justice.

INCARNATION, ACCORD, AND JUSTICE

Based on the scriptural foundation laid in part 2, it is by accord that Satan takes Christ as a substitute in exchange for all humanity. The realm of Satan's authority is over humanity, so the Incarnation becomes necessary for a substitutionary transaction to take place. A price must be paid, not because God requires it, but because Satan had gained the right to inflict the penalty that God instituted as a judgment on humanity.

Victorious substitution does not compromise God's justice, for God's transactions even with the powers of evil are evenhanded. As Gregory of Nyssa argued long ago, because humankind voluntarily sold itself, in order for the method of restoration to be consistent with justice a ransom price had to be paid.[33] Evil is overcome not by an external use of force but by the voluntary paying of a ransom price. Regarding the devil's rights, on the one hand the devil is an enemy, a beguiler, a usurper. On the other hand, he has gained certain rights over humankind. But this dualism is limited because the devil is not a power equal to God. Insofar

---

33. Gregory of Nyssa, *Catechetical Oration*, 73.

as he has power over humans, he ultimately derives this power from God, for it results from God's own judgment against humankind. God's way of delivering humankind through the payment of a ransom price is entirely just and moral because it respects the position gained by Satan through God's righteous judgment against humankind.[34] The Father and Son respond to the situation created by the fall by making a sacrifice in which Christ becomes a substitute so that humankind may go free.

THE MEANING OF PENALTY

Christ enduring the consequences of humankind's sin is, in reality, the same thing as Christ enduring the penalty for human sin. One must, however, be cautious in using the word *penalty* in describing what Christ endures. "The punishment that brought us peace" (Isa 53:5) is indeed upon Christ; he enters the penumbra of human penalty. But Christ's suffering the penalty does not mean there is a transfer of penalty from God.[35] The idea that he is punished by God, who is ever well-pleased with his beloved Son, must be rejected. However, rejecting entirely the word *penal* is difficult. Denying that Christ's sufferings are penal in the sense of God transferring punishment is not to say that they are in no sense penal.[36] Christ, who is innocent, may have suffered the penalty that humankind deserves,[37] but that does not mean that the action taken against him is from God. Nevertheless, Jesus' sufferings can be considered penal because death is the penalty appointed by God for sin.[38] When Paul says that Christ "[became] a curse for us," it is clear from the context that the curse is not the curse of God but of the law. Humankind's failure to keep the law of God placed us in a plight from which we needed deliverance.

The way in which Paul quotes Deuteronomy 21:23 in Galatians 3:13 demonstrates that God does not punish Christ. Paul says, "Christ redeemed us from the curse of the law by becoming a curse for us, for it is written: 'Cursed is everyone who is hung on a pole.'" Paul, however, is careful not to use the exact words of Deuteronomy, which read, "Anyone who is hung on a pole is under God's curse." Paul omits "under God's

---

34. Aulén, *Christus Victor*, 54–55.
35. Forsyth, *Cruciality of the Cross*, 41.
36. Brown, "Objective and Subjective," 260.
37. Packer, "Cross," 31.
38. Worrall, "Substitutionary Atonement," 353.

curse." To have done otherwise would have been misleading. Jesus is not accursed (judged) of his Father; he is doing the Father's will in becoming accursed, enduring the curse of death for humankind.[39]

God does not inflict pain and suffering. A fallen world of sinful humans and an evil enemy create pain and suffering. To say that God directly inflicts on Christ the torture of crucifixion as the kind of retributive punishment God deems appropriate for human sin is incongruous with his character. To say that he allows Christ to bear the consequences of human sin in enduring the evil that humans and Satan could invent is an entirely different perspective. Enduring crucifixion is a demonstration of an unfathomable love that takes the worst that evil can mete out. "Human and satanic cruelty being what it is, it is perhaps no surprise that Christ meets with a horrifying crucifixion."[40]

In summary, Christ's sufferings may be described as penal, but not in that he suffers punishment as a substitute for others because God has to punish someone. His death is penal in that he suffers the consequences (which could be described as penalties) of other people's sins. He submits to Satan's authority, which was derived from God, and endures the suffering that human sinfulness, under God's judgment following the fall, entails.[41]

Christ even endures, as a consequence of sin, the breaking of his personal relationship with God. The fundamental nature of God's original judgment against humankind is seen at Calvary when the Son, in bearing the full consequences of sin, experiences the feeling of separation from God (Mark 15:34).[42] God allows his Son to endure the cost of human sin so that whoever comes to him might never experience its full consequence. This is certainly substitution. Christ, in becoming humankind's substitute, bears its sin.[43] In doing so Christ reveals the heinousness of sin, the extent of human and satanic evil, and the depth of God's love.

"CHRIST BORE OUR SINS"

The concepts of penalty and substitution are also brought out in 1 Peter 2:24: "'He himself bore our sins' in his body on the cross, so that we

---

39. Worrall, "Substitutionary Atonement," 345.
40. Taliaferro, "Atonement," 90.
41. Gerrish, "Atonement and 'Saving Faith,'" 190.
42. Lee, *Romans*, 80.
43. Crawford, "Penal Theory," 272.

might die to sins and live for righteousness; 'by his wounds you have been healed.'" Advocates of penal substitution interpret this to mean that the sins of humankind were imputed to Christ by God, who then exacted punishment from him. However, these conclusions are not stated; they are conjectural, as they do not necessarily follow from the terminology.

New Testament scholar Peter Davids, in his commentary on 1 Peter, says of this verse:

> The use of tree for gallows, and (in the NT) therefore for a cross, is a typical euphemism (Deut 21:22; Acts 5:30; 10:39; 13:29; Gal 3:13). Because of its use in Deuteronomy 21:22, the idea that the one so hung was cursed by God cannot be far from the author's mind, but without explicitly mentioning this he points out that this death was vicarious, for it was "our sins" that he bore. This fact is further underlined in the last clause of the verse (now shifting to Isa 53:5) that his wounds . . . have brought healing to us.[44]

This book agrees with Davids' statement that Christ's death is vicarious. It is indeed "our sins" that he bore, and his wounds bring healing. Christ takes the consequences of "our sins." However, Davids' contention that "because of [the tree's] use in Deuteronomy 21:22, the idea that the one so hung was cursed by God cannot be far from the author's mind" is not supported. To say that Christ was "cursed by God" is clearly not stated in this verse or anywhere in Scripture. (As mentioned previously, in Galatians 3:13 Paul omits the phrase "cursed by God" ["under God's curse" NIV] when he quotes Deuteronomy 21:23 in reference to Christ's death.) To say that Christ being cursed by God "cannot be far from the author's mind" is conjecture and is based on the penal substitution theory's notion of satisfaction.

Some scholars interpret "in his body on the cross" with the sense of *motion toward* the cross.[45] The RV, RSV, and some others have as an alternate reading in a footnote, "He himself carried up our sins in his body to the tree," presenting an image of sacrifice with Jesus as high priest carrying sins to the cross.[46] However, 1 Peter 4:14 has another example of the same preposition being used to denote *place where*. "Upon the tree" ("on the cross" NIV) indicates the place where Christ bore sins.[47] This

---

44. Davids, *First Epistle of Peter*, 113.
45. Cranfield, *I & II Peter and Jude*, 85–86.
46. Michaels, *1 Peter*, 148. The "some" are cited as Bigg, 147, and Schelkle, 85.
47. Cranfield, *I & II Peter and Jude*, 85–86.

translation is preferred because, as Davids points out, "The idea of Jesus offering up our sins as a sacrifice that God accepts is intolerable in any known Jewish or early Christian context."[48] No Jew thought of sins being laid on the altar, because nothing unholy could come into God's presence (in 1 Peter 1:19, Christ is referred to as "a lamb without blemish or defect").[49] Those who interpret this verse to mean that Christ carried up our sins "to the altar of the cross" read into the passage ideas that do not belong to the context.[50] To "bear" sins, then, is not to offer sins, for Christ offered not our sins but himself.[51]

What does bearing our sins on the cross mean? The background for this expression is found in Isaiah 53:12, "He bore the sin of many."[52] Since "sin" or "sins" cannot be literally borne, to "bear the sin" means to bear vicariously the penal consequence of sin.[53] This use is rare, but a parallel is found in Numbers 14:33: "Your children will be shepherds here for forty years, suffering for [the penalty of] your unfaithfulness."[54] Christ suffered the "curse" of sins by enduring their penal consequences.[55] And this bearing of human sins is substitutionary because Christ suffered the punishment in humankind's place.[56]

The emphasis in this passage, however, is on the removal of sins achieved by Christ suffering the penal consequences. The "bore" in 1 Peter 2:24 simply means "carried away." A good translation is, "He himself carried [away] our sins in his body on the cross," the point being that he took them away.[57] Peter says Christ carried our sins away "so that we might die to sins and live for righteousness." Similarly, Romans 6:11 says, "Count yourselves dead to sin but alive to God in Christ Jesus." The Greek word translated "die" in 1 Peter 2:24 occurs only here in the NT and means not so much death as complete separation. The literal sense is "to be away from" or "to have no part in."[58] The contrast with "live" suggests

48. Michaels, *1 Peter*, 148.
49. Selwyn, *First Epistle of Peter*, 180.
50. Selwyn, *First Epistle of Peter*, 180.
51. Masterman, *First Epistle of Peter*, 116.
52. Selwyn, *First Epistle of Peter*, 180.
53. Cranfield, *I & II Peter and Jude*, 83.
54. Beare, *First Epistle of Peter*, 124.
55. Selwyn, *First Epistle of Peter*, 180.
56. Cranfield, *I & II Peter and Jude*, 86.
57. Michaels, *1 Peter*, 148.
58. Wand, *General Epistles of St. Peter and St. Jude*, 84.

the translation "die," but Peter does not use the common word for "die." He chooses the Greek word that means "to be away" or "to depart."[59] The point is that sins are departed, removed.

Parting with sins is not the end itself but the preliminary to living for what is right and doing good.[60] Isaiah 53:4 says prophetically of Christ, "Surely he took up our pain and bore our suffering." Matthew 8:16–17 interprets this passage to mean that Christ "bore" the people's spiritual infirmities and physical diseases by healing them, by *taking them away*. Therefore, in addition to Christ bearing the penal consequences of sin, it can be said that he bore sin away. The effect of the Atonement is an actual abandonment of sin and a redirection of life toward righteousness.[61]

First Peter 2:24 also emphasizes this positive purpose of Christ's death, that humankind, having abandoned sins, might live for righteousness. "Righteousness" here is not imputed righteousness but practical righteousness; that is, virtuous conduct, doing what is right. Finally, the sufferings of Christ result in healing. Peter returns to the second-person pronoun when quoting Isaiah 53:5, "By his wounds you have been healed," emphasizing the special application of his words to suffering slaves.[62]

Because Christ was wounded, "you have been healed." "Healed" suggests restoration to health from the wounds made by sin; namely, moral and spiritual healing. Davids says, "Like Isaiah before him Peter uses physical healing as a metaphor for religious conversion."[63] This interpretation is supported by the next verse: "For 'you were like sheep going astray,' but now you have returned to the Shepherd and Overseer of your souls" (1 Peter 2:25).[64] Conversion is the opposite of aimless wandering. When one is converted, their life has a purpose that is directed toward God.[65] Nothing in 1 Peter 2:24 should be interpreted to mean that *God* punished Christ for the sins of humankind, but that through Christ's substitutionary death the power of sin was broken. Peter's meaning is seen from the second part of the verse. Christ died (bore sin) to release humankind from their sins so that they could live in righteousness.

59. Michaels, *1 Peter*, 148.
60. Michaels, *1 Peter*, 148.
61. Selwyn, *First Epistle of Peter*, 181.
62. Vaughan and Lea, *1, 2 Peter, Jude*, 69.
63. Michaels, *1 Peter*, 149.
64. Michaels, *1 Peter*, 70.
65. Masterman, *First Epistle of Peter*, 117.

Particularly notable is the similarity between the physical sufferings of Christ and those of Peter's primary audience in this passage: slaves who suffer for doing good.[66] The context is not primarily doctrinal, for Peter is bidding Christians to follow Christ's example of sin-bearing (2:19–21).[67] The mention of wounds ("stripes" KJV) in verse 24 has particular relevance to slaves. Christ, too, was wounded, but because of his suffering there is healing for slaves.[68] Continual stripes were the lot of slaves under harsh masters, and death by crucifixion was the punishment for those determined to be insurrectionists. Peter's readers might easily fall under that condemnation. How could they endure such a life? Only by recognizing that Christ, who had called them, had himself suffered in this fashion, but that by his suffering he had broken the power of sin and thus made possible the imitation of his own humility in suffering.[69] Slaves bore physical suffering, and therefore Peter emphasizes the physical sufferings of Christ.[70] The phrase "in his [Christ's] body" stresses the fact that redemption was accomplished here on earth within the sphere and under the conditions of human life.[71] The phrase is reminiscent of Colossians 1:22: "But now he has reconciled you by Christ's physical body through death."

GOD'S WRATH IS NOT COMPROMISED

God's wrath is his response to sin, which results in judgment. God's wrath is not imposed on Christ, and as a result, it is certainly not exhausted but still functions as it always has.[72] The OT Scriptures are filled with examples of God punishing wrongdoing of both individuals and nations. One cannot read these books without acknowledging the plain references to the judgment of a God who brought a flood, rained fire upon Sodom and Gomorrah, destroyed the firstborn of Egypt, and excluded from the promised land Moses, Aaron, and nearly the whole generation that crossed the Red Sea. The testimony of the psalmists and the prophets is

---

66. Cranfield, *I & II Peter and Jude*, 83.
67. Selwyn, *First Epistle of Peter*, 180–81.
68. Beare, *First Epistle of Peter*, 124.
69. Cranfield, *I & II Peter and Jude*, 83–84.
70. Masterman, *First Epistle of Peter*, 117.
71. Vaughan, *1, 2 Peter, Jude*, 68–69.
72. Forsyth, *Cruciality of the Cross*, 41.

that God is on the side of justice and will punish evil. Sometimes they acknowledge the forbearance that delays the execution of punishment so sinful people might have time to repent. Sometimes they warn their own people and the nations that the wrath of God will only be more terrible if they do not forsake their sin.

The NT is just as clear on the subject of God's wrath as the OT. Christ said, "The Father judges no one, but has entrusted all judgment to the Son" (John 5:22). Christ refers to a time when "the Son of Man is going to come in his Father's glory with his angels, and then he will reward each person according to what they have done" (Matt 16:27). Peter puts the future judgment of the world by Christ as one of the basic truths the apostles had been called to proclaim: "He commanded us to preach to the people and to testify that he is the one whom God appointed as judge of the living and the dead" (Acts 10:42). Paul warned the Athenians that God "has set a day when he will judge the world with justice by the man he has appointed" (Acts 17:31), and he spoke with Felix about "the judgment to come" (Acts 24:25). The future judgment is spoken of for Christians as well: "We must all appear before the judgment seat of Christ, so that each of us may receive what is due us for the things done while in the body, whether good or bad" (2 Cor 5:10). Scripture speaks of the execution of future wrath on the unrepentant, that they "are storing up wrath against [themselves] for the day of God's wrath, when his righteous judgment will be revealed" (Rom 2:5). And Christ, who "is revealed from heaven in blazing fire, . . . will punish those who do not know God and do not obey the gospel of our Lord Jesus" (2 Thess 1:7–8). There will be a terrible sentence inflicted on the impenitent: "Depart from me, you who are cursed, into the eternal fire prepared for the devil and his angels" (Matt 25:41).[73]

To say that Christ becomes the substitute for humanity, bearing the consequences of human sin, does not mean that God's wrath is upon him or that no penalty remains to be paid by those who reject salvation. Eternal separation from himself is the penalty that God has decreed for unrepentant sinners. As Dale points out, "From the final judgment of God there will be no escape, and upon those who have resisted His authority and rejected His grace He will inflict the just penalties of their sins."[74] Crucifixion should not be viewed as God's execution of justice. To deny

---

73. Dale, *Atonement*, 383–89.
74. Dale, *Atonement*, 449.

that God's wrath is inflicted on Christ in his death is not to deny or in any way compromise God's wrath itself. The wrath of God is an active force in the world today and will certainly be seen in its full consequences in the future judgment. Calvary is not an act of God's wrath but of his love.

Although God's wrath is not inflicted on Christ at Calvary, his death becomes a necessity because of God's wrath (or judgment) that was imposed on humankind after the fall. The powers that opposed God became instruments of the divine wrath against the world.[75] "The power and right of Satan and his hosts are derived from the wrath of God."[76] From this power and right of Satan, the world, through God's sacrificial, substitutionary gift of his Son, is ransomed, set free, and offered salvation.

WAS CHRIST'S DEATH NECESSARY FOR ATONEMENT?

An important issue, and one on which atonement theories differ, is the question of necessity. If salvation is a matter of grace and sovereignty, it cannot be a matter of necessity. However, if it is given that God in his love intends to save a people (Titus 2:14), then it must be asked whether the Incarnation and suffering and death of the Son of God was an absolute necessity as the only method of atonement. Could God's love realize its end and fulfill its purpose through other means? Could God and humankind have been reconciled in any other way?[77]

The view known as "hypothetical necessity" maintains that God could have accomplished atonement through other means, for with God all things are possible. According to this view, God in his wisdom chooses the way that has the most advantages.[78] The moral-influence, exemplarist, and governmental theories all hold to hypothetical necessity.

The other view may be called "consequent absolute necessity." The word *consequent* points to the fact that salvation is an act of God's grace and sovereignty. The word *absolute* refers to a necessity arising from God's own nature. According to this view, God, intending salvation for humankind, has no other way to accomplish atonement. The penal

---

75. Kleinknecht, *Wrath*, 118.
76. Kleinknecht, *Wrath*, 118.
77. A. Hodge, *Atonement*, 234.
78. J. Murray, *Redemption*, 11.

substitution theory holds that absolute necessity is due to God's nature, which demands retributive justice.[79]

The victorious substitution theory also holds to consequent absolute necessity, but not based on the demand for satisfaction required by retributive justice. God's method of atonement is his just and necessary response to an actual historical and spiritual situation.[80] God, who is sovereign, for reasons that are not entirely revealed but are surely related to humanity's free choice, allows Satan to become "the prince of this world." Satan holds humankind in bondage because of their sin and because of God's judgment, and humankind is unable to free itself. If humanity is to be free, God must respond. And because God is just, he must accomplish this deliverance in a lawful and just way.[81] A sacrificial substitutionary ransom provides that way. When Peter objects to the necessity of Christ's suffering and death, his words are rebuked as satanic. Peter had become the mouthpiece of the Lord's tempter, and the sharpness of the rebuke indicates the reality of the temptation to turn away from what was unavoidable.[82]

Like the penal substitution theory, then, victorious substitution insists that God must act according to his nature. The theories differ, however, in their understanding of God's nature and in their perception of the situation that requires God's intervention. If humankind is in bondage to sin, death, and Satan, then redemption and deliverance are what is needed. The way of redemption requires the Incarnation and includes the payment of a ransom price, which involves suffering the consequences of sin at the hand of an evil enemy.

The necessity of substitution is related to humankind's need, not to God's need. James Denney, in recognizing this point, says:

> If I were sitting on the end of the pier, on a summer day, enjoying the sunshine and the air, and someone came along and jumped into the water and got drowned "to prove his love for me," I should find it quite unintelligible. I might be much in need of love, but an act in no rational relation to any of my necessities could not prove it. But if I had fallen over the pier and were drowning, and someone sprang into the water, and at the cost of making my peril, or what but for him would be my fate, his own,

---

79. J. Murray, *Redemption*, 12.
80. Forsyth, *Cruciality of the Cross*, 97.
81. Forsyth, *Cruciality of the Cross*, 97.
82. Hodgson, *Atonement*, 75.

saved me from death, then I should say, "Greater love hath no man than this." I should say it intelligibly, because there would be an intelligible relation between the sacrifice which one made and the necessity from which it redeemed. Is it making any rash assumption to say that there must be such an intelligible relation between the death of Christ—the great act in which his love for sinners is demonstrated—and the sin of the world?[83]

Would the death of Christ even be the supreme demonstration of love if there were no necessity for such suffering?[84]

Jesus dies "for our sins" because the sin of humanity and its consequent bondage makes the Atonement necessary.[85] If Christ does not die as a satisfaction for humankind's sins, and if he does not die for his own sins since he has none (2 Cor 5:21; 1 Pet 2:22), one could conclude, apart from the ransom concept, that Christ is handed over to die unjustly, undeservedly, and unnecessarily. This conclusion is unthinkable in light of Christ's prayer in Gethsemane. Three times Jesus prays, "If it is possible, may this cup be taken from me" (Matt 26:39). Surely absolute necessity exists. Apart from a demand for satisfaction, only the ransom concept makes God's action an absolute necessity and therefore understandable.

According to subjective theories of the Atonement there is no reason that reconciliation, any more than forgiveness, *has* to involve death.[86] This book agrees fully with this conclusion. However, victorious substitution holds to another reason for absolute necessity: humankind needs to be ransomed and the power of God's enemy needs to be broken.

VICTORIOUS SUBSTITUTION DOES NOT VIOLATE REASON, MORALITY, OR SCRIPTURE

The victorious substitution theory does not pose logical, moral, and theological dilemmas such as those created by the penal substitution theory. For God to pay a ransom to himself (or propitiate himself) is not logical. Yet it is logical for God to pay a ransom to the one who holds humankind in bondage. For the Son to take humankind's place in exchange for their freedom was an act of sacrifice and love on the part of both the Father

---

83. Worrall, "Substitutionary Atonement," 355–56.
84. J. Murray, *Redemption*, 17.
85. N. Robinson, *Jesus Christ Saves Men*, 140.
86. Hebblethwaite, "Doctrine of the Atonement," 66.

The Scriptural Foundations of Victorious Substitution

and the Son. No division is thereby created in the Godhead where the Son must appease the wrath of the Father.

In the penal substitution theory, God demands punishment for sins and then professes to freely forgive. No such contradiction exists in victorious substitution, for God is not punishing Christ. And since God is not punishing Christ, he cannot be punishing the innocent, an act that would violate his character. Under victorious substitution, God, who is "the same yesterday and today and forever" (Heb 13:8) judges the guilty and forgives the repentant just as he did in the past, does in the present, and will do in the future (Num 14:18–19; Ezek 18:21, 27, 30).

In the victorious substitution theory, God acts to free humankind from the power of Satan, sin, and death so that they may be reconciled to himself. This is consistent with Scripture, which teaches that God takes action to reconcile humankind. In the penal substitution theory, God takes action to reconcile himself. However, no Scripture indicates that God himself, in order to be reconciled, needs more than one's repentance and faith.

Advocates of penal substitution have a problem relating substitution and salvation. The theory's idea concerning substitution contains a contradiction:[87] if one does not hold to universal salvation they must believe that some (the unrepentant) whose sins are transferred to Christ will pay the penalty themselves also. Substitution viewed in light of the ransom concept has no such contradiction.[88] The victorious substitution theory, then, does not violate reason, morality, or any scriptural principle.

---

87. Packer, "Cross," 37.

88. Substitution for the elect only also has no contradiction. Cave points out that John McLeod Campbell was deposed from the ministry in 1831 by the Church of Scotland because he maintained that Christ died for all, in clear opposition to the Westminster Confession. His abandonment of the doctrine of predestination caused him to change his understanding of the Atonement. He recognized that the penal substitution theory finds its most consistent expression when the sins whose penalty Christ bore are regarded as the sins of the elect only. Since Campbell believed that Christ died for all, he saw a contradiction in the penal theory. He says, "That cannot be the true conception of the nature of the atonement which implies that Christ died only for an election from among men." Cave, *Work of Christ*, 262; Campbell, *Atonement*, 51.

CONCLUSION TO PART III—THE VICTORIOUS SUBSTITUTION THEORY OF THE ATONEMENT

Both the victorious substitution and penal substitution theories rely on the same scriptural facts concerning Christ's suffering and death: *Christ is humankind's substitute, enduring the penalty for sin that humankind deserves*. Given the dominance of penal substitution since the Reformation, it is necessary to remind the reader that both views remain in the realm of theory and should not be confused with the above fact. Below is a summary of how each *theory* approaches the reality of Christ's atoning death.

Penal substitution theory: Christ endures the penalty from the hand of God, who punishes him in humankind's place. Christ's life is a sacrifice that propitiates God's wrath and satisfies his requirement for retributive justice. The ransom payment is made by Christ to God to free humanity from God's judgment. God both inflicts and endures the penalty.

Victorious substitution theory: Christ endures the penalty from the hand of Satan who, as a result of the fall (human free choice) and God's judgment against sin, holds humankind in bondage and has the "power of death." In exchange for humanity, the ransom payment, Christ himself as humankind's substitute, is made to Satan. God endures the penalty. He does not inflict it.

PART IV

The Christian Experience of Victorious Substitution

PART 4 LAYS OUT an application of the victorious substitution theory to the life of the believer, which includes a discussion of free choice, justification, reconciliation, and exchanging one's life for the life of Christ. For those desiring to reign in life with Christ, there is a simple, if still difficult, way to participate in the victory of Christ over Satan, sin, and death through faith.

8

The Application of Atonement
A New Situation

A FINISHED WORK OF Christ precedes Christian experience, for Scripture states that "while we were God's enemies, we were reconciled to him through the death of his Son" (Rom 5:10). Second Corinthians 5:18–19 also makes this point: "All this is from God, who reconciled us to himself through Christ and gave us the ministry of reconciliation: that God was reconciling the world to himself in Christ, not counting people's sins against them. And he has committed to us the message of reconciliation." The English verb "to reconcile" does not mean exactly the same as the corresponding Greek verb. The English indicates that both parties are reconciled to one another, implying that humans have already entered into a state of peace with God apart from any response on their part to the work of Christ. But the Greek does not go this far, and this idea would clearly contradict even the immediate context. If reconciliation is complete there is no need for the "message of reconciliation." These verses do indicate, however, that Christ finishes the work of reconciliation (i.e., makes atonement) in some sense even before the preaching of the gospel. God acts apart from humanity without its involvement.[1] The human situation changes because of God's initiative and Christ's victory.[2] Jesus pays the price for the reconciliation of all humankind, providing for the liberation of all people, even the false prophets who are said to have

---

1. Worrall, "Substitutionary Atonement," 343.
2. Bloesch, *Jesus Is Victor!*, 49.

been "bought" by Christ (2 Peter 2:1). Forgiveness and reconciliation are waiting for every sinner that repents.

Because of the new situation created by Christ's sacrifice, people are free to become citizens of God's kingdom and experience the benefits of salvation if they so choose.[3] God's reason for acting on behalf of humanity is that he desires a people to be his own: he "gave himself for us to redeem us from all wickedness and to purify for himself a people that are his very own, eager to do what is good" (Titus 2:14). After God pays the price and wins the victory, is God's end accomplished? Not exactly. God does not violate free will and therefore each person chooses their allegiance freely. Although Christ pays the price for human freedom, a person does not join God's kingdom unless they choose to belong to the Lord. If one does not so choose, they remain under the divine judgment against sin and subject to its consequences of eternal death. The "message of reconciliation" to which Paul refers serves to bring people to God in repentance and faith. Paul calls on all people to choose reconciliation: "We are therefore Christ's ambassadors, as though God were making his appeal through us. We implore you on Christ's behalf: Be reconciled to God" (2 Cor 5:20). God does not remit guilt and receive the sinner into fellowship with himself apart from repentance and faith. Grace that would forgive the impenitent would deny God's righteousness and moral order. Justification takes place individually but only because Christ has already redeemed humankind. Saving faith does not receive the benefits of a completed work which itself atones, but rather a completed work that may *become* atonement for the individual. Atonement must involve this personal choice if God and the sinner are really to be "at one."[4]

THE APPLICATION OF ATONEMENT IS BOTH OBJECTIVE AND SUBJECTIVE

In one sense the Atonement is a historical event, and in this sense the word is most commonly used. Yet in another sense atonement takes place each time an individual repents and believes.[5] In order to have a relationship of fellowship with God, humans must make a subjective response (repentance and faith) to God's objective work (incarnation,

---

3. Worrall, "Substitutionary Atonement," 343.
4. Gerrish, "Atonement and 'Saving Faith,'" 185.
5. Macquarrie, *Principles of Christian Theology*, 324.

death, and resurrection). God's forgiveness is always waiting and longing to begin the process of reconciliation. The offer of forgiveness and fellowship with God, however, is not something that happens automatically or by just saying the right words.[6] The heart of the believer must long for communion just as God does.

The everyday experience of family life reveals that restoring a relationship requires deep commitment and cooperation. As Fiddes explains:

> A healing of relationship and personality cannot be accepted like a package, a ticket or even a contract. It must be created anew through the meeting of persons. Applied to the doctrine of reconciliation between God and humanity this means that human response must actually be part of the act of salvation, not merely a reaction to it afterwards.... Popular evangelistic preaching has often, for example, depicted a prisoner languishing in a condemned cell on the eve of execution, and then suddenly receiving a free pardon from the monarch or president. All the prisoner needs to do, it is urged, is to accept what is offered.... The picture of a pardoned criminal fails to communicate the painful relational experience which lies at the heart of forgiving and being forgiven. The mere issue of a pardon cannot touch a person deeply; in life a prisoner can accept a pardon and go free, hating the authorities who gave it and the judge who sentenced him—or perhaps laughing at them.[7]

> There is a great deal of difference between believing that God "saves" through Christ, and believing that we simply claim the benefits of a salvation that has already happened, a deal that has already been concluded. Salvation in the present tense has frequently been depicted as if it were merely picking up a ticket to paradise which was issued long ago, and which has been waiting through long ages on the counter of a celestial travel agent. But a transactional view of atonement like this is highly impersonal. If salvation is the healing of a broken relationship between persons, then it must actually happen now; it must involve the human response as an intimate part of the act of atonement.[8]

When one speaks of *the* Atonement, they often refer to a historical event that took place in which Christ died and was victoriously resurrected. Atonement takes place for individuals, however, as they come to God

---

6. H. Robinson, *Redemption and Revelation*, 218.
7. Fiddes, *Present Salvation*, 15.
8. Fiddes, *Present Salvation*, 14.

in repentance and faith. Atonement is also a process that continues after conversion, for believers grow in their "at-one-ment" with God.

The purpose of the Atonement, then, is the restoration of fellowship with God. Those who respond to Christ find undeserved acceptance and unconditional love—the beginning of a relationship with God in which a new and righteous life becomes possible.[9] The subjective element, an initial and sustained human response, is essential to the Atonement. Each soul is free to choose to be reconciled to God, free to repent and enter into a loving relationship of fellowship in which they become the "friend" of God (John 15:14). Christ can be humankind's substitute and win its freedom. He can draw individuals by his love, but he cannot achieve reconciliation alone. Each person must desire and choose to be "at one" with him.[10] This at-one-ment is implied when Scripture speaks of Christians as being "in Christ" and of Christ as being "in" believers.[11]

The theory of victorious substitution is entirely compatible with the above description of the divine-human relationship and subjective view of the Atonement. It is true that what God has done in Christ declares his unchanging love and draws the human soul to desire fellowship with him. His love and readiness to forgive have always been present. However, an understanding of the Atonement that only involves this subjective view is inadequate. The NT simply does not allow one to devise an atonement theory from faith and response alone. Such a theory would be much less than the mighty act of deliverance, victory, and new creation of which the NT authors speak.[12]

The Atonement is objective as well as subjective. It is a rescue accomplished by God in Christ on behalf of sinners.[13] The action of God invades human society. Christ is the king who comes to win victory over enslaving forces.[14] The objective act, the victory, makes individual reconciliation possible.[15] Humankind has to be freed from Satan and the consequences of sin, and Christ's sinless life and undeserved death accomplish this end. He is resurrected victorious, having taken our place.

---

9. Ziesler, "Salvation," 359.
10. Hodges, *Pattern of Atonement*, 55.
11. N. Robinson, *Jesus Christ Saves Men*, 153.
12. Barry, *Atonement*, 148.
13. Hart, "Anselm," 322.
14. Macquarrie, *Principles of Christian Theology*, 321.
15. F. Young, *Sacrifice*, 95.

The freedom that God wins for humankind is, however, a freedom that insists on response. God does not override this freedom, but the opportunity to respond is there for "whosoever will" (John 3:16).

The following sections are each directed toward the application of the objective, historical work of the Atonement in individual lives—in justification, reconciliation, exchange, and victory. These four areas of application do not involve theory, but the ongoing process of atonement within individuals and in the world.

THE APPLICATION OF ATONEMENT: JUSTIFICATION

This section will discuss how the scriptural concept of justification fits into atonement theory by contrasting the penal substitution view with the view of victorious substitution. It should be noted that the English words *just* and *righteous* are both used to translate the Greek adjective *dikaios*. However, "to justify" does not mean "to make righteous." The verb as used by Greek writers means "to put in right standing," or "to treat justly." The first definition would involve pardon.[16]

Paul declares that humans are "justified freely by his grace" (Rom 3:24–25). Through repentance and faith, persons are pardoned in God's law court. The term *justification*, then, refers to release from sin's penalty through the gift of eternal life. Colossians 2:14 states that God has "canceled the charge of our legal indebtedness, which stood against us and condemned us; he has taken it away, nailing it to the cross."

Yet Romans 4:5 claims that God "justifies the ungodly," a clear contradiction of civil justice. The contrast with conventional legality emphasizes God's incomparable act of grace. Paul's switch to the past tense "justified" indicates that God completely absolves the sinner (Rom 5:1).[17] They receive a new status as a result of a judicial pronouncement. The forensic background of this word group (just, justify, righteous, righteousness) indicates that the term *righteousness* in this context denotes a standing or a status and not the ethical quality of right living.[18] As Morris says, "[Rom 3:4] refers to God being justified, which is enough to show that the meaning of the word must be something like 'declare

---

16. Dodd, *Romans*, 51.
17. Quell, *Righteousness*, 61–63.
18. Morris, *Apostolic*, 250.

righteous, for it is impossible to think that the apostle meant that God was to be 'made righteous.'"[19]

The penal substitution theory maintains that God can justify the ungodly because he has already passed sentence on someone else; namely, Christ. God *does* pass the sentence that law requires, but he carries it out on a substitute. However, a theory of transferred penalty cannot be deduced from the metaphor of justification. Justification simply asserts that when summoned into God's law court, in spite of all the evidence and strict demands of the law, one is pardoned or accepted by God rather than condemned. Justification is the bare statement of acceptance into good standing and does not contain the idea of transferred penalty. Scripture makes no connection between the new status of a believer and penal substitution. Advocates of penal substitution assume the very *fact* of justification implies a process of substitution involving a transfer of penalty.[20] This book maintains that no such connection exists.

Neither does the metaphor of justification include the idea of transferred righteousness. Christians may say with Paul that Christ is their righteousness (1 Cor 1:30) just as he is their redemption (1 Cor 1:30), but it is quite another step to propose a doctrine of salvation by legal transfer in which God agrees to impute Christ's righteousness in exchange for human guilt and to impose a penalty upon Christ. Such a conclusion is not stated by Paul or other NT writers. It involves assumptions about the demands of law and the nature of divine justice which this book has already examined and denied in chapter 3.[21]

Traditional Protestantism emphasizes a doctrine of imputed righteousness, stating that God imputes Christ's merits to believers.[22] Calvin, for instance, says that "the Son of God, though spotlessly pure, took upon him the disgrace and ignominy of our iniquities, and in return clothed us with his purity."[23] This view, however, should be rejected, for if one holds to imputed righteousness "we have not emancipated ourselves from that very doctrine which Paul spent most of his life in combating—namely, that salvation is by righteousness. . . . The fact of the matter is that God does not require righteousness at all, in any shape or shadow, as

19. Morris, *Apostolic*, 259.
20. Morris, *Apostolic*, 272.
21. Fiddes, *Present Salvation*, 88–89.
22. Imputed righteousness is discussed further in the section entitled "The Application of Atonement: Exchange."
23. Calvin, *Institutes*, 132.

a condition of salvation. He requires faith. . . . It involves such repentance as the sinner is capable of at the time, and in that sense it involves 'true repentance.'"[24] Repentance and faith express the inner condition, whereas justification or righteousness expresses the outward standing.[25]

Justification, then, is essentially an expression of the status of a believer before God and describes only this aspect of the new life of a believer.[26] Justification means acceptance with God, "rightness" before him (Matt 12:37; Rom 9:30–32). The sinner is delivered from the consequences of their sins and receives God's forgiveness and approval.[27] The NT conceives of the one who is justified living a righteous life: "Dear children, do not let anyone lead you astray. The one who does what is right is righteous" (1 John 3:7).

How does justification, God's absolution of the repentant believer, relate to reconciliation or atonement? From God's point of view reconciliation takes place when he forgives, because sin is expiated and therefore a barrier to fellowship no longer exists. Before pardon, a person's communion with God is hindered by the sense of guilt produced by the conscience. However, when they believe in Christ and repent and accept Paul's statement that God forgives the guilty, they are able to move forward in the freedom of a clear conscience and the confidence of a restored relationship.[28] The following section will examine the nature of the reconciliation that takes place between the justified believer and God.

THE APPLICATION OF ATONEMENT: RECONCILIATION

In addition to being both a historical event and an event in the lives of individual Christians, atonement also involves a continuous process of reconciliation, of becoming "one" with God (John 17). What is the nature of this reconciliation that takes place between God and a person who chooses to be obedient to the Father? The answer depends on the nature of the divine-human relationship that needs restoring. Different theories of the Atonement perceive this relationship in different ways. In an article entitled "Atonement and Reconciliation," Vincent Brümmer

---

24. Snaith, *Old Testament*, 257.
25. Morris, *Apostolic*, 258.
26. Symonds, "Justification," 69–70.
27. Ziesler, "Salvation," 357.
28. Dodd, *Romans*, 53.

analyzes three basic models of relationship with God and their implications for the theories of atonement.[29] This outstanding analysis will be summarized to clarify the nature of the relationship that God desires and that Jesus dies to make possible.

Relationship with God is often understood in terms of relationships that people have with each other. Three distinct kinds of relationship exist: controlling relations, contractual relations, and fellowship. (In reality, human relations are almost always a combination of all three.)[30]

Controlling relationships are those in which one person tries to gain control over another person. These relationships are asymmetrical because one person is the object of another's control. The controlling person is able to establish, change, or terminate the relationship, whereas the object does not have the ability to establish, change, or prevent the relationship. The relationship is impersonal because only one in the relationship is functioning as a person—the other is an object.[31]

Contractual relationships are those in which persons relate to each other in terms of social agreements. Each party accepts certain rights and duties toward the other. People enter into such relationships looking to benefit from the terms. Such relationships are quite different from those of mutual fellowship in which each partner chooses to serve the interests of the other and not primarily their own, or in which one identifies with the other so completely they consider the interests of the other to be their own. In contractual relationships, goodwill toward another is conditional and limited. One person will keep their part of the bargain provided the other keeps theirs. A person's value is determined by their usefulness, and the good that one is prepared to do for the other is proportional to this usefulness. Another person who could provide the same services would do just as well. There are no commitments to a person as a person, only to them as a useful partner.[32]

In relationships of fellowship, however, a person is valuable for who they are, and the relationship has intrinsic value irrespective of usefulness. Neither another person nor another relationship can be a substitute because one cannot have *that* relationship with anybody

---

29. Brümmer, "Atonement and Reconciliation," 435–52.
30. Brümmer, "Atonement and Reconciliation," 435.
31. Brümmer, "Atonement and Reconciliation," 436.
32. Brümmer, "Atonement and Reconciliation," 437.

The Application of Atonement

else. That irreplaceability gives one personal value and identity in such relationships.[33]

All three types of relationship can be damaged, and the way in which each must be restored is different. In a controlling relationship it is up to the controlling partner to manage and repair the relationship. They therefore receive the credit for restoring the relationship or the blame if there is no improvement.[34]

In a contractual arrangement the relationship breaks down when one party fails in their duties or responsibilities to the other. The other is then no longer obligated to fulfill their part of the arrangement. There are three ways in which this kind of relationship can be restored. (1) The offending party could try again to do that which they failed to do, or render some kind of equivalent service. The other party's rights would be satisfied and the offender would be restored to a position in which they could expect to receive their rights. (2) If the offending party is unable or unwilling to make satisfaction, the offended party could restore the balance through punishing the offender by withholding the services that would have been due. If punishment is borne, then the debt is paid and the balance of rights and duties is restored to the relationship. Providing satisfaction or bearing punishment are therefore two ways that the guilty party could *earn* restoration. (3) A final way in which a contractual relationship could be restored is for the offended party to condone the wrong done by not requiring any reparation.[35] In this case the action becomes an acceptable part of the relationship or of the contract.

Relationships of fellowship are those in which persons relate to each other in such a way that they treat the interests of the other as their own. Their communion and union is such that one loves the other as themselves. Humans are not able to sustain this level of fellowship consistently. Because of selfishness they put their own interests above those of the other and therefore act in ways that cause the other injury. When this occurs the relationship has been damaged, and the offended party has grounds for resentment.[36]

There are two conditions that must be met for the relationship to be healed. The wronged party must become willing to forgive. They must

---

33. Brümmer, "Atonement and Reconciliation," 437–38.
34. Brümmer, "Atonement and Reconciliation," 439.
35. Brümmer, "Atonement and Reconciliation," 440–41.
36. Brümmer, "Atonement and Reconciliation," 440.

consider the breach in relationship a greater evil than the wrong done to them. This essential element for healing the relationship is characterized by suffering. The one who will forgive is the one who suffers; they pay the price for healing the relationship. As Horace Bushnell says, suffering is "the necessary correlate of forgiveness."[37] Yet, to forgive is not the same thing as to condone. The forgiven offense remains offensive; it does not become an acceptable element of the relationship.[38] Forgiveness is not simple. If it appears easy it probably involves the condonation of indifference, which implies that one does not care deeply about the character of the one who has wronged them. However, if one is betrayed by a family member or a friend, forgiveness is more difficult and painful.[39]

The second element that is essential for healing and restoration of fellowship is repentance on the part of the offending partner. Forgiveness is one's willingness to identify with the other in spite of their offense. If, however, the offending party refuses to acknowledge their wrong and does not repent of their actions, continued identification would entail acquiescence or condonation. Therefore the offending party *must* seek forgiveness, acknowledge their wrong, and have a change of heart in order for the relationship to be restored. Forgiveness from one party and repentance from the other are required for true restoration of relationship.[40]

Although repentance is a necessary condition for the restoration of fellowship, it cannot cause or earn forgiveness. Neither does it create the obligation to forgive. Forgiveness must be freely given from the heart. Both parties must be involved in restoring a relationship just as both parties must be involved in establishing it in the first place. Neither forgiveness nor repentance can be forced or earned. Bearing punishment or making satisfaction earns reinstatement in a contractual relationship, and what is earned the other party is required to give. Punishment or satisfaction makes forgiveness unnecessary.

Forgiveness cannot be demanded as a right; it can only be sought. In asking for forgiveness one acknowledges their dependence on the free decision of the other.[41] If there is both confession of wrong and forgive-

---

37. Bushnell, *Forgiveness and Law*, 48.
38. Brümmer, "Atonement and Reconciliation," 440.
39. Cave, *Work of Christ*, 280.
40. Brümmer, "Atonement and Reconciliation," 441.
41. Brümmer, "Atonement and Reconciliation," 441

ness, a relationship may not only be restored, it may be strengthened, as Burnaby suggests:

> We shall be to one another what we were before, save for one important difference. I know now that you are a person who can forgive, that you prefer to have suffered rather than to resent, and that to keep me as a friend, or to avoid becoming my enemy, is more important to you than to maintain your own rights. And you know that I am a person who is not too proud to acknowledge his fault, and that your goodwill is worth more to me than the maintenance of my own cause.... Forgiveness does not only forestall or remove enmity: it strengthens love.[42]

What are the implications of these three types of relationship for reconciliation between God and humankind? In a theology that describes the divine-human relation in terms of a controlling relationship, salvation is brought about exclusively by the action of an omnipotent God. Salvation is generally viewed in terms of deliverance from the consequences of sin rather than the healing of relationship. God is the only active partner in reconciling this type of relationship. Thus Calvin says:

> Before the first man was created, God in his eternal counsel had determined what he willed to be done with the whole human race. In the hidden counsel of God it was determined that Adam should fall from the unimpaired condition of his nature, and by his defection should involve all his posterity in sentence of eternal death. Upon the same decree depends the distinction between elect and reprobate: as he adopted some for himself for salvation, he destined others for eternal ruin.[43]

The theological benefit of this model is that it excludes any chance of salvation by merit. All glory belongs to God. However, there are serious disadvantages. This view does not consider Christ to have died for the salvation of all persons, compromises human free will, and even makes it difficult to see the need for the death of Christ.[44]

These disadvantages vanish when the divine-human relationship is described in terms of rights and duties in a contractual relationship. According to this view, God commits himself to provide humans with eternal happiness if they obey his will. However, humankind fails to keep

---

42. Burnaby, *Christian Words*, 87.
43. Calvin, *Theological Treatises*, 179.
44. Brümmer, "Atonement and Reconciliation," 444.

its end of the agreement by not giving God the obedience that is his right under the covenant. Humans have disturbed the balance of rights and duties; therefore, they forfeit eternal life. As previously mentioned, there are three ways in which this balance may be restored: punishment, satisfaction, or condonation. H. A. Hodges summarizes this contractual view:

> Our relation to God as sinners is this: we must pay a penalty appropriate and adequate to our wrong-doings, we must undergo punishment adequate to our guilt, we must make satisfaction adequate to the affront which we administer to God's honour, and by these means or by direct appeal to his mercy we must propitiate Him.[45]

God cannot condone human sin. God can restore the balance to the relationship by punishment, denying humans the eternal happiness that would have been theirs had they not broken the contract. This fate could be avoided if humans could make satisfaction by good works, which *earn* a restoration of balance and would merit eternal life. Sinners, however, do not have the ability to make adequate satisfaction. Christ's work is to make adequate satisfaction in the place of humankind. All credit for salvation goes to him, but it is still a salvation that is *earned* (by Christ rather than by humans). The satisfaction theory of Anselm employs this line of argument.[46]

The many weaknesses of this view of atonement were presented in chapters 2 and 3. An additional weakness is the relationship it assumes between God and humans. Each party is valued for the services they can provide for the other rather than for who they are as persons. God is not valued for himself alone, but for the eternal happiness he is able to provide. God does not love an individual for themselves, but for the obedience that brings him honor. In other words, God values his own honor more than he does the individual person. This view of the divine-human relationship presents a defective picture of the nature of God's love as well as human worth.[47] Individual worth is derived from God's love for the individual person. This love and the resulting relationship is what gives a person dignity and their life meaning.

In a relationship of fellowship, each partner identifies with the other, making the interests of the other their own. When applied to the

---

45. Hodges, *Pattern of Atonement*, 45.
46. Brümmer, "Atonement and Reconciliation," 445–46.
47. Brümmer, "Atonement and Reconciliation," 446–47.

divine-human relationship, God makes individual human salvation and eternal happiness his own concern. Individuals identify with God by making his will their own. Neither partner is compelled to consider the interests of the other. Each is free to give love. Individuals are not obliged to love God; neither is God obliged to love persons who have earned his love by doing his will. Salvation is entirely by grace. Any possibility of a theology of merit is excluded from this relationship of fellowship. God desires for humans to love him based on who he is and not on what he can provide for them. Individuals who seek their own interests in their relationship with God fail to identify themselves with his interests and his will. According to this understanding of divine-human relationship, sin is not something that requires the individual to be controlled or the guilt to be removed by punishment or satisfaction. Rather, sin is the cause of alienation and requires reconciliation. The essential conditions for reconciliation are repentance and forgiveness.[48]

One should remember that God's forgiveness is not earned by repentance. Scripture reveals that he will always forgive the repentant: "If we confess our sins, he is faithful and just and will forgive us our sins and purify us from all unrighteousness" (1 John 1:9). But this assurance does not mean that one can presume upon God's love and forgiveness, nor does it contradict the fact that it is free and unearned.[49] Neither does the fact that God knows each human heart remove the need to confess before God. As C. S. Lewis says, "By unveiling, by confessing our sins and 'making known' our requests, we assume the high rank of persons before [God]."[50]

The method of reconciliation in relationships of fellowship does not compromise the reality of the wrath of God. One is not obligated to choose between a God of wrath and a God of love, for wrath is the other side of God's love. Even in human love there is an analogy: the more a parent loves a child the more they hate seeing in them hypocrisy or lying or immorality. In this sense there can be wrath and at the same time great love.[51] God's love never varies and its constancy should not be doubted, but God's wrath is removed in reconciliation.

---

48. Brümmer, "Atonement and Reconciliation," 448.
49. Brümmer, "Atonement and Reconciliation," 449.
50. Lewis, *Letters to Malcolm*, 21.
51. Morris, *Apostolic*, 197.

THE APPLICATION OF ATONEMENT: EXCHANGE

The victorious substitution theory includes the idea that in the ongoing process of reconciliation between God and a believer, an exchange of lives takes place. This idea of life exchange is in contrast to the forensic view of the Atonement that adheres to an objective exchange referred to in traditional Protestantism as the doctrine of imputation.[52] The Reformers maintain that in the Atonement the sins of humankind are transferred to Christ, and in exchange, his righteousness is transferred to believers as a part of God's legal action (i.e., in an objective sense). The problem here is obvious: neither guilt nor innocence can be transferred.[53] This objective idea of imputed righteousness has been strenuously opposed in modern times, as it was by Socinus at the time of the Reformation. This section will refute the objective view of imputation and then present the victorious substitution view of exchange.

Scripture nowhere states that the righteousness of Christ is imputed to believers who are then regarded as innocent by God. It does say that faith is imputed as righteousness, and that believers have the righteousness of Christ. These two thoughts, however, are separate and are never connected in Scripture. Despite this, a number of verses are cited in support of the objective view of imputation. Romans 4:5–8, 11, for example, says:

> However, to the one who does not work but trusts God who justifies the ungodly, their faith is credited as ["counted for" KJV] righteousness. David says the same thing when he speaks of the blessedness of the one to whom God credits ["imputeth" KJV] righteousness apart from works: "Blessed are those whose transgressions are forgiven, whose sins are covered. Blessed is the one whose sin the Lord will never count against them.". . . So then, [Abraham] is the father of all who believe but have not been circumcised, in order that righteousness might be credited ["imputed" KJV] to them.

The idea of imputing righteousness here is clearly that of not counting a person's sin against them because of forgiveness (based on repentance and faith; see Rom 4:3, 5). To impute righteousness (to justify), then, is simply to regard as righteous or not to impute sins. Nothing is said of imputing the righteousness *of another*.[54] Imputation has the same mean-

---

52. Morris, *Apostolic*, 257.
53. Gerrish, "Atonement and 'Saving Faith,'" 182.
54. Godbey, "Socinus," 299.

ing in 2 Corinthians 5:19: "God was reconciling the world to himself in Christ, not counting [imputing] people's sins against them." Galatians 3:6 states that "Abraham 'believed God, and it was credited [imputed] to him as righteousness.'" Clearly Paul is not saying that the righteousness of another person was imputed to Abraham.[55]

Other passages that do not use imputation language, like 1 Corinthians 1:30–31, also may lead to the idea that Christ's righteousness is imputed, or transferred, to believers: "It is because of him [God] that you are in Christ Jesus, who has become for us wisdom from God—that is, our righteousness, holiness and redemption. Therefore, as it is written: 'Let the one who boasts boast in the Lord.'" In these verses, believers who are "in Christ" really have the wisdom, holiness, freedom, and righteousness of Christ and are not just *regarded* as having these attributes. All boasting should be about Christ, for it is his life that is in believers. There is no thought in these verses of a transfer of merit from Christ that effects salvation. Believers have the righteousness of Christ because they have Christ himself. They are able to live righteously *through* Christ.[56] The righteousness of Christ belongs to the believer not by "fictitious imputation or technical transfer," but by virtue of their real union with Christ.[57]

2 Corinthians 5:21—Christ "Made to Be Sin"

One verse that is difficult to interpret but often cited to support the idea of imputation is 2 Corinthians 5:21. Explaining how God through Christ reconciles the world to himself, Paul says, "God made him who had no sin to be sin for us, so that in him we might become the righteousness of God." Since it cannot be true that Christ literally becomes sin, some interpretation is necessary. The history of interpretation reveals that there arises around the time of the Reformation a markedly different understanding from the predominant thought of the preceding tradition.[58]

---

55. Godbey, "Socinus," 301. Morris also recognizes this, saying, "[Paul] never says in so many words that the righteousness *of Christ* was imputed to believers, and it may fairly be doubted whether he had this in mind in his treatment of justification, although it may be held to be a corollary from his doctrine of identification of the believer with Christ." *Apostolic*, 257.

56. Godbey, "Socinus," 305.

57. Dale, *Atonement*, 478.

58. Lyonnet and Sabourin, *Sin, Redemption, and Sacrifice*, 187. For a history of the interpretation of 2 Corinthians 5:21, see Lyonnet and Sabourin, *Sin, Redemption, and*

Historically, three interpretations have been proposed for the first half of the verse. For the early Reformers, "made to be sin" means that Christ is made to bear the guilt of sin as the object of God's wrath. Christ is treated in a penal substitutionary transaction as a sinner, the very personification of sin. This interpretation is theologically problematic and finds no expression in Scripture. It is usually proposed with reference to Galatians 3:13: "Christ redeemed us from the curse of the law by becoming a curse for us, for it is written: 'Cursed is everyone who is hung on a pole.'" The meaning of this verse in Galatians has already been discussed (see chapter 7, "The Meaning of Penalty") and it was noted that Paul, by not quoting all of Deuteronomy 21:23, carefully avoids saying that Christ is cursed by God.[59]

A second interpretation says that God makes Christ "to be sin" when Christ assumes human form. According to this interpretation, Christ being "made sin" is a reference to the Incarnation. Augustine, for example, combines the thought of 2 Corinthians 5:21 with that of Romans 8:3, which refers to Christ as having "the likeness of sinful flesh."[60]

A third interpretation, the one adopted here, views the reference to sin sacrificially. This interpretation was generally accepted until the time of the Reformation and has a solid basis for authenticity. Writing to the Romans, whom he had not evangelized, Paul uses the words *peri hamartias* ("for sin") when he refers to Christ being a sin offering (8:3). In writing to the Corinthians, Paul uses the shorter *hamartian* ("sin") instead of *peri hamartias*, perhaps to contrast literarily "sin" and the "righteousness of God" (2 Corinthians 5:21). It can be supposed that Paul had previously explained to the Corinthians how the sacrifices of the OT describe the sacrifice of Christ. In any case, it is reasonable to assume that even the Greek-speaking Jews would easily understand the significance of the phrase "God made him . . . to be sin" in this sacrificial sense.[61] Luther

---

Sacrifice, 189–245.

59. Lyonnet and Sabourin, *Sin, Redemption, and Sacrifice*, 250.

60. Lyonnet and Sabourin, *Sin, Redemption, and Sacrifice*, 250–51.

61. "When referring to 'sacrifice for sin' (*hatta't*), the LXX, it is true, generally uses the phrase *peri hamartias*. But the term *hamartia* is also used 'absolutely' to designate the sin-offering in various formulas: *hamartia estin*, 'it is a sin (-offering: Lev 4:24; 5:9, 12)'; *hamartia synagoges estin*, 'it is a sin (-offering) of the assembly" (Lev 4:21); *hamartias estin*, 'it is of a sin (-offering: Exod 29:14)'; *eis hamartian*, 'for a sin (-offering: Num 6:14)'; *houtos ho nomos tes hamartias*, 'this is the law of the sin (-offering: Lev 6:18–25).' These examples show that the independent use of *hamartia* in 2 Cor 5:21 to mean 'sacrifice for sin' does not contradict the usage of the Greek Bible."

gives this interpretation as well, saying that when Scripture calls Christ a "curse" or "sin" it means that he became a sacrifice for the curse or a sacrifice for sin.[62]

The interpretation of Christ as a "sacrifice for sin" in 2 Corinthians 5:21 reflects the Suffering Servant theology of Isaiah 53. The idea is that Christ, who has no sin, is made an offering for sin so that humans might be reconciled to God. The same is said of the Suffering Servant: though he has done no wrong, his life is given as a sin offering, and many shall be justified through a knowledge of him (Isaiah 53:9–11).[63]

A Proper Understanding of Exchange

Just as Christian thinkers err when they add to the text to represent Christ as a scapegoat or as the object of God's anger, they also err in their explanation of how Christ is "made to be sin" (2 Cor 5:21) and in what sense he becomes a "curse" (Gal 3:13). This is not to say that no exchange takes place in the Atonement. An exchange takes place in that Christ becomes the ransom substitute providing freedom for humankind. The result of this exchange is that Christ experiences the consequences of sin (the curse) that were due to human choice, and believers have the opportunity to experience the blessings that result from Christ's life of perfect obedience.

This interpretation of the Atonement clearly involves substitutionary exchange, but Christ dying on behalf of humans as their substitute is only part of his work. There is also a victorious exchange. The exchange he offers as a living victor is equal in significance to that which he offers as a dying substitute.

The following section will consider the results of the completed work of Christ as well as his ongoing work in the lives of individual Christians, both of which are substitutionary and victorious.

THE APPLICATION OF ATONEMENT: VICTORY

The Atonement is both a work of substitution and a work of victory. These two aspects are inseparably linked because Christ's substitutionary

---

Lyonnet and Sabourin, *Sin, Redemption, and Sacrifice*, 251–53.

62. Pelikan, *Lectures on Galatians*, 288.

63. Lyonnet and Sabourin, *Sin, Redemption, and Sacrifice*, 254.

death is the culmination of his victory over evil. The nature of Christ's substitutionary work as a ransom has already been examined. But what are the results of this vicarious and victorious work? What is the situation to which Christ's work responds, and how does his being a substitute and a victor change this state of affairs? How does Christ's victory apply in the life of a believer? What is the character of the battle that was fought and is still ongoing? The victorious substitution theory seeks to answer all these questions.

Before Christ's living substitutionary and victorious work can be examined (the subject of chapter 9), we must first consider the state of affairs to which the Incarnation responds and how his substitution and victory change this situation.

Four results of the fall of humanity will be evaluated in this section, and Christ's work will be considered as a corrective response to each.[64] These four results are: (1) Satan gains a position of authority and power, (2) humankind experiences spiritual death and alienation from God, (3) futility is introduced into life, and (4) creation was subject to corruption and decay.

Satan Gains a Position of Authority and Power

After creating humankind, God, from whom comes all authority, delegates to humans authority over all the earth (Gen 1:26–28; 2:19). Satan, however, is able to usurp this authority by causing Adam to follow him in disobedience and rebellion against God. By believing and choosing to follow Satan rather than God (Gen 3:1–7; Rom 5:12; 1 Tim 2:14), humankind aligns itself with Satan, giving him a place of power and authority in God's creation. The reality of Satan's authority is seen in the temptation of Jesus, in which he offers Jesus "all the kingdoms of the world" (Luke 4:5). Satan claims "all their authority and splendor; it has been given to me, and I can give it to anyone I want to" (Luke 4:6). The phrase "it has been given to me" translates a Greek word meaning "to give over to" (Young's Concordance) that can also be translated "betrayed" (it is the same word used of Judas). In other words, the authority God gave to Adam is betrayed to Satan, and he thereby gains a position of influence in the world. Jesus does

---

64. Parts of this section examining the results of the fall, primarily the selection of Scripture verses, come from the author's notes on a series of audiocassettes by Derek Prince entitled *Spiritual Conflict* (1971).

not challenge this claim of Satan. In fact, three times in John's Gospel Jesus refers to Satan as the "prince of this world" (12:31; 14:30; 16:11).

Paul calls Satan "the ruler of the kingdom of the air, the spirit who is now at work in those who are disobedient" (Eph 2:2). In 2 Corinthians 4:4 Satan is called "the god of this age." Hebrews 2:14 specifically says that Satan has the "power of death." It is clear from these verses that Satan has some ability to influence and some authority in this world, including the "power of death." That is not to say, however, that God is not sovereign, for this power or authority exists because of God's judgment against sin. Scripture insists on God's sovereignty, saying "his kingdom rules over all" (Ps 103:19). Still, Satan's authority, betrayed to him by Adam and resulting from God's judgment, is actual, even if limited and ultimately controlled by God.

A transfer of power takes place after the resurrection of Jesus. Before his death, Jesus declares, "Now the prince of this world will be driven out" (John 12:31). After his resurrection, Jesus says, "All authority in heaven and on earth has been given to me" (Matt 28:18). Paul refers to this conquest, saying that Christ "disarmed the powers and authorities" and "made a public spectacle of them, triumphing over them by the cross" (Col 2:15). Paul also speaks of the authority given to Christ by the Father, who "raised Christ from the dead and seated him at his right hand in the heavenly realms, far above all rule and authority, power and dominion, and every name that is invoked, not only in the present age but also in the one to come. And God placed all things under his feet and appointed him to be head over everything" (Eph 1:20-22).

These verses speak of the defeat of Satan and of his consequent loss of authority. How does this defeat come about? What does Christ do that makes him the victor? The progress of the narrative in Luke 4 illustrates that Christ's victory is achieved by obedience. It begins with the temptation of Jesus, which represents the opening engagement in a struggle destined to culminate in Gethsemane and at Calvary. The outcome of Jesus' refusal to succumb to temptation, seen in the description of the opening of his ministry, is that "his words had authority" (verse 32). Jesus' refusal to give in to temptation is the source of his power, for he went out "in the power of the Spirit" (verse 14) to wage successful war against those very forces that hold human life in subjection. He is even victorious over the demonic forces that are part of human bondage (verses 33–41). Mark's account puts even greater emphasis on the ministry of Jesus as the assertion of lordship over demonic forces. The divine victory over the forces of evil, then, begins in the human ministry of Jesus and continues until its final crisis.[65] As a man, putting himself in humanity's place, he was "tempted in every way" (Heb 4:15). But because he is without sin, Satan cannot defeat him (John 14:30) and death cannot hold him (Acts 2:24).

As a result of Christ's victory Satan loses all authority. An exchange, or ransom substitution, first takes place in which Satan forfeits humankind, enabling Jesus to proclaim "freedom for the prisoners" (Luke 4:18). Satan is then defeated in the battle for Christ himself because Christ never succumbs to Satan's temptations. As Gunton says, Christ's life is a "submission which consists of a refusal to submit."[66] He endures all that the power of evil can bring against him in suffering a horrendous death, but he never disobeys the Father even when he feels forsaken. Satan loses the battle at the moment when he seems to be victorious.[67] Sin, death, and the devil still exist, but their power is broken once and for all.[68] Christ, though stronger than Satan, submits to his power and thereby breaks it. The book of Revelation can therefore interpret the triumph of the Lion of the tribe of Judah in terms of the slaughter of the Lamb of God (Rev 5:5–9).[69] In this manner, as a sinless substitute, Jesus triumphs,[70] and God is revealed as one who would rather bear the power of evil than punish those who have come under it.[71]

The deliverance of humanity from the power of the devil comes about in a way that takes Satan's authority seriously, because humanity's captivity resulted not only from its own free choice given by God but also from God's forewarned judgment of that choice. God's work of redemption in which he overcomes the forces holding humanity in bondage is at the same time the suffering of the consequences of his judgment on sin.[72] God takes seriously his own judgment against evil, for he accepts and bears evil's destructive consequences. He also takes evil itself seriously, for he engages it in battle and defeats it at great cost.[73]

---

65. Gunton, *Actuality of Atonement*, 58–59.
66. Gunton, *Actuality of Atonement*, 77.
67. Gunton, *Actuality of Atonement*, 55.
68. Gunton, *Actuality of Atonement*, 59.
69. Gunton, *Actuality of Atonement*, 77.
70. Gunton, *Actuality of Atonement*, 76.
71. Gunton, *Actuality of Atonement*, 84.
72. Aulén, *Christus Victor*, 57.
73. Gunton, *Actuality of Atonement*, 161.

As a ransom payment, a substitute, Christ restores to humankind the freedom it lost. Like the psalmist who declares, "I am forced to restore what I did not steal" (Ps 69:4), his work involves more than that of a substitute; he triumphs over Satan and sin and death.[74] The victorious life he lives he offers to all who believe and are reconciled to God. "I have come that they may have life, and have it to the full" (John 10:10). Christ's victory continues in the life of a Christian so that Paul can say, "In all these things we are more than conquerors through him who loved us" (Rom 8:37) and John can say, "For everyone born of God overcomes the world. This is the victory that overcomes the world, even our faith" (1 John 5:4). Christ's victory, seen in the way he lives his life and verified in his resurrection from the dead, is not to be isolated from the continuation of his victory in the life of believers.[75] As Greathouse says, "It is this understanding of Christ's work which furnishes the most solid basis for a dynamic biblical doctrine of sanctification."[76]

Spiritual Death and Alienation from God

The second result of the fall is that humankind experiences spiritual death and becomes alienated from God. Sin causes fellowship with God to be broken (Isa 59:2). For the first time there is fear of the presence of God, for "the man and his wife . . . hid from the Lord God among the trees of the garden" (Gen 3:8). God had warned Adam that disobedience would result in death, saying, "You must not eat from the tree of the knowledge of good and evil, for when you eat from it you will surely die" (Gen 2:17). A spiritual death takes place when Adam sins, into which all humankind is born: "You were dead in your transgressions and sins. . . . All of us also lived among them at one time, gratifying the cravings of our flesh and following its desires and thoughts. Like the rest, we were by nature deserving of wrath" (Eph 2:1, 3). Because of the fall and God's resulting judgment, humans are born in a state of alienation from God and in a state of spiritual death. This is the state of affairs to which God responds in the Atonement. "Sin, when it is full-grown, gives birth to death" (Jas 1:15), but "when you were dead in your sins and in the uncircumcision of your flesh, God made you alive with Christ. He forgave us all our sins"

---

74. Gomes, *Jesu Christo Servatore*, 254.
75. Gunton, *Actuality of Atonement*, 57.
76. Greathouse, "Sanctification," 49.

(Col 2:13). Jesus is "obedient to death" (Phil 2:8), being "made lower than the angels for a little while, now crowned with glory and honor because he suffered death, so that by the grace of God he might taste death for everyone" (Heb 2:9) and "free those who all their lives were held in slavery by their fear of death" (Heb 2:15).

Jesus' obedience to death not only eliminates spiritual death but also restores humankind to communion with God. By his life Jesus demonstrates to humankind how they are to live in union with God. He says, "I live because of the Father" (John 6:57) and "I and the Father are one" (John 10:30). One of his last utterances, however, indicates that he felt his communion was broken: "My God, my God, why have you forsaken me?" (Matt 27:46). In experiencing the consequences of God's judgment, Jesus for the first time feels separation from his Father. Because of Christ's substitutionary work, humans need not ever experience separation from their heavenly Father (Heb 13:5). "The punishment that brought us peace was upon him" (Isa 53:5). In exchange for his bearing the consequences of sin, separation from God, humans may have "peace." This exchange is stated eloquently by Mather:

> Christ has not only done for men what they cannot do for themselves, but in doing so He has undergone an experience into the depths of which they need not enter. As a Christian matures he may feel poignantly the suffering of Christ and the sin of men. He may have to experience persecution and even become a martyr. But nevertheless there is an experience that he does not need to know, a pain which he is not required to endure. That is the bitterness of death that Christ experienced, the sense of desolation that He knew before His physical life had come to a close. The cry of dereliction from the cross points to this conclusion. In this expression of anguish, which has so perplexed interpreters, man catches a glimpse of an infinite depth of suffering. The exact nature of this experience is not known, nor does it need to be known. Into it the Christian is not called to enter. However sharp and severe may be the task of discipleship, however much the sense of discouragement may at times come close around the Christian, he at least need never believe himself forsaken by God.[77]

God intends that a believer never again experience separation from himself and that they experience a life in his fellowship: "Our fellowship

---

77. Mather, "Atonement," 271.

is with the Father and with his Son, Jesus Christ" (1 John 1:3); Jesus "died for us so that, whether we are awake or asleep, we may live together with him" (1 Thess 5:10); "God is faithful, who has called you into fellowship with his Son, Jesus Christ our Lord" (1 Cor 1:9).

Because a believer will not experience spiritual death or separation from God and because the body will be resurrected, he or she does not need to fear physical death:

> When the perishable has been clothed with the imperishable, and the mortal with immortality, then the saying that is written will come true: "Death has been swallowed up in victory. Where, O death, is your victory? Where, O death, is your sting?" The sting of death is sin, and the power of sin is the law. But thanks be to God! He gives us the victory through our Lord Jesus Christ. (1 Cor 15:54–57)

The first two effects of the fall Jesus puts right through his work as a substitute. First he frees humankind from the power of Satan. Second, he provides the way for humans to experience spiritual life, communion with God, and eternal life. God's grace calls them to reconciliation and to a relationship of fellowship that will satisfy their soul.

Those who do not repent and believe, however, continue in a state of alienation from God and will suffer eternal death (Rev 20:6, 14–15). The horror of death reveals the seriousness in God's sight of the sin from which it results.[78] The theory of victorious substitution does not compromise or eliminate God's wrath. Sin still lies under the judgment of God.

The work of Jesus in the Atonement reverses this condition of alienation from God, because when a person is born again, the old, sinful nature dies and a new nature is given to them (Rom 6:1–14).[79] This new nature is the gift of Christ's own life through a new covenant ratified in his blood. Jesus not only redeems humankind from bondage to Satan but also breaks the bondage to sin in the lives of believers. Through the gift of Christ's life the believer is able to obey God, do his will, and overcome

---

78. Worrall, "Substitutionary Atonement," 352.

79. A good point is made by Dale: "It is far less difficult to apprehend the fact that we live in the life of Christ, than the fact that we died in His Death; but the teaching of St. Paul seems to be explicit. The destruction of evil within us is the effect and fulfillment in ourselves of the mystery of Christ's death, as the development of our positive holiness is the manifestation of the power of His life. . . . In [Christ's] death our sin dies, and in His life the very life of God is made our own. How the death of Christ effects the destruction of our sin we may be unable to tell." *Atonement*, 485, 487.

sin. This aspect of the atoning work of Christ continues the victorious life that he lived on earth. Christ gives his life to believers so that they may be born again (John 3:5–7), may become new creatures (2 Cor 5:17), and may experience his victory over temptation (Rom 6:14). The believer overcomes sin through a relationship of fellowship and mutual identification in which the believer is "in Christ" and Christ is in the believer. Christ's nature is the source of victory for believers, for the sin within individuals cannot be conquered by an external atoning act.[80]

How is this victorious aspect of the work of atonement made effectual in the life of a believer? One begins by receiving their liberation and by being restored to a proper relationship with God.[81] Following repentance and faith, believers receive justification, and they experience new beginning and belonging.[82] But the victory of the Atonement does not end there. Believers enter a new covenant relationship in which victory over sin *during life* is meant to be the experience of all who would come under this covenant (Rom 6).

Why does God make a covenant with humans? And, more importantly, why does he choose to make two covenants with humans? God responds to human weakness and need by making a covenant in order to relate with people in a way that helps them to have faith in his faithfulness: "Know therefore that the Lord your God is God; he is the faithful God, keeping his covenant of love to a thousand generations of those who love him and keep his commandments" (Deut 7:9).[83] By making a covenant, God seeks to encourage faith. His covenants reveal his purpose: providing a security and guarantee as an aid to faith in all that he wills.[84] What God wants from a person is faith, for what one believes, moves and rules their being. Just as humankind could not redeem itself from the power of Satan, it cannot overcome sin. If redemption is to take place God must do it all, but humans must have a desire to overcome and believe that it is possible. New covenant salvation is a gift to be accepted by faith, but its chief purpose is to restore humans to that close fellowship

---

80. F. Young, *Sacrifice*, 95.
81. F. Young, *Sacrifice*, 95.
82. Ziesler, "Salvation," 358.
83. A. Murray, *Two Covenants*, 1.
84. A. Murray, *Two Covenants*, 4–5.

with God for which they are created (true "at-one-ment")[85] and to give them a new life that overcomes sin.

Why did God initiate two covenants? Through the first covenant humans discover their impotence and captivity under the power of sin. Human desire and effort must be proven insufficient in spite of outward instruction and miracles. The old covenant attains its object only if it brings people to a sense of their sinfulness and their inability to overcome sin (Gal 3). Seeking to conquer sin through keeping the law is a mark of the old covenant. It fails to grasp the deep humility and spirituality of a faith that depends on God for all.[86]

How are believers to enter into the new covenant of which Jesus is the mediator? What is needed for believers to understand all that the new covenant in Christ's blood offers? First, they must have a knowledge of the power of sin and a certainty of their inability to overcome in their own strength (old covenant). Paul urges the Galatian believers to live in the new covenant rather than the old. He says there are two covenants, one characterized by bondage and the other by freedom (Gal 4:24–31), but they are told: "Stand firm, then, and do not let yourselves be burdened again by a yoke of slavery" (Gal 5:1). In the new covenant God reveals that liberty from sin and self is found only in absolute dependence on his being and doing everything within a person.[87] Second, they must understand that God's way of salvation in the new covenant is *his life* working within the believer to effect all that is pleasing in God's sight.[88] Third, they must believe in the possibility of living in holiness. If they believe the holiness offered in the new covenant is unattainable, excusing sin because obedience is considered impossible, then life in the spirit of bondage will continue.[89] In this case the fullness of the Atonement, for which Jesus suffers and dies, will not be realized.

Scripture says concerning the new covenant:

> "This is the covenant I will make with the people of Israel after that time," declares the Lord. "I will put my law in their minds and write it on their hearts. I will be their God, and they will be my people. No longer will they teach their neighbor or say to

---

85. A. Murray, *Two Covenants*, 8.
86. A. Murray, *Two Covenants*, 37–46.
87. A. Murray, *Two Covenants*, 13–14.
88. A. Murray, *Two Covenants*, 26.
89. A. Murray, *Two Covenants*, 23.

> one another, 'Know the Lord,' because they will all know me, from the least of them to the greatest," declares the Lord. "For I will forgive their wickedness and will remember their sins no more." (Jer 31:33–34)
>
> I will give you a new heart and put a new spirit in you; I will remove from you your heart of stone and give you a heart of flesh. And I will put my Spirit in you and move you to follow my decrees and be careful to keep my laws. (Ezek 36:26–27)
>
> I will make a covenant of peace with them; it will be an everlasting covenant. (Ezek 37:26)

The new covenant serves to remedy evil in the human heart. The inscription of God's law in human minds and hearts is identical with liberation from servitude to sin.[90]

The central promise of the new covenant is a heart delighting in God's law and capable of experiencing fellowship with him. God will be for his people all that they need. Personal fellowship with God is the privilege of every member of the new covenant. The pardon of sin ("I will forgive their wickedness and will remember their sins no more") occurs first and is the root of all. But the other part of the covenant, the law written on the heart and the direct divine teaching and fellowship, is too often not fully apprehended because it is not fully believed. What God has joined should not be separated. The objective, outward work and the subjective, inward work are both part of the Atonement.[91]

What are the characteristics of the Christian life to be lived in the new covenant? The following is a partial list, briefly stated. First, this life overcomes sins. Jesus came to "save his people from their sins" (Matt 1:21), "to bless [them] by turning each of [them] from [their] wicked ways" (Acts 3:26). This is especially clear in Paul's statements to the Romans: "What shall we say, then? Shall we go on sinning so that grace may increase? By no means! We are those who have died to sin; how can we live in it any longer?" (Rom 6:1–2). "Sin shall no longer be your master, because you are not under the law, but under grace" (Rom 6:14). "Through Christ Jesus the law of the Spirit who gives life has set you free from the law of sin and death" (Rom 8:2). This being freed from the "law of sin and death" is what Christ did when he redeemed us from the curse of the law (Gal 3:13).

---

90. Godbey, "Socinus," 129.
91. A. Murray, *Two Covenants*, 28–35.

A second characteristic of life in the new covenant is that the believer may live in intimate communion with God. "And our fellowship is with the Father and with his Son, Jesus Christ" (1 John 1:3). Third, the new covenant life is full satisfaction with the Lord. Jesus proclaims to the woman at the well, "Whoever drinks the water I give them will never thirst. Indeed, the water I give them will become in them a spring of water welling up to eternal life" (John 4:14).

Fourth, through the life of Christ, the believer, regardless of circumstances, overcomes sin. Paul refers to this victorious aspect of the new covenant life: "Who shall separate us from the love of Christ? Shall trouble or hardship or persecution or famine or nakedness or danger or sword? . . . No, in all these things we are more than conquerors through him who loved us" (Rom 8:35, 37).

> St. Paul's conception of the Atonement or as he would call it reconciliation to God (2 Cor 5:18–20) is seen to be much larger than that of later theologians and quite different from it. So far from confining his treatment of the subject to Romans 3:21–31 . . . St. Paul treats it directly through the next four chapters of Romans. The glowing description of the triumphant life in Christ in Romans 8 is as much a part of his theory as the reference to Christ's death in Romans 3:24–26. Indeed, it is the climax of his exposition of it.[92]

Triumph does not mean that because one has faith and is obedient that life will always be pleasant. Outward circumstances *will* be difficult or perhaps even horrendous. It is "in all these things" that one conquers; that is, endures without sin or separation from God. In spite of life's harsh circumstances this "triumph in Christ" is to be the common experience of Christians: "Thanks be to God, who always leads us as captives in Christ's triumphal procession and uses us to spread the aroma of the knowledge of him everywhere" (2 Cor 2:14).[93]

Fifth, good works characterize the new covenant life. In speaking of salvation (Eph 2:8–9) Paul says, "We are God's handiwork, created in Christ Jesus to do good works, which God prepared in advance for us to do" (Eph 2:10). Sixth, the new covenant life is full of light: "I am the light of the world. Whoever follows me will never walk in darkness, but will have the light of life" (John 8:12). Finally, this life is completely set apart

---

92. Barton, "Romans," 92–93.
93. A. Murray, *Two Covenants*, 17–24.

for God: "May God himself, the God of peace, sanctify you through and through. May your whole spirit, soul and body be kept blameless at the coming of our Lord Jesus Christ" (1 Thess 5:23).[94]

God prepares in the new covenant a full salvation that includes victory over sin, communion with God, contentment in the Lord, victory over one's circumstances (meaning they cannot destroy us or cause us to sin), a life of revelation, and the ability to do good works. Jesus came to undo the results of the fall, and nothing less than Christ's own victorious life experienced by Christians accomplishes this end. "God has given us eternal life, and this life is in his Son. Whoever has the Son has life; whoever does not have the Son of God does not have life" (1 John 5:11–12). "Praise be to the God and Father of our Lord Jesus Christ, who has blessed us in the heavenly realms with every spiritual blessing in Christ" (Eph 1:3).[95]

Futility

Thus far two results of the fall have been considered and the correction to each that the Atonement provides: Satan gains a position of authority and power, humans experience spiritual death and alienation from God. The third result of the fall is the loss of meaning and purpose in life—futility. One entire book in the Bible, Ecclesiastes, is devoted to the theme of "vanity," or futility, which is the state of affairs "under the sun." Even one who possesses unlimited wealth and power and experiences the most refined pleasures of life knows only "vanity" if life is lived apart from the purposes of God (Eccl 1:1—2:16). The Teacher, in summarizing this state of affairs, declares, "So I hated life, because the work that is done under the sun was grievous to me. All of it is meaningless, a chasing after the wind" (Eccl 2:17).

The perspective of Christians, however, is not limited to life "under the sun." They can say with Paul that "our light and momentary troubles are achieving for us an eternal glory that far outweighs them all. So we fix our eyes not on what is seen, but on what is unseen, since what is seen is temporary, but what is unseen is eternal" (2 Cor 4:17–18). God intends for Christians to live with an eternal perspective. Just as Jesus was the personal representative of the Father sent to earth to show his

---

94. Nee, *Life That Wins*, 17–25.
95. Nee, *Life That Wins*, 26.

likeness (John 14:9), Christians are meant to live as the personal representatives of Christ on earth today. Jesus tells his disciples that "as the Father has sent me, I am sending you" (John 20:21). Just as Christ lived by the Father, believers are to live by Christ (John 6:57). Christ did the will of the Father (John 6:38), spoke the words of the Father (John 14:24), and did the works of the Father (John 14:10). In this context he said to his disciples: "Whoever believes in me will do the works I have been doing, and they will do even greater things than these, because I am going to the Father" (John 14:12).

Christians are not only to show Christ to the world (Gal 1:16) by living in the power of his life, but they are also to partner with God in all that he purposes. Accordingly, Christ says to his disciples, "I no longer call you servants, because a servant does not know his master's business. Instead, I have called you friends, for everything that I learned from my Father I have made known to you" (John 15:15). And Paul says to the Corinthians, "We are co-workers in God's service . . . this, then, is how you ought to regard us: as servants of Christ and as those entrusted with the mysteries God has revealed" (1 Cor 3:9; 4:1). As a part of the Atonement, Christian are "redeemed from the empty way of life" (1 Pet 1:18), for their works have eternal meaning and value. They are not to strive but to live in peace with God, abiding in Christ (John 15:5), trusting in the Father to lead them into the good works prepared for them before the foundation of the world (Eph 2:10). The Atonement, in reversing the effects of the fall, means that life in Christ is not lived in vain. Futility is not to be the experience of those who have responded to God's call to live and work with him.

Creation Is Subject to Corruption and Decay

Scripture refers to another kind of bondage that will be undone in the future: "the bondage to decay." While this book does not address whether "decay" was in effect before the fall, Scripture reveals that, in the future, all creation "will be liberated from its bondage to decay and brought into the freedom and glory of the children of God" (Rom 8:21). The deliverance of creation from the bondage of decay is part of God's work in reconciling all things to himself. It will not be complete until the time of the resurrection of the body, when creation itself will be delivered.

The righteousness of God, then, will be seen when God redeems humankind within and with the cosmos. The justification of the sinner is only part of what is meant by "the righteousness of God," which includes the redemption of the whole created order as the outcome of God's loyalty to his creation. The Atonement takes place in order for God to complete what he began in creation itself.[96] The benefits of Christ's victory extend to all parts of the created order so Scripture can say that through Christ "all things" are reconciled (Col 1:20) and that "when the times reach their fulfillment" God will "bring unity to all things in heaven and on earth under Christ" (Eph 1:10).[97]

Although the victory of Christ is complete, its full realization is still to come. Thus the eschatological nature of the victory is seen in 1 Corinthians 15, where Paul says that the risen Christ "must reign until he has put all his enemies under his feet" (verse 25). Yet Paul justifies the proclamation by an appeal to a victory that has already taken place: "For he has put everything under his feet" (verse 27). The past victory is the guarantee of the future consummation. Scripture expresses the tension of the "now but not yet" concerning the Atonement in that there is a victory won, being won, and to be won. Christ's victory will be complete "when the times reach their fulfillment" in spite of those forces that oppose it, and God's world will become that which he intended it to be.[98]

---

96. Gunton, *Actuality of Atonement*, 102–3.
97. Gunton, *Actuality of Atonement*, 79–80.
98. Gunton, *Actuality of Atonement*, 81–82.

9

How to Enter into the Victorious Life Provided through the Atonement

THE VICTORY INTENDED FOR the Christian as a part of the redemption in Christ Jesus is not so much a *changed* life as it is an *exchanged* one. Paul states this truth clearly to the Galatians: "I have been crucified with Christ and I no longer live, but Christ lives in me. The life I now live in the body, I live by faith in the Son of God" (Gal 2:20). The source of victory in Paul's life is the person of Christ within and not a reformation of his own person.[1] This exchange can only occur through death. Christ's death is necessary that he might be the mediator of the new covenant (Heb 9:16–17), bringing about the transference of the property. Christians must die to self that Christ might live in them. Just as Adam died to God and humans have a nature that is dead to God, so in Christ believers die to sin and inherit a nature that is dead to sin (incapable of sin—1 John 3:9) and its dominion. Before one can come to God in complete impotence and surrender and accept as one's only deliverance Christ's life within, one must see that self is incurable and therefore must die. Only death makes an end of all self-effort.[2]

In Christ's death he is seen in complete surrender, allowing and counting upon God to deliver him and give him life. Believers are to do

1. Nee, *Life That Wins*, 29–30.
2. A. Murray, *Two Covenants*, 68–70.

the same. Only as they give themselves to death, ceasing from self and its works, can God "through the blood of the eternal covenant . . . equip [them] with everything good for doing his will, and may he work in us what is pleasing to him, through Jesus Christ" (Heb 13:20–21). The purpose of this "eternal covenant" is to restore humans out of the fall and into the life in God for which they are created.[3]

The resurrection life of Christ is his gift and not a reward: "Thanks be to God! He gives us the victory [over sin, verse 56] through our Lord Jesus Christ" (1 Cor 15:57). Victory is a gift and is not attained through self-effort. Just as one is not saved by works, one does not overcome by works. Christ died at Calvary to deliver "whoever will" from the consequences of sin, and he now lives within the believer to deliver "whoever will" from sin itself. He gives his endurance and his holiness, indeed all of his virtues, to the believer through the gift of his own life.[4]

The Christian does not develop and perfect their own life. Rather, they are constantly receiving and appropriating the life and power of Christ. The Christian does not *attain* but *obtains*, as a gift, the victorious life of Christ. Paul states that righteousness is a gift to be received: "If, by the trespass of the one man, death reigned through that one man, how much more will those who receive God's abundant provision of grace and of the gift of righteousness reign in life through the one man, Jesus Christ" (Rom 5:17).[5] The ability to "reign in life" comes about only through the "gift of righteousness." But this gift of righteousness is not speaking of imputed righteousness, which refers to justification or being regarded as righteous (see chapter 8, "The Application of Atonement: Justification"). Reigning in life is meant to be the actual experience of believers, for in Scripture, to be righteous means "to live in a righteous manner," or, as John says, one "does what is right" (1 John 3:7; Ezek 33:1–20; Prov 10:11; 11:1–31).[6] Righteousness is the moral uprightness that avails before God and is recognized by him (Jas 1:20; 5:16; 1 Pet 2:24; 3:12, 14; 2 Pet 3:13).[7] James can say that believers are justified by works because works reveal an exchanged life. Christ's life must inevitably do good works. Those who claim righteousness on the basis of a supposed

---

3. A. Murray, *Two Covenants*, 71.
4. Nee, *Life That Wins*, 33–35.
5. Nee, *Life That Wins*, 37.
6. Godbey, "Socinus," 340.
7. Godbey, "Socinus," 455.

legal transfer while at the same time living in an unrighteous way are deceived, are misusing Scripture, and are subverting God's purpose in the Atonement.[8]

To live righteously is to express the life of Christ within. This way of life does not result from a suppression of natural life but is an expression of the victory of Christ.[9] One does not overcome sin through a combination of self-control and help from God. Self-effort must cease and faith must depend on the gift of Christ's righteous life within (Gal 2:20). But, God's giving waits for our taking. Each person must seek God for wisdom and guidance as to what that victory looks like within the circumstances of their life. It must always be remembered that the victory is over sin, not suffering (just like Christ's own victory). In fact, it is suffering without sin that demonstrates Christ's victory in one's life. This kind of victory is often not what people seek, and God never forces a person to receive spiritual blessings. He gives in proportion to a person's desire and faith to receive.[10] The Christian's part is to abide in Christ: "Remain in me, as I also remain in you. No branch can bear fruit by itself; it must remain in the vine. Neither can you bear fruit unless you remain in me. I am the vine; you are the branches. If you remain in me and I in you, you will bear much fruit; apart from me you can do nothing" (John 15:4–5).

THE "OLD SELF" MUST DIE

The first condition for entering into a life that overcomes sin is indicated by Paul's words to the Galatians, "I have been crucified with Christ" (2:20). The second condition follows in the same verse: "The life I now live in the body, I live by faith in the Son of God." What does being "crucified with Christ" mean? In what sense must a person be "crucified with Christ"? When a person becomes a Christian, Christ gives his life to them: "Do you not realize that Christ Jesus is in you?" (2 Cor 13:5). There are two lives within the Christian: their own life and the life of Christ. Freedom from sin comes only from the life of Christ. The "old self," the nature that inevitably sins, is crucified with Christ (Rom 6:1–14). Christ dies not that the old self should undergo a reformation but that the old self should die also, "so that the body ruled by sin might be done away with, that we

---

8. Godbey, "Socinus," 342–43.
9. Nee, *Life That Wins*, 42–45.
10. A. Murray, *Two Covenants*, 162.

should no longer be slaves to sin" (Rom 6:6). In order to live in Christ's victory, Christians must accept God's requirement for the death of their old nature. The "old self," according to God's estimation, is beyond repair or improvement or hope. The new, divine nature that is given to Christians provides the only hope of living a godly life: "His divine power has given us everything we need for a godly life through our knowledge of him who called us by his own glory and goodness. Through these he has given us his very great and precious promises, so that through them you may participate in the divine nature, having escaped the corruption in the world caused by evil desires" (2 Pet 1:3–4).

Paul evaluates himself according to God's evaluation: "I know that good itself does not dwell in me, that is, in my sinful nature" (Rom 7:18). Resolutions do not solve the problem, for, as Paul continues, "I have the desire to do what is good, but I cannot carry it out." Like Paul, Christians must accept God's evaluation and verdict before they are able to depend solely on the life of the Lord as their holiness and victory.[11] James Denney says, "In childhood men repent of what they have done; but at a more mature stage they repent of what they are. At first they feel that they must make amends; but when they come to know themselves, they feel that they must be born again."[12]

As long as Christians are struggling to be holy they will not overcome. The first step is to let go of one's struggle to overcome and to commit oneself to Christ knowing that victory is his work.[13] A new life is necessary in order to overcome sin, and that new life, his own life, is Christ's gift. It is absolutely essential to let go, admit inability, and cease effort, for as long as one is struggling to improve the flesh, they cannot crucify it (Gal 5:24).

Christ, in his life on earth, exemplifies this complete dependence on the Father:

> Some twelve times and more [Jesus uses] the word *not* and *nothing* of Himself. *Not* my will. *Not* my words. *Not* my honor. *Not* mine own glory. I can do *nothing* of myself. I speak *not* of myself. I do *nothing* of myself. Just think for a moment what this means in connection with what He tells us of His life in the Father. "As the Father hath life in Himself, so He hath given to the Son to have life in Himself" (John 5:26). "That all men should honor

---

11. Nee, *Life That Wins*, 47–52.
12. Denney, *Studies in Theology*, 83–84.
13. Nee, *Life That Wins*, 54–55.

the Son, even as they honor the Father" (verse 23). And yet this Son, who has life in Himself even as the Father has, immediately adds (verse 30): "I can of mine own self do nothing." We should have thought that with this life in Himself He would have the power of independent action as the Father has. But no. "The Son can do nothing of Himself, but what He seeth the Father do." The chief mark of this Divine life He has in Himself is evidently unceasing dependence, receiving from the Father, by the moment, what He had to speak or do.... The infinite importance of this truth in the Christian life is easily felt. The life Christ lived in the Father is the life He imparts to us. We are to abide in Him and He in us, *even as* He in the Father and the Father in Him. And if the secret of His abiding in the Father be this unceasing self-abnegation—"I can do nothing of Myself"—this life of most entire and absolute dependence and waiting upon God, must it not far more be the most marked feature of our Christian life, the first and all-pervading disposition we seek to maintain?[14]

OVERCOMING THROUGH FAITH

The first condition, then, for entering the victorious life is recognizing one's sinfulness and inability to change, as well as God's plan for the death of the flesh. The second condition for a life of victory is total dependence based on faith: "The life I now live in the body, I live by faith in the Son of God" (Gal 2:20). There must be faith in the Son of God for one's present life. This verse is not speaking of eternal life but how to live in the present. What does this "faith in the Son of God" believe? Scripture says that Christians are joined to Christ. Therefore, "at-one-ment" means more than reconciliation of two persons. Faith must believe that the mystery of union is God's work by which all of Christ's virtues may be expressed in the life of a believer. One receives eternal life through faith alone. Likewise, one overcomes sin through faith alone.[15]

If someone enters the victorious life by believing that the nature of Christ is given through the Atonement, how do they continue in this new covenant life? As long as one lives the Christian life there will be a continuous battle for victory, but it is with faith, not self-effort, that

---

14. A. Murray, *Two Covenants*, 184–85.
15. Nee, *Life That Wins*, 58–60.

a Christian is to fight. "Fight the good fight of the faith [or 'of faith']."[16] Take hold of the eternal life to which you were called" (1 Tim 6:12). The "good fight" is one "of faith," faith in the triumph of Christ and the power of his life. "The righteous shall live by faith" (Rom 1:17). Anyone who would be righteous must fight from a position of faith rather than a hope that is uncertain of the possibility of overcoming. "Faith is confidence in what we hope for" (Heb 11:1), the certainty that Christ's own life is able to overcome.

The Bible does not teach that all sin will be eliminated in the experience of a believer. Yet because of Christ's provision in the Atonement, no believer should practice sin. Christians should be "more than conquerors" and manifest Christ daily. If they fall they are immediately restored through confession and repentance (1 John 1:9).[17] As one confesses their sin they should also confess that they can never be changed and that they are not going to try to change themselves. Rather, they should "glory" in weakness so that the life of Christ may come forth, for God's "power is made perfect in weakness" (2 Cor 12:9).[18]

As long as one continues in the Christian life they will continue to "grow in the grace and knowledge of our Lord and Savior Jesus Christ" (2 Pet 3:18). Growth in the Christian life involves "growing in grace," learning to depend more on the grace of God. It also involves "growing in knowledge," because one can overcome only the sins of which they are aware. Jesus, praying for his disciples, asks God to "sanctify them by the truth" (John 17:17). Christ is asking God to reveal more and more of his truth about holiness. An increased understanding of holiness leads to an increased capacity for holiness, which in turn calls for increased dependence on God's grace (what God does for a believer). To "grow in grace" is to allow God to do more as the believer's understanding of truth increases. First, truth reveals an area of failure in the life of a believer, and

---

16. The Greek *pisteōs* is in the genitive, suggesting to some that the battle the Christian fights is one "of faith," or fought using one's faith (so translated in KJV, NASB, NCV, etc.). It also is preceded by the definite article, indicating to others that the fight is one of "the faith," or a fight to defend Christian doctrine (so in NIV, ESV, LEB, NABRE, NRSV, etc.). The concept of overcoming through faith in Christ's victory is consistent with other statements by Paul concerning the victorious Christian life (see Gal 2:20, Eph 6:16, and 1 Thess 5:8).

17. Nee, *Life That Wins*, 115.

18. Nee, *Life That Wins*, 120.

then grace supplies the ability to correct it. Although the victory of Christ is complete, the scope of his victory in the believer is ever enlarging.[19]

The author of Hebrews speaks of Jesus as the guarantee of a better covenant: "And it was not without an oath! Others became priests without any oath. . . . Because of this oath, Jesus has become the guarantor of a better covenant. . . . Therefore he is able to save completely those who come to God through him, because he always lives to intercede for them" (Heb 7:20, 22, 25). Because the priesthood of Jesus is confirmed by the oath of God, Jesus becomes the guarantee of a better covenant. The oath is intended to show that "it is impossible for God to lie" and to ensure that believers "who have fled to take hold of the hope set before us may be greatly encouraged" (Heb 6:18). In order to encourage belief and confidence God gives (1) a covenant with certain specific promises, (2) Jesus as the guarantee of the covenant, and (3) an oath, all of which show that the one thing that God wants is faith that he will do all he has promised. Jesus is "able to save completely" those who draw near to God through him, for "he always lives to intercede for them." He is ceaselessly engaged in watching their needs and presenting them to the Father. Christians are to be assured of the sufficiency of Christ's finished redemption. Christ accomplishes all that is needed for freedom from the power of sin. Christians too often speak of the great work of Christ at Calvary but fail to expect him to do great things in their hearts. Yet it is in the heart that the consummation of Christ's work takes place. In the heart the Atonement has its full triumph, but this triumph can only be experienced in weakness and in faith.[20]

CHRIST'S VICTORY BECOMES OUR OWN

The eternal purpose of God in creating and redeeming humans is that they would manifest the life of his Son and share in his Son's glory. To this end, believers are "born again," receiving a new nature, the very life of Christ. Before the foundation of the world God purposed to have many sons; therefore, "those God foreknew he also predestined to be conformed to the image of his Son, that he might be the firstborn among many brothers and sisters" (Rom 8:29). God purchases humans and sets them free that they may become his people. According to the right of

19. Nee, *Life That Wins*, 118–23.
20. A. Murray, *Two Covenants*, 94–101.

redemption, humanity belongs to God, but he will not coerce them. One becomes a servant (bondslave) of God only by choice, by "[offering themselves] as a living sacrifice" (Rom 12:1) to be "set free from sin" and to "become slaves of God," to have holiness and eternal life (Rom 6:22).[21]

In summary, through the new covenant Christ gives to believers a new nature, a new life, his own life. Christians express Christ's victory in their lives by (1) recognizing their inability to overcome, (2) recognizing that it is not God's purpose to reform the old self, and (3) by believing in (depending upon) the life of Christ within them. As Christ's life is lived out in the lives of believers, his victorious work continues and God's enemy continues to be defeated (Rom 16:20). Christ dies in place of humankind to free us from the penalty of sin, but he lives in place of humankind to free us from sin itself. He is both a substitutionary ransom and a substitutionary victor.

The theory of victorious substitution views Christ's work as naturally carrying forth into the life of the believer. Sincere Christians are not just concerned about justification or eternal standing but about living a holy life pleasing to the Lord who bought them. For one whose desire is to be "blameless . . . when our Lord Jesus comes" (1 Thess 3:13), Christ's substitutionary life is just as essential as his substitutionary death. Andrew Murray speaks of these two aspects of Christ's work from Galatians 4:5–6:

> This passage brings into view that which is the distinctive blessing of the new covenant. In working out our salvation God bestowed upon us two wonderful gifts. We read: "God sent forth His Son, that He might redeem them that were under the law, that we might receive the adoption of sons. And because ye are sons, God sent forth the Spirit of his Son into your hearts, crying, Abba, Father." Here we have the two parts of God's work in salvation. The one, the more objective, what He did that we might become His children—He sent forth His Son. The second, the more subjective, what He did that we might live like His children: He sent forth the Spirit of His Son into our hearts. In the former we have the external manifestation of the work of redemption; in the other, its inward appropriation; the former for the sake of the latter. These two halves form one great whole, and may not be separated.

---

21. A. Murray, *Two Covenants*, 144–45.

> God sent Christ to accomplish a redemption by which man's heart would be won back to Him; nothing but that could satisfy God. And that is what is accomplished when the Holy Spirit makes the heart of God's child what it should be. The whole work of Christ's redemption—His Atonement and Victory, His Exaltation and Intercession, His glory at the right hand of God—all these are only preparatory to what is the chief triumph of His grace: the renewal of the heart to be the temple of God.... If we look carefully at what the new covenant promises mean, we shall see how the "sending forth of the Spirit of His Son into our hearts" is indeed the consummation and crown of Christ's redeeming work.[22]

Christ's victory for believers in the Atonement becomes Christ's victory in believers by the indwelling Spirit (Rom 8:1–11). Christ's triumph over sin is reproduced in the lives of Christians, thus Christ himself becomes the believer's sanctification (1 Cor 1:30). This sanctification involves spiritual warfare in which victory over sin is assured as Christ is permitted to live moment by moment in the believer (John 15:1–6; Eph 6:10–18; Col 1:18–23; Rom 8:12–13, 26–39; 13:11–14).[23] The reign of sin in human nature is ended.

---

22. A. Murray, *Two Covenants*, 59–61.
23. Greathouse, "Sanctification," 51–53.

Conclusion

THE FIRST TWO PARTS of this book prepare the way for the explanation, emphasis, and affirmation of the victorious substitution theory. Parts 3 and 4 present the victorious substitution theory itself, setting forth the nature of the Atonement and the nature of the Christian life produced by atonement. The goal is not to criticize but to introduce a positive, victorious view of the Atonement that does justice to all the scriptural teaching and is true to each NT metaphor. The theory of victorious substitution will be briefly summarized in four points: the motivation for the death of Christ, the reason for the necessity of the death of Christ, the character of the death of Christ, and the effect of the death of Christ.[1]

THE MOTIVATION FOR THE DEATH OF CHRIST

The NT throughout reveals the motivation for the death of Christ to be not only God's desire to restore "all things" but also God's love for humankind. Only God's love could have willed his Son to suffer and die as a sacrifice for sin (John 3:16). "God demonstrates his own love for us in this: While we were still sinners, Christ died for us" (Rom 5:8). "Greater love has no one than this: to lay down one's life for one's friends" (John 15:13).

---

1. Marshall, "Death of Jesus," 20–21.

THE REASON FOR THE DEATH OF CHRIST

Since the Atonement is by its very nature a transaction or an event in which God enters into his creation, one must seek, in carrying out a doctrinal search for the reason for this intervention, a larger viewpoint from which the Atonement originated. A proper understanding may only be found from the standpoint of God, not of humanity. What was present in God's heart when he created a perfectly ordered world and when he determined to restore that perfect order to a fallen world?[2]

According to the theory of victorious substitution, the reason for the death of Christ is the fallen condition of God's creation. The state of the world necessitates God's intervention, for God's enemy has usurped a position of authority and power in God's realm for his own sinister purposes. Humankind has defied God by acting in direct disobedience to him. Humans, unable to free themselves from the tyranny that resulted from their choice, must have God's involvement to liberate them from the kingdom of Satan, the sway of sin, and their own condition of spiritual death.

The drama of spiritual battle ensues and will be final only when "all things" are reconciled to God, whether in heaven or on earth (Col 1:20). The reality of evil in the world and God's coming forth to triumph over that evil is the dominant theme of the Atonement.[3] This theme runs throughout the NT, reminding one constantly that the victory of Christ has cosmic dimensions.

THE CHARACTER OF THE DEATH OF CHRIST

The triumph of Christ results from his sinless life given in sacrifice as a substitutionary ransom payment. He endures the penalty for human sin that results from God's original judgment of humankind. Christ comes to do spiritual battle with hostile powers and to establish his kingdom, asserting his claim against a rival kingdom in a fallen world. He comes as "the *de jure* Sovereign challenging to mortal combat the *de facto* ruler."[4] He fights humankind's battle, entering the conflict at humanity's side and opening the way to victory by enduring the enemy's spears. Victory

---

2. H. Clark, *Cross and Eternal Order*, 1–4.
3. Aulén, *Christus Victor*, 159.
4. H. Clark, *Cross and Eternal Order*, 53–55.

requires his vicarious suffering.⁵ He is tried to the uttermost, never losing a battle; he perseveres without sin and is therefore triumphant forevermore. The redemption that Christ provides *is* substitutionary, for Christ pays the price that humankind owes and suffers their penalty in their stead to set them free. There is a judgment to be faced and he faces it; there is a price to be paid and he pays it; there is a penalty to be borne and he bears it; there is a victory to be won and he wins it.⁶ This is surely a sacrifice for both Father and Son. Christ's life and death can be described as sacrificial, substitutionary, and victorious. Jesus is at once the Lamb of God, the sacrifice for human sins, and the Lion of the tribe of Judah (Rev 5:5), triumphant over Satan as sin's source, death as sin's consequence, and sin itself.⁷

THE EFFECT OF THE DEATH OF CHRIST

The effect of Christ's death is multifaceted. His resurrection and exaltation demonstrate his victory over the evil to which he submits himself. God's enemy, who had deceived God's people and so damaged God's creation, receives the decisive, if not final, blow in Christ's death. Satan may still be an "enemy" and a "a roaring lion" (1 Pet 5:8), but his power is vanquished. His human captives are liberated and called to be reconciled to the God who loves them and gave himself for them. A lifetime of intimate fellowship begins for those who answer the call in repentance and faith and are thereby reconciled to God. They are redeemed in two ways. They are free from the penalty of sin, for their sins are forgiven, meaning they are free from death and given eternal life. But more, through faith, they are free from sin itself through the gift of Christ's triumphant life; they now draw upon his life rather than their own sinful and selfish life. The work of the Atonement involves not only what Christ has done *for* humans but also what he continues to do *in* humans. As Paul says:

> But God demonstrates his own love for us in this: While we were still sinners, Christ died for us. Since we have now been justified by his blood, how much more shall we be saved from God's wrath through him! For if, while we were God's enemies, we were reconciled to him through the death of his Son, how much

---

5. N. Robinson, *Jesus Christ Saves Men*, 143.
6. Morris, *New Testament*, 405.
7. Bloesch, *Jesus Is Victor!*, 48.

more, having been reconciled, shall we be *saved through his life*! Not only is this so, but we also boast in God through our Lord Jesus Christ, through whom we have now received reconciliation. (Rom 5:8–11, emphasis added)

This passage reveals three aspects of the Atonement. First, there is the objective atonement that God accomplished when the world was still alienated from him (verse 8). This reconciliation denotes simply a change of situation, for it was accomplished "while we were still sinners." Second, there is the subjective atonement that takes place when an individual believes and is "justified by his blood . . . saved from God's wrath" (verse 9). Third, there is the ongoing atonement or reconciliation with which Paul is most concerned in this passage, for he is making an argument by degrees. He argues that if God undertook reconciliation when humankind was in the enemy camp, "how much more," for one who is now justified (in right standing with him), will he give his life to finish the salvation that he died to accomplish.[8] "How much more, having being reconciled, shall we be *saved through his life*!" (verse 10).

Verse 11 speaks of the rejoicing that follows for those who are reconciled. The Son of God has given himself to be where they are so that they may be where he is (John 17:24), experiencing the life of God. Just as Christ gives himself freely they are to freely give their lives as a "living sacrifice, holy and pleasing to God" (Rom 12:1).[9] There follows an overcoming life. Scripture teaches that this life is only realized in faith and in complete dependence on the life of Christ within.

The effects of the death of Christ are "now but not yet." The full experience of salvation for believers and the full redemption of creation are yet future. Therefore, "the Spirit and the bride say, 'Come!' And let the one who hears say, 'Come!' Let the one who is thirsty come; and let the one who wishes take the free gift of the water of life" (Rev 22:17).

FINAL THOUGHTS

The argument and analysis put forth in this book expresses a theory of the Atonement that is logical, moral, theologically sound, and based on careful exegesis. However, no effort is made to call theory fact. The author is content for victorious substitution to remain a theory, but argues

---

8. Bushnell, *Vicarious Sacrifice*, 446–47.
9. Gunton, *Actuality of Atonement*, 140.

that it is a good theory, for it weaves together in a proper (if not perfect) balance the elements of necessity, God's judgment against sin, ransom, substitution, penalty, reconciliation, and victory.

In revealing the positive aspects of victorious substitution it has been necessary to refute the penal substitution theory. This refutation in chapters 2 and 3 intends to highlight what this book considers a better theory. It involves a unique combination of ideas into a slightly divergent conception of the Atonement and its application in the lives of Christians. The victorious substitution theory has advantages over other theories because it includes the scriptural insights of other theories. It incorporates the insight of the subjective theories in that Christ's dying to deliver humanity from the kingdom of darkness involves, in part, his drawing and arousing individuals to himself and to a holy life. Victorious substitution goes beyond this, however, in insisting that only by the very life of Christ can one live righteously.

Victorious substitution gives weight to the conviction that Christ's work is not inspirational alone. Humankind needs a real deliverance, which involves a real cosmic struggle. The concept of retributive justice and God's wrath against sin is retained by holding that those who reject Christ are still subject to God's wrath and the resulting punishment as their just wage. Victorious substitution also holds that divine forgiveness of sins is not enough for full at-one-ment. God's purpose is intimate communion and dependence on him.

When the believer lives by faith in the promise of the new covenant, dependent on Christ's life, they too may experience victory over sin, carrying forth Christ's victory until "all things" are reconciled and all enemies defeated. Victorious substitution relates the Atonement to real human need—deliverance from the kingdom of darkness, deliverance from the judgment of God, deliverance from the power of sin, and deliverance from spiritual death.

Beneath all the differences of interpretation there is the common Christian experience that Christ does save. Uncertainty about theories may exist alongside the certainty of that which the various theories seek to explain. Yet differences in atonement theories are not unimportant, for every interpretation of Christ's work is ultimately a conception of the character of God.[10]

10. Cave, *Work of Christ*, 278.

Acknowledging that "now we see only a reflection as in a mirror" (1 Cor 13:12), the author has sought to present a clear theory of the Atonement—one that inspires believers to embrace all that Christ dies to provide them and to go forth to complete the victory of Christ in evangelism, social and political involvement, in altruism, and in care for others. May God "rescue us from the hand of our enemies" and "enable us to serve him without fear in holiness and righteousness before him all our days" (Luke 1:74–75).

Appendix A

Romans 3:21–26
Context, Terminology, and Exegesis

ROMANS 3:21–26: CONTEXT AND TERMINOLOGY

ADVOCATES OF THE PENAL substitution theory consider Romans 3:25–26 to be the proof text for their theory. Indeed, they often do not consider it a theory at all, believing this passage to be so clearly an expression of their concept of atonement. A careful analysis of the context and terminology of these verses (expanded to include 3:21–26), however, does not support the penal substitution interpretation. Instead, a scripturally faithful reading of these verses simply presents God's activity in redemption.

> But now apart from the law the righteousness of God has been made known, to which the Law and the Prophets testify. This righteousness is given through faith in Jesus Christ to all who believe. There is no difference between Jew and Gentile, for all have sinned and fall short of the glory of God, and all are justified freely by his grace through the redemption that came by Christ Jesus. God presented Christ as a sacrifice of atonement, through the shedding of his blood—to be received by faith. He did this to demonstrate his righteousness, because in his forbearance he had left the sins committed beforehand unpunished—he did it to demonstrate his righteousness at the present time, so as to be just and the one who justifies those who have faith in Jesus. (Romans 3:21–26)

Context

Romans 3:21–26 occurs at a crucial moment in Paul's letter to the Romans, gathering up what has gone before and pointing ahead to much of what he will say in the ensuing chapters. Paul's continuing argument must be kept in mind when considering this passage.[1] The message of Romans 3:21–31 closely corresponds to that of 1:16—3:20, for both passages seek to protect divine impartiality. In chapters 1–2 Paul shows that God is impartial in judging on the basis of works; in 3:21–31 he shows that God is impartial in saving on the basis of faith. The opening argument reveals God's fairness with respect to Jews and Gentiles in judgment, while Romans 3:29–30 repeats this message in the new context of the proclamation of grace. Romans 3:9–20 insists that all—Jew and Gentile alike—stand condemned before God, while 3:22 reveals that all can be saved. Thus, the concept of impartiality introduced in 2:11 is central to all of chapters 1–3.[2]

At the beginning of chapter 3 Paul is wrestling with the problem of the allegedly special status of the Jews before God. He has argued in the previous paragraph that the Jew has no reason to boast of his possession of the law, because real circumcision is a matter of the heart, spiritual and not literal (Rom 2:29). That statement leads him into difficulty, however, because it seems to imply that Jewishness is meaningless. Paul is unwilling to accept that conclusion for very definite theological reasons, since Jewish identity is rooted in claims about God's dealings with his people in history. If the Gospel somehow annuls this special relationship, it means that God's past dealings with his people were false dealings, that he made promises from which he is now backing out. But Paul is committed to the revelation that the God who raised Jesus from the dead is the same God who gave the promises to Israel; consequently, the trustworthiness of the God who made these promises must be established. The concern is God's integrity, and this is the issue which drives the discussion in Romans 3.[3] In broad outline, the movement of the argument in chapter 3 is as follows:

1. Verses 1–8—Has God abandoned his promises to Israel? Is he inconsistent or unjust?

---

1. Ziesler, "Salvation," 356.
2. Bassler, "Divine Impartiality," 55.
3. Hays, "Logic of Romans 3," 109.

2. Verses 9–20—All such objections are invalid; humanity, not God, is guilty of injustice.
3. Verses 21–26—God has not abandoned his people; he has now revealed his justice/righteousness in a new way, overcoming human unfaithfulness by his own power and proving himself faithful and just.[4]

How does this argument in chapter 3 relate to what has come before? In 1:16–17 Paul summarizes what he believes the Gospel to be: "For I am not ashamed of the gospel, because it is the power of God that brings salvation to everyone who believes: first to the Jew, then to the Gentile. For in the gospel the righteousness of God is revealed—a righteousness that is by faith from first to last, just as it is written: 'The righteous will live by faith.'" The Gospel is the power that saves (liberates) all who respond to (have faith in) God's provision in Christ. It reveals God's saving righteousness that enables those who believe to be righteous. Because the Gospel is received solely by response (faith), it cuts across all distinctions, in particular the distinction between Jews and Gentiles. From 1:18 to 3:20 Paul seeks to demonstrate the universal problem of sin and the universal need for salvation. It is the revelation of the righteousness of God (3:21–26) that answers this problem and meets this need.[5]

The Righteousness of God

What is the meaning of the revelation of God's righteousness (Rom 1:17; 3:21), which Paul views as the heart of the Gospel? Paul uses the full phrase "the righteousness of God" in his most solemn and striking utterances on the subject of salvation; elsewhere, he speaks simply of righteousness.[6] It is a key phrase not only in this passage (Rom 3:21, 25, 26), but also in Paul's "theme verse" of the epistle (Rom 1:16–17). Paul uses the phrase eight times in Romans (1:17; 3:5, 21, 22, 26; 10:3, twice) and only once outside of Romans (2 Cor 5:21); therefore, the phrase should give a clue to the distinctive message of Romans.[7] How is this phrase to be interpreted?

---

4. Hays, "Logic of Romans 3," 113.
5. Ziesler, "Salvation," 356.
6. Quell, *Righteousness*, 42.
7. Moo, *Romans*, 71.

Righteousness as Right Standing

Interpretations fall into three main categories. The first understands "the righteousness of God" as "righteousness that is from God." This view sees God's righteousness as a gift from God that renders believers acceptable, or not guilty, in his sight. It does not denote the infusion of righteousness, but rather it is a forensic term declaring a person not guilty before God because of the gift of God's righteousness (right standing).[8] In this view, Paul is declaring that the Gospel reveals the righteous *status* God gives believers.[9]

What are the arguments supporting this view? First, the frequent connection of righteousness with faith suggests to some a person's standing before God (Rom 3:21–22; 4:3, 5–6, 9, 11, 13, 22–24; 9:30–31; 10:3–4, 6, 10; Gal 2:20–21; 3:6, 21–22; 5:5; Phil 3:9).[10] But in every case except Romans 3:21–22 (which will be considered later) it is not "the righteousness of God" that is related to faith; rather, it is human righteousness or right standing before God that depends on faith. Second, Scripture speaks of faith being "reckoned" ("credited" NIV) as righteousness, showing that a status is ascribed to a believer by their faith (Rom 4:3, 5, 6, 9, 11, 22, 24; Gal 3:6).[11] This is certainly one way Paul uses the word righteousness, but again, it is human righteousness that is in view, not God's righteousness. Third, Paul speaks of the "gift of righteousness" in Romans 5:17.[12] The righteousness of humankind, their right standing, is God's gift. But, the right standing granted to the believer does not define God's own righteousness. Finally, 1 Corinthians 1:30 speaks of the righteousness that believers have because they are "in Christ Jesus." Righteousness in this verse probably does not refer to right standing but to Christ's own righteousness or uprightness. Believers have Christ's righteousness because they have his very life, not because it was granted to them by God. Clearly Paul uses the word *righteousness* in Romans to refer to God's gift to believers of right standing before him by faith. But should this righteousness given to humans define "the righteousness of God" in Romans 3:21–26? There are many reasons to believe that the phrase is much broader.

---

8. Schreiner, *Romans*, 63.

9. Moo, *Romans*, 71. Moo adds that this is the view of Nygren, Ridderbos, Cranfield, Ladd, Seifrid, Gultmann, Conzelmann, Klein, and Zeller.

10. Schreiner, *Romans*, 64.

11. Schreiner, *Romans*, 64.

12. Schreiner, *Romans*, 64.

Righteousness as Divine Action

The second interpretation understands "the righteousness of God" more broadly in terms of God's saving power.[13] In this view God's righteousness is an activity, "the saving action of God"[14] that effects reconciliation or a right relationship. Several arguments support God's righteousness as a divine action. Two verbs used by Paul, translated "revealed" in Romans 1:17 and "made known" in 3:21, are used to refer to the activity of God in bringing about his redemptive plan (Rom 1:18; 2:5; 8:18, 19; 1 Cor 1:7; Gal 1:16; 3:23; 2 Thess 1:7; 2:3, 6).[15] A proper understanding of this usage fits well with the view that the righteousness of God is his saving activity, for it is more logical to speak of a divine action being revealed than of a new standing being disclosed.[16] Second, this understanding also parallels the meaning of "revealed" in 1:18: "The wrath of God is being revealed [i.e., being inflicted] from heaven..."[17] Just as "the wrath of God" refers to a divine activity, so "the righteousness of God" portrays a divine activity. Both reveal God's actions in history.[18] Romans 1:16 describes the Gospel as "the power of God that brings salvation." Third, since verses 16 and 17 are connected by the conjunction "for," a connection should also exist between "the power of God" (verse 16) and "the righteousness of God" (verse 17). "The power of God" describes his action; therefore, "the righteousness of God" should describe God's action as well.[19]

Fourth, the strongest argument for interpreting "the righteousness of God" as his saving activity in history is the OT understanding of the phrase. Psalm 98:2 says, "The Lord has made his salvation known and revealed his righteousness to the nations." The parallel between salvation and righteousness is clear. In Psalm 71 the psalmist asks for God's deliverance "in your righteousness" (verse 2). If God answers his prayer, he promises to "tell of your righteous deeds, of your saving acts all day long" (verse 15). God's decree in Isaiah 51:8 also parallels salvation with righteousness: "My righteousness will last forever, my salvation through

---

13. Schreiner, *Romans*, 63.

14. Moo, *Romans*, 71. Moo adds that this is the view of Dodd, Michel, Barrett, and Dunn.

15. Schreiner, *Romans*, 65; Moo, *Romans*, 69.

16. Schreiner, *Romans*, 65.

17. Schreiner, *Romans*, 65; Moo, *Romans*, 69.

18. Schreiner, *Romans*, 65.

19. Schreiner, *Romans*, 66.

all generations." Other examples of God's righteousness as divine action include Psalm 22:31; 31:1; 35:24; 40:10; 69:27–29; 88:12; 119:123; Isa 42:6, 21; 45:8, 13; 51:5–8; Mic 6:5; 7:9. The evidence is abundant and indisputable: in the OT God's righteousness is one way of describing his saving action. In light of the OT meaning of "the righteousness of God," then, it is doubtful that Paul could be using the term in only a forensic sense.[20]

Righteousness as an Attribute

A third interpretation argues that the expression could refer to an attribute of God. An attribute of righteousness could have one of two meanings. The righteousness of God could be God's justice. Contemporary scholars who give this meaning to the phrase in Romans 3:5 and 25–26 rarely do so in 1:17 or 3:21, for the latter context necessitates a positive and broader meaning for the phrase.[21] But if the righteousness of God is interpreted as an attribute, then it is still a further interpretation to maintain that this attribute of righteousness refers in Romans to punitive justice.

As an attribute, the righteousness of God could just as well refer to his faithfulness, expressed in his saving activity, especially for his covenant people.[22] This meaning of God's covenant faithfulness is closely connected to God's saving activity in the OT (Exod 15:13; Ps 35:24; 36:5–6, 10; 51:14; 71:2; 89:16; 103:17; 111:3; 119:40; 143:1, 11; 145:6–7; Isa 62:1–2; 63:7), and the two are sometimes difficult to distinguish.[23] Paul picks up this idea of both covenant faithfulness and saving activity in Romans 3:26: "He did it to demonstrate his righteousness [saving activity] at the present time, so as to be just [true to his covenant] and the one who justifies those who have faith in Jesus."[24]

God's covenant faithfulness in the OT also includes his actions as a judge on behalf of his people. Psalm 50:5–6 says, "Gather to me this consecrated people, who made a covenant with me by sacrifice. And the heavens proclaim his righteousness, for he is a God of justice." In Psalm 72:1–2, 4 it is God's righteousness that the king must have so that he will be able to "defend the afflicted among the people and save the children of

20. Schreiner, *Romans*, 66–67.
21. Moo, *Romans*, 70.
22. Käsemann, *Romans*, 27; Moo, *Romans*, 70.
23. Moo, *Romans*, 82.
24. Hunter, *Paul and His Predecessors*, 122.

the needy; may he crush the oppressor" (verse 4). Other OT Scriptures also say that God will judge in righteousness (Ps 67:4; 94:15; 89:14; 97:2), meaning he will do what is right. He will keep his covenant promises. When associated with righteousness, God's attribute of doing what is right as a judge is most often manifested in his deliverance of his people. His righteousness naturally takes on a negative judgmental aspect, however, when Israel's enemies are in mind or when Israel fails to keep the terms of the covenant (Isa 5:16; 10:22).[25]

The righteousness of God is a theme developed in the OT prophets that often moves beyond justice and proper ethical conduct to a specific concern for the helpless, to rescue them from those who are more powerful.[26] God's righteousness, in accordance with his covenant promises, means his disposition to do for humans what they need but cannot do for themselves. The context of Romans 3:21–26 makes this meaning especially appropriate.[27] The following discussion relates this book's interpretation of the term "the righteousness of God."

God's Righteousness Is More Than an Attribute

If the righteousness of God refers merely to an attribute, then a revelation of the righteousness of God (1:17) would only mean a revelation that God is righteous. One can reason, then, that the revelation of God's righteousness is more involved. It is a revelation, not of a self-contained righteousness, but of one that flows out from God to meet the needs of humankind.[28] Paul's use of the phrase must be understood in light of his Jewish background and training. In Hebrew thought, righteousness is essentially a concept of relation. Righteousness is not something that an individual possesses alone; it is something one has in one's relationships. When the phrase is used of God, it refers to his covenant relationship with his people.[29]

In Paul's vocabulary, righteousness undoubtedly is an attribute of God, as in ordinary English and Greek usage, but one must recognize that it also stands for an act or an activity in Hebrew usage. Whereas

25. Moo, *Romans*, 83.
26. Snaith, *Old Testament*, 70.
27. Lunceford, "*Ilaskomai* Cognates," 86.
28. Lee, *Romans*, 62–63.
29. Dunn, *Romans*, 40–41.

much of God's activity is hidden and mysterious (Rom 11:33), when Paul says that God's righteousness is being revealed (Rom 3:21) he means that God is taking action that can be observed by humankind.[30] Thus Isaiah speaks of God's righteousness as going forth (Isa 51:5).[31]

The background for Paul's thinking and vocabulary is the OT. He read the OT in the Septuagint, but he also understood the original Hebrew. Frequently, the meaning of a Greek word used by the Septuagint translators is determined for Paul by the meaning of the Hebrew that it translates. The Greek word used in Romans 3:25 and 26 (*dikaiosynē*) is the ordinary term for "righteousness" or "justice." But the corresponding Hebrew terms (*tsedheq*, *ts'dhaqa*), although often identical in meaning with the Greek terms, attain that meaning along a specific line of development. They are derived from a verb (*tsadhaq*) whose primary meaning is "to be in the right" rather than "to be righteous." Its causative form (*hitsdiq*), generally translated "justify," means not "to make righteous" but "to put in the right," and very often, "to vindicate" or "give redress to" a person who has been wronged. Thus, a judge or ruler is thought of as righteous not so much because they observe and uphold a perfect standard of justice but because they vindicate the cause of the wronged; their righteousness is revealed in the justification of those who are the victims of evil.[32]

This shade of meaning can be seen in the OT when God acts as judge to see that right is done, that those who are in the right are vindicated. In Judges 5:11, the "righteous acts of the Lord" (KJV; literally "the righteousnesses") refer to the acts of vindication or deliverance that God has wrought for his people in delivering them from their enemies.[33] God is "righteous" when he meets the obligations he took upon himself to be Israel's God, that is, to rescue Israel and punish their enemies (e.g., Exod 9:27; 1 Sam 12:7; Dan 9:16; Mic 6:5). His righteousness is his covenant faithfulness.[34] This meaning is also apparent in Psalm 35:24–28: "Vindicate me in your righteousness, Lord my God; do not let them gloat over me . . . may those who delight in my vindication shout for joy and gladness; . . . my tongue will proclaim your righteousness, your praises

30. Quell, *Righteousness*, 43; Dodd, *Romans*, 10.

31. Lee, *Romans*, 63.

32. Dodd, *Romans*, 10.

33. Dodd, *Romans*, 11. Consistent with this meaning, the NIV renders "the victories of the Lord."

34. Dunn, *Romans*, 41.

all day long." Here the righteousness of God is his divine nature preventing him from allowing wrong to triumph over right. When his people are wronged, it is in virtue of his righteousness that he vindicates or, as it may be expressed, justifies them. Therefore, in the OT, God's people appeal to his righteousness not as something to be feared but as their one sure hope. "In you, Lord, I have taken refuge; . . . deliver me in your righteousness" (Ps 31:1). "For your name's sake, Lord, preserve my life; in your righteousness, bring me out of trouble" (Ps 143:11).[35]

When the word *righteous* is used to describe God, it is a word that belongs to the terminology of relationship. In the OT, he is righteous by doing justice to claims made upon him in the name of relationship. Thus God's righteousness is manifested first in that he rules according to the covenant relationship that he has with his people. It is a concrete rather than abstract way of conceiving God's righteousness, and it includes both juridical and rescuing elements. The judicial righteousness, with its retribution, rewards, and punishments, cannot be separated from the actions, on behalf of his people, of a God who is both king and judge. This is especially seen in Isaiah 40–55 where the argument is often couched in the language of a lawsuit (e.g., "prove they were right" [justified] in 43:9; "state the case for your innocence" in 43:26). Yahweh's judicial righteousness ("He who vindicates [justifies] me is near. . . ; Isa 50:8–9) secures justice for his oppressed people against their conquerors. This concept directly leads to the idea that God's judgment and righteousness bring help and salvation (Deut 32:4, 35–43; Hos 2:19; Mic 7:9).[36] Hence also the frequent combination of righteousness and salvation found in the latter half of Isaiah: "I am bringing my righteous near, it is not far away; and my salvation will not be delayed" (Isa 46:13). "My righteousness draws near speedily, my salvation is on the way, and my arm will bring justice to the nations. . . . my salvation will last forever, my righteousness will never fail" (Isa 51:5–6).[37]

In passages such as these, God's righteousness is not retributive justice, but is instead essentially gracious. It is not that justice must be done so that grace may be free to act; it is grace itself in action for vindication or justification.[38] Therefore, when the people of God are wronged, it is

---

35. Lee, *Romans*, 65.
36. Quell, *Righteousness*, 29–30.
37. Lee, *Romans*, 66.
38. Lee, *Romans*, 66.

to God's righteousness that they appeal. Like Christ, who was reviled and insulted, they commend their souls and bodies to God who judges righteously (1 Pet 2:23) and trust in him for their cause. Paul says to the persecuted Thessalonians, "God is just: He will pay back trouble to those who trouble you" (2 Thess 1:6). There is a relationship between God and his people that involves obligations of both, and God's righteousness is his faithfulness to the covenant he has made.[39]

Particularly in Psalms and Isaiah, righteousness and salvation are seen as virtually synonymous. The "righteousness of God" involves his action to restore and keep his own within the covenant (Ps 31:1; 35:24; 51:14; 65:5; 71:2, 15; 98:2; 143:11; Isa 45:8, 21; 46:13; 51:5–6, 8; 62:1–2; 63:1, 7). It is this concept of God's righteousness that Paul is using in Romans when he refers to the righteousness of God as the power of God for salvation, and it provides the key to understanding 3:5, 21–22, 25–26; and 10:3. Any attempt to say that God's righteousness denotes only an aspect of the divine nature that demands punishment denies the clear thrust of the evidence.[40]

God's faithfulness is revealed most strikingly when his people have failed to meet their obligations, yet he does not forsake them. Thus the psalmist can say, "Deliver me from the guilt of bloodshed, O God, you who are God my Savior, and my tongue will sing of your righteousness" (Ps 51:14). Righteousness here refers to God's faithfulness to his promise to forgive those who repent of their sin. In the same way, John can say, "If we confess our sins, he is faithful and just [righteous] and will forgive us our sins" (1 John 1:9); that is, he is true to the obligations involved in relating to us as Christians. Passages like these undoubtedly speak of a "righteousness of God" that is gracious and is exhibited in the forgiveness of sins. The question is, Can this righteousness be identified with "the righteousness of God" found in Romans?[41]

During the two or three centuries before Christ, Judaism thought that in this present age the cause of right does not prevail. Although "the Most High is sovereign over all kingdoms on earth" (Dan 4:17), for reasons known only by himself, he permits evil to have its way. But in the

---

39. Lee, *Romans*, 66.

40. Dunn, *Romans*, 41; Cranfield objects, saying that "there is no reason to assume that [Paul] must have used the language he took over in precisely the same way as that in which it had been used. We must allow for the possibility of his having used what he took over with freedom and originality." *Romans*, 22.

41. Lee, *Romans*, 67.

age to come, the strength of the Lord will be revealed for the defeat of evil and the establishment of good. It is then that his righteousness will be fully revealed. The Gospel that Paul says he is proud to proclaim is that the righteousness of God is now revealed (Rom 3:21). This is directly linked to the OT expectation of God's righteousness or salvation. Paul proclaims that the age to come has arrived and the vindication of right is taking place. The present tense of the verb (which the NIV renders "has been made known") would be better translated "is being revealed," for the Greek present is primarily a tense of continuous action. Although the revelation is not yet complete, it is now a reality in progress.[42] The righteousness of God in Romans 3, then, is a gracious righteousness like that spoken of so often in the OT.

But there is nevertheless a striking difference in this new revelation of God's righteousness. In the OT the righteousness of God is always seen in relation to the covenant people of God. God does right by his own people who are in covenant relation with him. It may be by achieving their deliverance from oppressors, which is often called his salvation, or it may be in forgiving the sins of which they repent. This righteousness of God is sometimes spoken of as being revealed to the world: "The Lord has made his salvation known and revealed his righteousness to the nations" (Ps 98:2). But this is not what Paul refers to in Romans when he speaks of the Gospel in terms of a divine righteousness that is now available for all people. The OT covenant righteousness refers to God's deliverance of *his people* from their enemies; there is nothing to suggest that such righteousness is available for those who are not already part of the people of God. When Scripture says, "All the ends of the earth have seen the salvation of our God," it means that they have seen the salvation that God has "remembered . . . to Israel" (Ps 98:3).[43]

In contrast, Paul is not declaring the Gospel to people who have a right to claim a covenant relationship with God; he is preaching to those who are hopelessly wrong before God. They have, as far as they know, no reason to count on God's faithfulness toward them. The righteousness Paul reveals is more than the vindication of the good who are wronged, or the faithfulness of God to his own people who have sinned. It is a righteousness that is astonishing and profound, a righteousness by which the ungodly are put in the right before God (Rom 4:5) and by which those

---

42. Dodd, *Romans*, 12–13.
43. Lee, *Romans*, 67–68.

who are alienated from him become the people of God (Rom 3:29). Although the OT concept of the righteousness of God is in the background, this righteousness reveals more of his purpose and plan than had been previously understood. Therefore this new revelation of God's righteousness is indeed "good news" for Jew and Gentile alike.[44]

The "righteousness of God" in Romans 1:17 and 3:21–26, then, is not God's insistence on retributive justice. The context of Romans 3:21–26 indicates that the righteousness of God is much more, for it is the very theme being developed in the epistle.[45] First, the epistle addresses the state of the world under the dominance of sin, which creates the need for God's righteousness. Next, it reveals God's righteousness in justifying all who believe, putting them in the right before him (Rom 3:21—4:25). God's righteousness is further displayed in the salvation of people from the power of sin (Rom 5–8). Finally, after an excursus that seeks to justify the ways of God with humankind, Paul's letter reveals the righteousness of God in the living of a good life by the people he has saved (Rom 12–15). Thus, in "the righteousness of God" Paul sees the fulfillment of all that the prophets desired for God's people—a salvation that includes justification and deliverance from evil (Isa 45:25; 46:13; 51:5, 7–8; 55:7). In the life, death, and resurrection of Jesus, and the creation of the Church through his Spirit, God's plan of salvation surpasses what the Jews had come to expect because it is for all humankind. His righteousness is manifested not only as his just judgment of sinful humanity, but also as his provision of salvation to all who believe the Gospel.[46] God's righteousness is therefore not simply an attribute, but an activity whereby the right is revealed in a new and more complete way, in the liberation from the power of evil for all who believe.[47] God still comes to the rescue of his oppressed people, but his people now include the Gentiles and the oppressor is now sin.[48]

It is then only one narrow interpretation of the phrase "the righteousness of God" that can be used as a foundation to build the penal substitution theory. Such theorists say the phrase means that God is righteous/just and therefore must punish sin and so punished Christ. But the necessity of retribution because of God's justice is not a statement made

---

44. Lee, *Romans*, 68.
45. Price, "Righteousness," 265.
46. Price, "Righteousness," 263.
47. Dodd, *Romans*, 11–12.
48. Ziesler, *Romans*, 108.

in Romans 3:21–26 or indeed anywhere in Scripture. It is a theory about why Christ had to die.

Faith

The second term to be considered is "faith" (Rom 3:22, 25). The theme of Romans is that the revelation of God's righteousness is a matter of faith (1:16–17), and to corroborate this claim, Paul quotes Habakkuk 2:4, "The righteous [just] will live by faith" (Rom 1:17). Paul, however, means more than Habakkuk meant. Habakkuk is saying that the righteous live in faithfulness or fidelity while they wait for God's deliverance. The life of the righteous one is preserved by sheer character, by honesty, integrity, trustworthiness. Galatians 3 indicates that Paul extends this meaning. Paul, quoting this same Habakkuk passage, asks the Galatians whether their Christian experience came to them because they obeyed the law or because they believed the Gospel message (Gal 3:2). The question indicates that faith is more than obedience (faithfulness) to a code of commandments. Paul continues, "Abraham 'believed God and it was credited to him as righteousness'" (Gal 3:6). Romans 4 discusses Abraham's faith at length, and Paul concludes by saying that Abraham gave glory to God and believed that he was able to do what he had promised (4:20). In Galatians, Paul says that God's promise to Abraham was that in him all nations would be blessed (3:8). They cannot be blessed by the law, though, because the law brings a curse (judgment) upon disobedience (Gal 3:10–11). The question then becomes, How can someone "live"? Paul answers by quoting Habakkuk, "The righteous will live by faith" (3:11). Paul therefore interprets Habakkuk to mean that it is impossible to gain life by obeying the law. It is possible only by, like Abraham, relying on God in the conviction that he is able to give the blessing he has promised. By the word *faith*, then, Paul means an attitude in which, acknowledging complete insufficiency for life, one relies entirely on the sufficiency of God.[49] It describes the attitude of pure receptivity and dependence by which the soul appropriates what God has provided.[50] Faith is not an outlook on our part that forces God to right wrong, but it is an acceptance of what God does through the death of Jesus in righting wrong.[51]

49. Ziesler, *Romans*, 14–15.
50. Ziesler, *Romans*, 56.
51. Best, *Romans*, 40.

Justify

The terms *righteous, just, righteousness, justice,* and *justify* all translate words from a single Greek root. However, the adjective *righteous* has no corresponding English verb. The Greek verb rendered "justify" means "to account or pronounce right," or "to treat justly." It also may be translated "to acquit." It does not signify "to make righteous."[52]

Therefore, to get the full flavor of the word *justify* as Paul intended it, the Hebrew must be taken into account. Justification means for them an act by which a wronged person is given their rights, is vindicated, or is delivered from oppression. When Isaiah looks forward to the coming of the "righteousness of God," he thinks of it in terms of the justification of his people; that is, their deliverance from the oppressive power of evil. This is the Hebrew background that colors the Greek terms. Paul's usage includes both their wider Hebrew and their narrower Greek connotations. When he says believers are justified, the foremost idea is that they are delivered, but because it is being stated in legal terms, deliverance takes the form of a pardon in court.[53]

Ransom

The Greek word translated "ransom" or "redeem" is commonly used with reference to the emancipation of slaves or prisoners of war, frequently accomplished by the payment of a sum of money as a ransom price. Although the word can be used in the sense of liberation without any explicit reference to the payment of money, the cost should be kept in mind, as Scripture says humankind was "bought at a price" (1 Cor 6:20). Clearly a cost was involved.

Once again the term's OT associations elucidate its meaning. When the children of Israel were liberated from bondage in Egypt, they were slaves redeemed by the Lord (Deut 7:8). In like manner, the later prophets spoke of the liberation from captivity in Babylon as redemption (Isa 60:2). Galatians 4:4–5 tells us that Paul perceives the work of Christ as being an emancipation for the people of God from bondage, which also is the thought of Romans 3:24.[54]

---

52. Dodd, *Romans*, 51.
53. Dodd, *Romans*, 51–52.
54. Dodd, *Romans*, 53–54.

Romans 3:24 refers to the "redemption that came by Christ Jesus." This redemption and the righteousness of God belong together (as in 1 Cor 1:30). The use of the word *redemption* recognizes humanity's condition in the former age, our slavery to the powers of destruction. "In Christ" that condition has completely changed. "The redemption that came by Christ" has entered into human history at a precise point: the death and resurrection of Christ. The power of the forces that oppose God was broken once for all.[55]

Blood

Finally, something must be said regarding "blood" in verse 25. There is little doubt that when Paul uses the word *blood* in conjunction with the word for expiation he is speaking in sacrificial terms. In the OT sacrificial system, defilement from sin could be annulled by the offering of a sacrifice and particularly by the shedding of blood. Why, in the sacrificial rites, was value attached to sacrifice and especially to the blood of that sacrifice? The answer is revealed in Genesis 9:4, Leviticus 17:11, and Deuteronomy 12:23: the blood is the life. Thus, when Paul speaks of the blood of Christ, he is referring to Christ's life given in obedience (Rom 5:19) and in sacrifice.[56]

Having defined the necessary terms, Paul's statement in Romans 3:21–26 should be more readily understood.

GOD'S RIGHTEOUSNESS SHALL PREVAIL: EXEGESIS OF ROMANS 3:21-26

The following exegesis of the passage will challenge the assumption that Romans 3:21–26 is a proof text for the penal substitution theory as well as present an interpretation that is true to the context of the passage.

Righteousness Apart from Law

> But now apart from the law the righteousness of God has been made known, to which the Law and the Prophets testify.

55. Nygren, *Romans*, 155.
56. Nygren, *Romans*, 55–56.

Romans 1:16—3:20 expounds the fallen human condition that the Gospel seeks to amend. A revelation of "the righteousness of God" addresses this condition; that is, a revelation of the way in which God would save and deliver humankind.[57] Paul, in this preliminary argument, has shown that apart from the Gospel there is nothing to be found in the world but sin and its retribution: the wrath is revealed but not yet the righteousness of God.[58] In 3:21 Paul begins "But now . . ." because the way of salvation had not been previously made known. The temporal dimension emphasizes the historical shift between the old covenant and the new. God's saving righteousness is not an attribute but an activity in history.[59] It is a righteous action of God, rather than an attribute, that is spoken of in verse 21.[60] The action delivers his people in fulfillment of his promises.[61] Paul's examination of the Gentile world, enlightened by the law of nature but breaking that law, and the Jewish world, enlightened by the Law of Moses but equally breaking that Law, lays bare the need for further action. He therefore returns to his original thesis: God's righteousness is now revealed by faith and for faith (Rom 1:17). In a world given over to sin and retribution, the righteousness of God is made known first in justifying sinful people on the basis of faith (3:21–25) and second by saving them out of the sinful order of the world into a new order of life lived in faithfulness (Rom 5–8).[62] The revelation of God's righteousness is a revelation of his saving activity previously unknown.[63] It includes not only his just judgment of sinful humanity, but also his offer of salvation to all who believe the Gospel concerning his Son.[64] It answers the dual problems of sin—the need for cleansing from its defilement and liberation from its power (3:9). As in the OT examples, the righteousness of God, more often than not, is simply his salvation, his coming to deliver his people when they are oppressed. Now, however, it includes not just his covenant people, but all who are oppressed. God's righteousness is his coming to their rescue.[65] God's righteous acts manifested from the

57. Lee, *Romans*, 61.
58. Fitzmyer, *Romans*, 343.
59. Schreiner, *Romans*, 180.
60. Shedd, *Romans*, 76.
61. Moo, *Romans*, 222.
62. Dodd, *Romans*, 49.
63. Hays, "Logic of Romans 3," 111.
64. Price, "Righteousness," 263.
65. Ziesler, "Salvation," 356–57.

earliest days (Judg 5:11; 1 Sam 12:7) attest to what Paul is about to teach, that God has acted to save and deliver.[66]

The relationship of this manifestation of God's righteousness to the OT is indicated by two phrases that show the continuity and discontinuity in salvation history.[67] The first is that this new revelation of God's righteousness is "apart from the law." This phrase might mean "apart from doing the law" and could be part of what Paul intends, but its significance is greater. As Paul will show in chapter 4, justification has always been by faith, apart from the law, so such a revelation says nothing new. Furthermore, verse 21 discusses the *manifestation* of God's righteousness and not the *receiving* of God's righteousness. The law was a stage in God's unfolding revelation, but there has been a basic shift in salvation history.[68] The law could not accomplish the necessary rescue or restoration. Instead, it identified the problem and what ought to be.[69]

Paul balances the discontinuity in salvation history with a statement of its continuity, for the continuity of divine purpose runs right through Scripture.[70] Although not a part of a system of commands, this new revelation is nevertheless related to the law in that it, too, is a part of God's self-revelation. Paul constantly appeals to the OT for confirmation of his teaching, and in verse 21 he maintains that his words are consistent with the revelation of the Law and the Prophets; that is, the OT as a whole.[71] In chapter 4 Paul uses the story of Abraham as proof that the law attests to salvation by faith.[72] The whole of biblical drama and the whole of biblical literature bear witness to God's revelation of himself. It is important to recognize the unity of purpose that runs throughout the Old and New Testaments; the unique relationship of the living God to Israel prepares for the unique redemptive act in Christ Jesus.[73] Any acceptable interpretation of "apart from the law" must give adequate attention to the assertion that the law bears witness to this revelation.[74]

---

66. Lee, *Romans*, 70–71.
67. Moo, *Romans*, 222.
68. Moo, *Romans*, 222–23.
69. Moo, *Romans*, 357.
70. Moo, *Romans*, 223; Dunn, *Romans*, 165.
71. Dodd, *Romans*, 49–50.
72. Fitzmyer, *Romans*, 344.
73. Lee, *Romans*, 72.
74. Dunn, *Romans*, 177.

Righteousness through Faith

> This righteousness is given through faith in Jesus Christ to all who believe. There is no difference between Jew and Gentile, . . .

In verse 22, Paul enlarges the scope of God's saving activity to include all humankind.[75] Paul has already shown that the Prophets (Hab 2:4, quoted in Rom 1:17) testify to this, and he will show that the Law (Gen 15:6, to be quoted in 4:3–16) also points in advance to God's intended solution to the human dilemma. God himself would provide the way out for humans willing to accept it (i.e., have faith). The way to human righteousness is now revealed to be faith in God's righteousness, faith in his provision through Christ as the means of salvation.[76]

Some have argued that the first reference to faith in verse 22 (literally, "through the faith of Jesus Christ") is to the faithfulness of Jesus rather than the faith of the believer. In place of the usual translation ("through faith in Jesus Christ to all who believe"), the alternative would be "through the faithfulness of Jesus Christ to all who believe." Paul may have been thinking ahead to the contrast he would draw between Adam and Christ in chapter 5: as one man's trespass led to condemnation for all, so one man's faithfulness leads to a favorable judgment for all who believe.[77] The faithfulness of Christ would then be interpreted as his obedience to the Father, even to death.[78] The evidence in favor of this interpretation is impressive. Constructions of the kind found here always refer to the faith *of* the individual, never faith *in* the individual. Scholars universally agree that Romans 3:3 refers to "the faithfulness *of* God" ("God's faithfulness"

---

75. Dunn, *Romans*, 177.

76. Ziesler, "Salvation," 357.

77. "Grammatically, the personal noun *Jesus* may stand in either a dative or genitive case. But the context, as well as Paul's usage elsewhere, supports the genitive. Before and after our text the apostle employs the term 'faith' with a personal noun where a genitive construction is clearly demanded, 3:5 and 4:12. In Hellenistic Greek, 'faithfulness' more often that 'faith' conveys the sense of the term Paul uses. Moreover, his use of the preposition *through* in 22b, "through (the) faith," ordinarily suggests the alternative translation and the genitive construction also, since it would be more in accord with the apostle's theology to affirm that Jesus' faithfulness, and not man's faith, is the instrument or cause of salvation." Price, "Righteousness," 271.

78. Fitzmyer, *Romans*, 345. Fitzmyer notes that commentators who support this view are Haussleiter, Kittel, Howard, Price, Willims, Johnson, Ramaroson, and Hooker. Those who understand the genitive as objective "through faith in Jesus Christ" are Luther, Cranfield, Käsemann, Kuss, Moo, Schlier, and Wilckens.

NIV), not "faith *in* God." Romans 4:12 and 4:16 speak of "the faith that our father Abraham had" and "the faith of Abraham," respectively, no doubt referring to the faith of Abraham and not faith in Abraham. Proponents also point out that the objective interpretation (Christ is the object of faith) is redundant. To say that the righteousness of God is "through faith in Christ to all who believe" is akin to saying "through faith in Christ to all who have faith in Christ." To say that the saving righteousness of God is made known by the faithfulness of Jesus Christ, however, would certainly fit the context. Also, Paul uses the personal name "Jesus" in verse 26 rather than "Jesus Christ" or "Christ Jesus," which signals his faithful human life of obedience. Faith and obedience are closely connected in Paul (Rom 1:5; 16:26). In Romans 5:19 the gift of righteousness is associated with the obedience of Jesus, which cannot be separated from his faithfulness. Finally, and perhaps most important of all, for the objective view (Jesus as the object of faith) there is the problem of explaining how the faith of humans in Christ reveals God's righteousness. But if the verse explains what Christ has accomplished on behalf of humankind through his faithfulness/obedience, "the righteousness of God" is indeed revealed in God's saving action.[79]

The view of this book is that the arguments supporting Christ's faithfulness are convincing and that strong contextual reasons exist for rendering the phrase "through the faithfulness of Jesus Christ." The manifestation of God's righteousness centers upon the coming of Christ, as indicated by the "but now" of verse 21. Righteousness by faith was previously revealed in the OT, as Paul makes clear in chapter 4. In fact, he equates the gift of righteousness that Abraham received with the righteousness that is available to his readers. Therefore, if righteousness was obtainable by faith before Christ, there is little, if any, climactic force in the announcement that *now* righteousness has been manifested by faith in Jesus to all who believe.[80] However, if God's righteousness is manifested in salvation through the faithfulness of Christ for all who believe, the full force of this historical revelation is realized. For *now*, something

---

79. Schreiner, *Romans*, 181–82.

80. Davies, *Romans*, 108. Davies also points out that "the force of the argument is not mitigated by seeing the newness of faith now being available for *all*. For, as Paul has persistently advocated throughout chapter 2, God's salvation has always been available for all, to the Jew first and also the Greek."

has been disclosed that had previously not occurred—the vindication of God's righteousness in the fulfillment of his covenant promise to save.[81]

Whether one interprets Jesus to be the subject or object of faith, Paul maintains that the saving "power of God" (1:16) is found in Jesus Christ, not the law; it is realized by faith, not by works. Both the preceding (3:9–20) and following (3:27—4:25) contexts make clear that these contrasts are intentional. Faith is thus the opposite of trusting oneself to establish a right relationship with God; it is trusting Jesus Christ as the means of reconciliation provided by God.[82] Paul's assertion that "there is no difference between Jew and Gentile" picks up the conclusion of 3:9–20 that different ways of establishing a right relation to God do not exist for those inside and outside the old covenant.[83]

All Fall Short of God's Glory

> For all have sinned and fall short of the glory of God . . .

No difference lies between Jew and Gentile regarding God's means of salvation because no difference exists in their condition and need; "all have sinned" is their common background. The Jewish Christians in Rome are not to see themselves as superior to the Gentile Christians.[84]

To "fall short of the glory of God" is ambiguous but commentators present several possibilities: (1) fail to give God the glory or fail to do what is to the praise of his glory (Luke 17:18; Acts 12:23; Rom 4:20; 1 Cor 10:31; 2 Cor 4:15; 8:19; Phil 1:11; 2:11; Rev 4:9, 11; 11:13; 14:7; 16:9); (2) not receiving the glory, honor, or approbation that God grants (John 5:44; 8:50; 12:43; Rom 2:7, 10; Heb 3:3; 1 Pet 1:7); (3) come short of reflecting the glory of God; that is, of conforming to his image (1 Cor 11:7; 2 Cor 3:18; 4:6).[85]

Regardless of how one understands glory, to fall short of the glory of God is a reference to sin. It is humanity's sin that has caused us to depart from the likeness or glory of God, that has caused us to be unfit to receive

---

81. Davies, *Romans*, 108–9.
82. Songer, "New Standing," 416.
83. Songer, "New Standing," 416.
84. Songer, "New Standing," 417.
85. J. Murray, *Romans*, 112–13.

God's approval and to give God glory. That which was lost through Adam is being restored in Christ.[86]

Because the context is justification, it is most logical to think of God's glory as his approval. In other words, when one stands before God's tribunal they cannot expect divine approbation through their own efforts, as "all have sinned."[87] Therefore some other grounds of justification are needed.[88] The verses that follow (24–26) describe God's approach to this condition of humankind.[89]

Justification Is a Gift

> And all are justified freely by his grace through the redemption that came by Christ Jesus.

The phrase "the redemption that came by Christ Jesus" refers to an act of God affecting the human race as a whole (Rom 1–3).[90] In contrast to the universal fall in 1:18—3:20, the universality of the redemption is emphasized even though it is received only by believers.[91] Justification as a free gift of God's grace, which comes through the redemption provided by Christ (verse 24), *is* "the righteousness of God [that] has been made known" in verse 21. Verses 22 and 23 are parenthetical, with verse 24 resuming the exposition of the revelation of the righteousness of God.[92] Verse 24 also explains verse 22, which asks implicitly how sinners who believe in Jesus Christ are redeemed and justified. What is this justification that is God's free gift and this redemption that is provided in Christ?

There have been many debates concerning whether justification means "to make righteous" or "to treat as righteous." Perhaps the best solution is to conclude that "to justify" means "to make righteous" (for this is more in keeping with Paul's teaching as a whole), but at the same time recognize that righteous does not mean virtuous, but right, clear, or pardoned in God's court of law. Justification, then, is no "legal fiction" but

---

86. Schreiner, *Romans*, 187.
87. Morris, *Romans*, 177.
88. Stuart, *Romans*, 162.
89. Dodd, *Romans*, 50–51.
90. Quell, *Righteousness*, 43.
91. Käsemann, *Romans*, 94.
92. Dunn, *Romans*, 179.

refers to reconciliation (right standing) resulting from an act of pardon on God's part, described in terms of the proceedings of a law court.[93]

God takes the necessary action and justifies—that is, accepts and restores to right relationship—those who are sinners. He does this "freely by his grace" for all who are willing to believe in their acceptance and turn to him. The judicial meaning should not be pressed too far, though, because in Jewish tradition the verb translated "justify" is used much more widely than in a strictly judicial sense and refers to the restoration of relationship.[94]

Clearly something more than acquittal or amnesty is involved in justification, for there is a restoration of right relationship that includes receiving grace and approval. A more literal translation may be suggested, such as "being granted favorable judgment" by God and "restored to fellowship" with him (reconciled, or at peace). The fact is, many words are needed for a single term describing the incomparable consequences of God's gracious action.[95]

Nevertheless, to say that the guilty are justified before the divine tribunal is a paradox, and Paul intended it to be so. If the dealing of God with sinful humanity can be described in legal terms at all, then it can be described only in terms of paradox. The use of legal terms requires one to say that God justifies the guilty, a thing unacceptable in law. In the OT, the phrase "to acquit the guilty" is something only an unjust judge would do (Isa 5:23; Prov 17:15; Exod 23:7). Paul was fully aware of what a daring thing he was saying in attributing such an action to God. The lesson is that the personal relation of God to humankind cannot be described in legal terms. The revelation of his righteousness is indeed "apart from law altogether."[96] It is the revelation of his grace in choosing to act through Christ.[97]

Paul continues to explain this gift that enables humankind to be right with God by saying that it takes place by means of, or on the basis of, "the redemption that came by Christ Jesus."[98] The word *redemption* indicates that something more takes place than just restoration to proper

---

93. Lee, *Romans*, 72–73; Moo, *Romans*, 227.

94. Ziesler, "Salvation," 357; for a discussion of justification in this broader, life-giving sense see Bushnell, *Vicarious Sacrifice*, 406–22.

95. Price, "Righteousness," 273.

96. Dodd, *Romans*, 52.

97. Moo, *Romans*, 228.

98. Lee, *Romans*, 73. Dunn, *Romans*, 179.

relationship; redemption is, above all, a word for liberation, for change of ownership, or for transfer from one lordship to another. Those who have been under sin's power (Rom 3:9) are redeemed and transferred into the possession and lordship of Christ. Henceforth they are "in Christ"—they are his possession and live in his power. Their freedom has been bought by an act of God. It was a costly act, and it is a costly gift which God offers. Verse 24 indicates that the righteousness of God provides both liberation and justification for those who believe.[99] Justification is not an arbitrary act of acquittal, for there was a cost, a ransom to be paid.[100] The idea of a cost cannot be separated from the concept of redemption in the NT, for other texts indicate that the price was the blood of Christ (Eph 1:7; 1 Pet 1:18–19; see also Matt 20:28; Mark 10:45). However, in this passage the focus is on deliverance.[101] This saving act of redemption, the "righteousness of God made known," is a historical act that occurred at a particular place and at a particular time. The death of Christ marks the end of the way of the Law. This event is the mighty act of God in history on behalf of all humanity.[102]

Jesus Our Expiation

> God presented Christ as a sacrifice of atonement, through the shedding of his blood—to be received by faith.

The following verses (25–26), in which Paul explains how redemption takes place, are the most controversial of the passage.[103]

"God Presented Christ"

The words "God presented Christ" emphasize that God is the one who acts.[104] This is an idea Paul will develop further in chapters 5 and 8: "But God demonstrates his own love for us in this: While we were still sinners

---

99. Ziesler, "Salvation," 357.
100. Dunn, *Romans*, 180.
101. Schreiner, *Romans*, 190.
102. Quell, *Righteousness*, 43.
103. Ziesler, "Salvation," 358.
104. Lee, *Romans*, 76.

Christ died for us" (5:8); "He who did not spare his own Son, but gave him up for us all . . ." (8:32).[105]

"Presented" here means either "set forth publicly" or "purposed." The immediate context favors the first possibility since it contains several terms denoting publicity. In this case Paul's point would be that Christ's death was something that was accomplished publicly. However, in its two other NT uses, both in the Pauline Epistles (Rom 1:13 and Eph 1:9), the verb clearly means "purpose"; and in eight of its twelve NT occurrences, the cognate noun means "purpose." A good reason seems required for deviating from such a meaning in Romans 3:25. No good reason is apparent. The revelation of God's eternal purpose is also appropriate to the context. This redemption originated with God and was planned by him in his eternal purpose of grace. It is not a new idea on God's part, but it is a new revelation of his purpose."[106]

Another possible meaning of "presented" is as a technical term for the bringing of a sacrifice. In view of the phrases that immediately follow, this sacrificial meaning is also a possibility.[107]

"As a Sacrifice of Atonement"

God himself, then, puts forward or presents the means whereby the guilt of sin is removed.[108] Christ, through whom comes justification (verse 24), is "a sacrifice of atonement ['an expiation' RSV] through the shedding of his blood." In Judaism, expiation was an act of annulment that resulted in the removing of the stain of sin. The case for expiation rather than propitiation has already been presented (see chapter 3). Most modern English translations follow or slightly modify the KJV's "a propitiation."[109]

Another translation, with a history going back to both Luther and Tyndale, is "mercy seat," reflecting the OT concept of atonement.[110] This is what the word means in its one other NT occurrence (Heb 9:5) as well as in 21 of its 27 LXX occurrences. It is attractive because it gives to *hilasterion* a meaning derived from its normal biblical usage and creates a

---

105. Lee, *Romans*, 80.
106. Cranfield, *Romans*, 72–73.
107. Ziesler, *Romans*, 112.
108. Dodd, *Romans*, 55.
109. Morris, *Romans*, 180.
110. Lee, *Romans*, 74–75.

fitting analogy between a central OT ritual and Christ's death. *Hilasterion* is best understood against this background of its LXX usage relating to the Day of Atonement. Christ is the new mercy seat, the place where God forgave (expiated) the sins of the people.[111]

The contrast between the old mercy seat and the new could be indicated by the words "God presented." The old mercy seat was concealed behind the curtain separating the holy of holies from the outer sanctuary and was seen only by the high priest on the Day of Atonement. But in Christ the mercy seat is no longer kept in seclusion; it is brought out into the midst of the world and set forth for all to see. This idea supports the rendering "mercy seat," with mercy seat being a metonym for "atoning sacrifice" (as in the NIV's "sacrifice of atonement").[112] Jesus, as the true mercy seat, is the fulfillment of the sacrificial system at its most vivid point of expression.[113]

The death of Christ, appropriated by faith, is the means by which God does away with his people's sin—not symbolically, as in the Day of Atonement with its physical mercy seat, but *literally*. The sin is removed from the conscience of the believer and from the presence of God (Heb 8:12, quoting Jer 31:34), making reconciliation a reality.[114] Sin, the cause of God's wrath and judgment, is no longer present. As in the OT, it is God who provides the means, it is God who initiates, and it is God alone who can remove or expiate sin.[115] The LXX never uses *hilasterion* to express the influence of humans on God, but always the atoning activity of God.[116]

"Through the Shedding of His Blood"

The phrase "through the shedding of his blood" refers to the sacrificial death of Christ as the means by which atonement for sin is effected.[117] (NEB translates "by his sacrificial death.") God reveals his righteousness (saving activity/covenant faithfulness) by providing a sacrifice.[118] The use

111. Fitzmyer, *Romans*, 350.
112. Bruce, *Romans*, 101.
113. Songer, "New Standing," 418.
114. Bruce, *Romans*, 100.
115. N. Young, "Hilaskesthai," 72.
116. Lunceford, "*Ilaskomai* Cognates," 101.
117. Bruce, *Romans*, 100.
118. Dunn, *Romans*, 173.

of the word *blood* is also a reminder that God initiates a new covenant. Consider the words of Jesus at the Last Supper: "This is my blood of the covenant, which is poured out for many" (Mark 14:22). The sacrificial aspect of Jesus' death was discussed in detail in chapter 6.

"Received by Faith"

The phrase "received by faith" is an interpretation of the words "through faith." It is possible to interpret "faith" as either the faith of the believer or the faithfulness of Christ (see previous discussion under heading "Righteousness through Faith"). If the reference is to the faith of the believer, it declares that although the mercy seat is accessible to all through the blood of Christ, it is effective only for those who have faith. God's mighty act of salvation is to be appropriated by faith. The necessity of faith always accompanies the most objective statements concerning the righteousness of God (Rom 1:17; 3:22–28; 4:5). Faith is the indispensable condition of the salvation offered through the righteousness of God.

On the other hand, "through faith" could mean that expiation of sin, or atonement, is available to all through the faithfulness of Christ. Accordingly, Romans 3:25 would read something like: "Whom God put forward as a mercy seat (means of atonement), through (Jesus') faithfulness by means of his blood."[119] The reference would then be to Christ's perfect obedience to the Father and to the absence of sin, which constituted the victory of Christ over Satan, sin, and death.

A reference to Christ's faithfulness, not to the faith of believers, best explains the meaning of these words, as they are located adjacent to two references to Christ's atoning work: "a sacrifice of atonement, through the shedding of his blood." Since both "sacrifice" and "blood" refer to what Christ has done, it would be awkward to insert a reference to the faith of believers in the middle. Rather, the whole unit refers to what Christ has done on behalf of humankind.[120] In the epistles of Paul, the word "blood" occurs at least thirteen times and the word "faith" at least 112 times. Nowhere in these epistles (unless Rom 3:25) or anywhere else in the NT, for that matter, does the phrase "faith in his blood" or any similar phrase occur.[121]

---

119. Longenecker, "Pistis in Romans 3:25," 479.
120. Schreiner, *Romans*, 182.
121. Lunceford, "*Ilaskomai* Cognates," 78.

Paul has thus far in this passage used the language of the law court ("justified"), the slave market ("redemption"), and the altar ("mercy seat," "expiation," "means of atonement") in describing God's gracious act in Christ. Pardon, liberation, and reconciliation are all made available by God's initiative and may be appropriated by faith.[122] All three metaphors emphasize the pure objectivity of what God has done for humanity. It is not until Romans 5–8 that Paul will show the subjective, inward effect of atonement in the lives of individuals.[123]

God Demonstrates His Righteousness

> He did this to demonstrate his righteousness, because in his forbearance he had left the sins committed beforehand unpunished—he did it to demonstrate his righteousness at the present time, so as to be just and the one who justifies those who have faith in Jesus.

Verses 25b and 26 cannot be separated from verses 21–25a; from the last phrase in verse 22, "There is no difference . . ." to the end of verse 26 is one sentence in the Greek.[124] The three metaphors of verses 24–25a (justification, redemption, and mercy seat/expiation) are referred to by "this" in verse 25 and "it" in verse 26. It is the redemption of humankind and the provision for the expiation of sin and justification of the believer that demonstrates God's righteousness (his saving activity/covenant faithfulness). According to the penal view, "this" in verse 25b refers to propitiation rather than expiation, and "the righteousness of God" would no longer have its saving connotations but would refer to strict justice that demands punishment.[125] Evidence has been presented that "propitiate" is an incorrect interpretation and translation, and that "the righteousness of God" should not be interpreted in this narrow, forensic sense. As a rule the penal interpretation assumes translations of "passing over" rather than "remission" in verse 25b and "proves" rather than "shows/demonstrates" in verse 26.[126] However, in these two phrases one presumes ideas

---

122. Bruce, *Romans*, 101–10.
123. Dodd, *Romans*, 57.
124. O'Neil, *Romans*, 71.
125. Ziesler, *Romans*, 115.

126. Kümmel, "Justification," 8–9; Nygren, *Romans*, 160. The same Greek word translated "show" (verse 25) and "demonstrate" (verse 26) can also be translated

(that God must prove his righteousness and that he had hitherto let sins go unpunished) that directly contradict Paul's teaching.[127]

"He Did This to Demonstrate His Righteousness"

The penal substitution view is that the vicarious punishment of Christ satisfies God's punitive justice and therefore "proves" God's righteousness. There is not, however, sufficient evidence to interpret the righteousness of God as supporting that premise, in part because that interpretation would differ from Paul's normal usage.[128] "Righteous" and "just" are only different English translations of the same Greek word, as are "righteousness" and "justice." The justice of God in verse 26 is the same thing as the righteousness of God in verse 21. It has already been shown that the righteousness of God, according to the prophets who provide the background to Paul's thinking, is his deliverance of his people from the power of evil; it is the victory of good. Thus, as a demonstration of God's righteousness he delivers humankind from the power of evil and "justifies" them in the OT sense of the word. Paul asserts that the life and death of Christ demonstrate God's justice (righteousness) at the present time, showing that God is just (righteous) himself, and that he justifies (vindicates or delivers) those who believe.[129]

"prove"; only context reveals the correct meaning. Translating "prove," which suggests that God wanted or needed to prove his righteousness, should be rejected for several reasons. (1) The "righteousness of God" must then mean something different than it did in the preceding verses, yet still somehow express God's attribute of justness. A change of meaning within the same sentence is not warranted. (2) The context involves God's gracious saving act. There is no need for God to prove anything, and it is unclear before whom God would offer such proof. (3) There is no logical connection between "prove" and the phrase "at the present time." Why would God want to prove his righteousness "at the present time"? One must assume that God's righteousness had been questioned, but this is not indicated in the text (as it is in Romans 9:19). The translation "show" or "demonstrate," on the other hand, connects well with "at this time," for it was at the then-present time that God had shown or demonstrated his righteousness (saving activity/covenant faithfulness) in Jesus Christ and his atoning death. "Demonstrate" is probably the best translation according to the context, which speaks not to what God does to justify himself but what he did to justify humankind.

127. Kümmel, "Justification," 2.
128. Ziesler, *Romans*, 115.
129. Bruce, *Romans*, 59.

"In His Forbearance ... Left the Sins Committed Beforehand Unpunished"

There is general agreement that "sins committed beforehand" ("former sins" RSV) refers to sins committed before the coming of Christ. Beginning in 3:19, Paul speaks of the reality before and after Christ and not of the turning point in an individual Christian's life. The same references to human history before and after Christ are found in 1 Corinthians 1:21 and Galatians 4:3-5. It is by no means Paul's opinion, however, that God passed over or failed to judge sins prior to Christ.[130]

Scholars dispute the meaning of the rare word *paresis* ("left... unpunished" NIV). In the NT it is found only in Romans 3:25 and not at all in the LXX. Some interpreters understand it to mean "pardon" or "remission."[131] This is the most common extrabiblical use of the word.[132] According to this interpretation Christ's death would demonstrate God's righteousness/salvation that pardoned the sin of humans of past times, sins that awaited this great day of expiation (Acts 13:38-39; Heb 9:15). The clause would not be understood as "righteousness *despite* his leaving the sins committed beforehand unpunished" but "righteousness *observed in* his leaving the sins committed beforehand unpunished."[133] *Paresis* can also be used in the sense of "passing over"; context must be the deciding factor.[134]

There are two arguments against a translation of "remission." First, had Paul been thinking of remission or forgiveness, it would have been natural to use the same word he uses in Colossians 1:14 and Ephesians 1:7. The choice of a rarer word probably indicates a different meaning.[135] Second, it is difficult to contrast God's forgiveness of sins in the time before Christ with the present revelation of his righteousness *in* Christ. The verse appears to contrast God's past and present dealings with the problem of sin. If *paresis* is translated "remission" there is little to contrast; therefore, the idea of remission does not seem to fit the context.

---

130. Kümmel, "Justification," 9-10.

131. Fitzmyer, *Romans*, 351. These commentators include Luther, Calvin, Bultmann, Cerfaux, Käsemann, Kümmel, Letzmann, and Stuhlmacher.

132. Kümmel, "Justification," 4.

133. Ziesler, *Romans*, 115.

134. Ziesler, *Romans*, 115.

135. Taylor, "Great Texts," 298. Taylor also discusses the grammatical issues that he believes makes "remission" an unlikely translation.

The majority of scholars understand *paresis* as "pass over'" or "let go," but they do not necessarily interpret its usage here in the same way. According to a propitiatory interpretation, "passing over" would refer to a failure to punish sin. In this case God would have given the erroneous impression that he did not care about right and wrong. The death of Jesus would "prove" that such an impression was indeed erroneous because the necessary punishment was inflicted upon Christ.[136] There are two objections to this interpretation. The first, previously discussed, is that God does not vindicate himself (Rom 9:19–20). In addition, it is difficult to understand how anyone could read the OT and think Paul is suggesting that God must prove he was not indifferent to sin in the OT. God's abhorrence of sin and resulting wrath is a pervasive OT theme.

The second reason for rejecting this interpretation of *paresis* (that God formerly did not judge sin), is that this cannot be Paul's meaning in chapter 3 without directly contradicting what he said in chapters 1, 2, and elsewhere. In Romans 1:24–32 he plainly states that God let humans sink increasingly deeper into the results of their disobedience, and in 1 Corinthians 10:5, 8–10 he indicates repeatedly and just as clearly that the fathers with whom God was not pleased "were killed." Finally, he believes that all humans had to die as a result of their sins (Rom 5:12–14) and that death was the wages of sin for all who were under the law (Rom 6:23; 7:13). Therefore, God's leaving sins unpunished in the time before Christ cannot refer to overlooking sin.[137] Any overlooking of sin certainly does not fit the context of Romans, for the lengthy section of 1:18—3:20 views the world as under the wrath of God. Paul asserts that God's anger against sin is already revealed in the period before Christ.

Another interpretation of passing over former sin does not contradict the context and specifically relates it (as the sentence does) to the phrase "in his forbearance." The normal extrabiblical meaning of forbearance is "holding back" or "delaying." The word translated "forbearance" in Romans 3:25 appears in only one other verse in the NT, Romans 2:4. In both cases the meaning of delaying is appropriate. This interpretation accords well with Paul's statement in Romans 5:6 (emphasis added): "*At just the right time*, when we were still powerless, Christ died for the ungodly." There was a delaying on God's part while he waited for the right time, "when the set time had fully come" (Gal 4:4), before intervening to

---

136. Ziesler, *Romans*, 115.
137. Kümmel, "Justification," 10.

bring about complete salvation.¹³⁸ According to this third view, "passing over" does not refer to either overlooking sin or forgiving sin. Rather, leaving sins "unpunished" should be understood in the sense of "neglecting." The question involves God's want of action against sin in previous generations. Although God punished the sins of former generations, he nevertheless can be said to have passed over sins in that the moral problem of sin was not dealt with.¹³⁹ Christ's death would demonstrate God's righteousness/salvation/deliverance in dealing with the power of sin (Rom 6–8), in contrast to his previous forbearance.¹⁴⁰

Dunn's thinking parallels this idea. He says:

> Paul presumably at least meant that while the sacrificial system was a legitimate way of dealing with sin in the past, it did not constitute an adequate or final answer to the problem of sin and sinning. Only the sacrifice of Christ could do that (presumably because with his resurrection came the possibility for the power of sin to be countered through union with him).¹⁴¹

This book agrees with Dunn's reasoning. The best translation of *paresis* is "passing over" because the word is connected to God's forbearance. "Passing over" refers to the fact that until Christ's death God's righteousness was not fully revealed because God had not fully dealt with sin. This interpretation fits perfectly with the chapters that precede Romans 3 as well as with those that follow in which Christ's death and resurrection are said to deliver believers from the power of sin (Rom 6–8).

Daniel Bailey, whose dissertation argues for a translation of *hilasterion* as "mercy seat," suggests that the idea of Jesus being put forward as the new mercy seat forms a conceptual parallel with Leviticus 16. Bailey maintains that the reference to Jesus as the new mercy seat helps explain the meaning of the phrase "he had left the sins committed beforehand unpunished." Although Leviticus does not have a technical term for it, he describes a temporary passing over of sins that were accumulating throughout the year leading up to the Day of Atonement. But did God really overlook the sins of the year? Chapters 1–15 of Leviticus describe

---

138. Wilson, "Romans 3:25, 26," 472–73.

139. Taylor, "Great Texts," 300.

140. Fitzmyer, *Romans*, 351. The commentators who hold this view include Althaus, Barrett, Blackman, Boylan, Cranfield, Dodd, Huby, Kuss, Lagrange, Michel, Prat, and Schlier.

141. Dunn, *Romans*, 173.

the sacrificial system and give no hint that it is inadequate and must be supplemented by a special Day of Atonement. Romans 3:25 reveals the provisional nature of Leviticus 16 in the same way that Leviticus 16 reveals the provisional nature of chapters 1–15. In other words, the Day of Atonement was to the other days in the Jewish year what Good Friday is to the entire preceding age of redemptive history.[142]

Bailey's interpretation fits the context of the new age mentioned in verses 21 and 26 ("but now . . . at the present time"). In the OT the blood had to be applied to the mercy seat by the priest because the sins of the people had been passed over during the previous year. But in the present age, God himself, in order to display his saving righteousness according to the pattern attested in the Law and the Prophets (Rom 3:21), has set out a new mercy seat in the person of Christ and established it by Christ's blood (Rom 3:25a). This follows not just a year but an entire age of human sin. God's public display of Jesus in his death as the mercy seat involves forgiveness of sins and access to God, even though both are mentioned explicitly only later (Rom 4:7).[143] Also explained later (Rom 6–8) is the understanding that the death of Christ provides not just for forgiveness of sins but for victory over sin as a power.

"To Demonstrate His Righteousness at the Present Time So as to Be Just and the One Who Justifies"

Verse 26 says that "at the present time" there is a divine intervention that demonstrates finally that God is righteous/just in that he makes righteous/justifies humans.[144] Now God's power is operative: God shows himself to be righteous; that is, overcoming wrong, reconciling humanity to himself, and granting favorable judgment to all who have faith in Jesus.[145] It would be better to translate the words "so as to be just and the one who justifies" as "so as to be righteous and the one who makes righteous" to preserve the kinship with the word *righteousness*, which occurs four times in this passage prior to 26b (verses 21, 22, 25, and 26a). Also, there is no opposing relationship between the clauses, as if it read "just *and yet* the one who justifies." According to this understanding, Christ has so exactly satisfied

---

142. Bailey, "Mercy Seat," 213–14.
143. Bailey, "Mercy Seat," 214.
144. Dodd, *Romans*, 59–60.
145. Price, "Righteousness," 277.

God's immutable justice by his sufferings that God appears to be just as ever, even though he justifies, or passes judgment in favor of, those who deserve nothing but punishment.[146] The passage, however, does not speak of a conflict between God's justice and God's mercy. It does not ask how God can be both just and justifier. Rather, it does the opposite, stating that because he is righteous/just, God acts in righteousness to redeem, and this action is in Jesus Christ.[147] As Fitzmyer states:

> Earlier commentators, who understood *dikaiosyne theou* [the righteousness of God] of God's retributive or vindictive justice, often gave concessive force to the [participle] *dikaiounta*, "in order to be just, even though he justifies." ... Such an interpretation, however, involves the demand that Jesus died in satisfaction for human sins. This understanding of the clause would tie in with the meaning of *hilasterion* as "appeasing" or a "means of propitiation." The context, however, seems to be all against such an interpretation, which is really born of later theological considerations, especially those of Anselm. Paul is saying instead that the recent divine intervention in human history proves that God is upright; he even makes human beings upright through faith in Christ's expiatory death.[148]

Nygren draws a conclusion similar to that of Fitzmyer:

> One could certainly apply the Anselmic judgment [to this passage]. It is a consistent demonstration of the necessity of the death of Christ, if we start from God's punitive righteousness. But it suffers a double weakness. It lacks support in the text and its meaning is not true to Paul's thought. Paul is not trying to give a rational demonstration of the necessity of Christ's death. He speaks of what God *has* done, not of what He *had* to do. He does not talk about something that God did to justify himself, but about what God has done to justify us. Men have looked here for a theodicy, a defense of God's dealings with humanity before Christ.... The text does not say that God wished to show that He really is righteous, as some translators would understand it. Paul says rather that God put forward Christ as a mercy seat thereby to let his righteousness openly appear. The righteousness of which verse 25 speaks is no other than that spoken of in verse 21. It is the same righteousness which is

---

146. Bushnell, *Vicarious Sacrifice*, 343–45.
147. Songer, "New Standing," 418.
148. Fitzmyer, *Romans*, 353.

affirmed throughout the epistle. It is always "the righteousness of God," with all that that implies. And when verse 26 sums up the purpose of God when He gave us Christ as a mercy seat, Paul does not say "that God might be found to be righteous," but simply that in so doing "he himself is righteous and that he justifies him who has faith in Jesus."[149]

"Those Who Have Faith in Jesus"

Verse 26 repeats and summarizes what has been stated in the previous verses. At the "present time" God's saving righteousness/justice is revealed by his justification of all (Jew and Gentile) who believe in Christ. The first reference to the revelation of the righteousness of God is in verse 21, and the first reference to the justification of the believer is in verse 24. The previous discussion of the meaning of justification ("Justification Is a Gift") mentions its relational aspect. That aspect deserves to be emphasized and expanded in order for this concluding thought in verse 26 to have its full impact.

First, it must be reemphasized that justification and justice are connected ideas being derived from the same root in Hebrew and in Greek. The separation that has developed between the English words *righteous*, *justify*, and *justice* obscures the fact that the biblical concept of justification arises out of the biblical concept of justice.[150] When Paul brought the language of righteousness/justification into his epistle to the Romans, he was raising an important OT theme: the key to understanding righteousness/justice, which includes the related idea of justification, is to recognize that it involves the concept of relationship. This recognition requires a conscious effort on the part of those whose thinking about justice comes from a Greco-Roman background. The Greco-Roman idea of righteousness/justice is an ethical standard against which actions can be measured. According to this understanding, a just or righteous act or person is one who meets that standard of right. Failure to measure up involves liability and guilt. "Justice" is a divine principle that must be upheld or satisfied lest disorder and injustice prevail. Hebrew writers, however, did not understand justice in this way. In Hebrew thought, righteousness is a concept of relation, something one has in one's relationships

---

149. Nygren, *Romans*, 160–61.
150. Dunn and Suggate, *Justice of God*, 39.

as a social being. In the Greco-Roman understanding, righteousness is something one may have on their own, independent of anyone else. But in Hebrew thought, one is righteous when they meet the claims others have on them by virtue of their particular relationships.[151]

For example, the king is considered righteous when he meets his responsibilities to his subjects, and the servant is righteous when he serves his master. First Samuel 24:17 provides a good example. King Saul admits that David is more righteous than he because David remained faithful to his responsibilities toward Saul, as subject to God's anointed ruler, whereas Saul abused the responsibility of his position as king. Another example is the particular responsibility of judges in Israel to recognize the various obligations of parties and judge accordingly. In these examples, righteousness/justice and relationship are inseparable ideas.[152]

The same is true of God's relationship with humankind. In Hebrew thought, God is righteous/just because he sustains his creation and makes it thrive. Humans are righteous when they recognize their creaturely status and honor and worship God accordingly, an idea to which Paul alludes in Romans 1:18–23. In addition, God had established a particular relationship with Israel, for he chose it to be his own people out of all the nations on earth. His righteousness meant his faithfulness to the covenant that he made with Israel. He supported Israel, defended Israel, and saved Israel even from its own failures. Israel's righteousness was to live in accordance with the terms of that relationship, which God set out in the law.[153]

The connection between law and righteousness that has created so much confusion begins at this point. Israel's righteousness is seen in her relationship with God. Righteousness is not a means of achieving that relationship but the expression of that relationship. God took the initiative to choose Israel and deliver this inconsequential, enslaved people. He gave the law at Mount Sinai *after* he chose them and *after* he delivered them in the exodus. The human righteousness expected and provided for (through sacrifice and atonement) is the response to divine righteousness. This relationship is described in Deuteronomy 5:1—29:1.[154]

---

151. Dunn and Suggate, *Justice of God*, 32–33.
152. Dunn and Suggate, *Justice of God*, 33.
153. Dunn and Suggate, *Justice of God*, 34.
154. Dunn and Suggate, *Justice of God*, 34.

Jewish thought emphasizes the indispensability of God's righteousness/justice on behalf of his people. The book of Psalms and the second half of Isaiah contain a strong consciousness of Israel's failure to maintain its righteousness in relationship to God. Therefore, in these books the idea of God's righteousness merges naturally into the idea of God's salvation. God continued to uphold his side of the relationship even when Israel did not. Thus the psalmist calls on God to deliver or vindicate him in accordance with his (God's) righteousness (31:1; 35:24; 71:2; 143:11). Modern translations regularly translate the Hebrew and Greek words for righteousness/justice as "deliverance," "acts of salvation," "vindication," "righteous deeds," etc. (Ps 51:14; 65:5; 71:15; 98:2; Isa 46:13; 51:5–8; 62:1–2; 63:1, 7). This saving action is the background for Paul's concept of divine righteousness/justice. The God who delivered, saved, and vindicated unfaithful Israel when the people repented and called upon him is the God who saves the sinner when he or she repents and believes.[155] It was not Luther, or even Paul, who first made the discovery of God's justification by faith, but the great spiritual writers of the OT.[156]

This OT background of Paul's teaching on divine righteousness leads to two important conclusions. First, the Jewish and early Christian understanding of God's justice put the primary emphasis on God's initiative and his ability and desire to do for humans what they could not do for themselves. The concept of justice is not one of an inflexible rule or standard, where failure has to be punished uncompromisingly, where the law must take its course. In the law court, strictly speaking, there is no provision for forgiveness. Rather, in the biblical concept of God's justice and of divine righteousness, the fundamental idea is sustaining a relationship through difficult circumstances and healing relationships damaged by human sin.[157]

Second, recognizing that righteousness is a matter of relationship and not of the independent individual helps resolve some of the problems that have plagued discussions of justification by faith. Is God's righteousness something he has as an attribute, or something he bestows on others as a status? Does God simply count someone as righteous even when that person is unrighteous, or does he actually make that person righteous? These questions arise out of the Greco-Roman context, which shaped the

---

155. Dunn and Suggate, *Justice of God*, 35.
156. Dunn and Suggate, *Justice of God*, 16.
157. Dunn and Suggate, *Justice of God*, 35–36.

post-biblical discussion of righteousness and justification. They are based on the assumption that when the NT speaks of God's justice or righteousness it is referring to God's verdict against sin and his sentence against the sinner. Once the relational character of the biblical concept is grasped, however, these become non-questions. God's righteousness is his acting out of the obligation he took upon himself in creating humankind and in choosing Israel to be his people. It consists primarily in drawing humans into a relationship of fellowship with himself and in sustaining them in that relationship.[158] Therefore, when verse 26 says that God "justifies," the meaning is that he restores the one who has faith to a right relationship with himself.

In Romans 5:18 this righteous act of God results in "justification and life" ("justification of life" KJV and others), a phrase indicating that justification involves receiving a life source. Where is the "life" of a mere acquittal granted on the grounds that a bad account is made even? In Romans 4:25 Christ is declared to have been "delivered over to death for our sins and . . . raised to life for our justification." If the matter of justification depended on what Christ suffered for our sins, one would be justified, or have their account made even, even if Christ did not rise. Doubtless, however, the resurrection has immense significance when justification is understood to be the renewing and sustaining of relationship based on receiving the life of Christ.[159]

To summarize, no one (Jew or Gentile) is justified apart from faith. The way is open to all and is the same for all. When one repents and believes in Christ, God pardons them and wipes away their sin. The result is the restoration of relationship. This justifying of believers has taken place because of the righteousness/justice (saving action) of God in Christ. God's justice is a saving justice.

There is a touch of tenderness in the last phrase of verse 26 in the use of the name "Jesus," which suggests the intimacy of personal relationship to the Savior.[160] All who "have faith in Jesus" are restored to fellowship with God; they will become righteous in Christ and will share in his glory. The Gospel is now God's standard of judgment as it will be at

---

158. Dunn and Suggate, *Justice of God*, 7, 36–37.
159. Bushnell, *Vicarious Sacrifice*, 355.
160. J. Murray, *Romans*, 121.

the end of time.[161] Faith is the means whereby the individual receives the benefits of God's act of righteousness.[162]

But is Paul here referring to this human faith? There is no question that Paul speaks of Christians' faith *in Christ* in Galatians 2:16, Philippians 1:29, and Colossians 2:5. The question is whether he does so in this case. Two other times in Romans 3:21–26 Paul has spoken of faith (verses 22 and 25), and in both cases there is good reason to think that Paul is speaking about the faith (faithfulness) of Jesus rather than the faith of the believer in Jesus. In verse 22, the most natural understanding is that God's righteousness is revealed "through the faith of Jesus Christ for all who believe." In verse 25, the expression "by faith" is found between two phrases referring to Christ, and it qualifies the manner of Jesus' death. God put forward Jesus as the means of atonement through Jesus' faithful death ("through the shedding of his blood"). The final phrase in 3:26, "those who have faith in Jesus" could be translated "those who share the faith of Jesus." In 4:16, precisely the same phrase is translated "those who have the faith of Abraham." It can be argued that it is significant that Paul uses only the personal name of Jesus, because when Paul does this elsewhere he seems to be intentionally referring to Jesus' humanity (Rom 8:11; 1 Thess 1:10; 2 Cor 4:10–14). The point of the reference to Jesus' human faithfulness is that his faithfulness can be shared by others. The emphasis, then, in Romans 3:21–26 is not on the human reception of God's gift through faith (although that is clearly stated in 3:22) but on the faithfulness of God and the faithfulness of Jesus, which is God's gift to believers.[163]

Suggested Paraphrase and Conclusion

The following expanded paraphrase expresses what this book considers to be a correct understanding of Romans 3:25–26: "God purposed Christ to be a mercy seat through his faithfulness; to reveal, by giving his life, God's [saving] righteousness [because God delayed to fully deal with sins in the past]; that is, to show openly God's [saving] righteousness at the present time, that he is righteous and the one who makes righteous everyone who has faith in [or the faith of] Jesus."

161. Price, "Righteousness," 266–67.
162. Quell, *Righteousness*, 46.
163. Johnson, *Reading Romans*, 59–60.

Advocates of the penal substitution theory of the Atonement often consider Romans 3:25–26 as conclusive proof of their position. Calvin's statement of the meaning is that "God has set forth Christ, as a propitiation, to make it plain that he is just, or righteous, in the forgiveness of sins." God's pardoning mercy is then seen as vindicated from all appearance of violating the demands of justice.[164] This is only an interpretation, for in no way do these verses directly state the penal theory. It is one view of "the righteousness of God," the "passing over" of sins, and the "forbearance" of God. In other words, only one interpretation supports the theory that God's justice requires satisfaction. The passage makes no reference to "the demands of justice," and as modern translations show, "propitiation" is not the proper translation of the Greek. The NT never says that God punishes Christ. In fact, the verbs and nouns for "punish" or "punishment" are only used several times in the whole of the NT, and *never* of God or Christ.[165] In fact, it is not easy to extract from Romans 3:25 *in its context* any indication that God is being placated by the death of Jesus.[166]

The emphasis on the righteousness of God in Romans 3:21–26 is not related to any alleged demands for punishment to satisfy justice, but rather proceeds from the context. In three chapters Paul has announced that all, Jew and Gentile alike, are equal before the divine tribunal; all are condemned, and all can equally be saved by faith.[167] The central points of the passage are: (1) the righteousness of God answers the plight of all humankind under sin in the gift of Christ as a ransom and expiatory sacrifice; (2) this saving act of God is in complete continuity with and in fulfillment of his covenant promises to Israel; and (3) salvation comes to all in the same way, through faith.[168]

Regardless of perspective, one thought in these verses rings loud and clear: God in Christ has done whatever necessary for humankind to be freed from the guilt of sin and able to start a new life in the strength of divine grace.[169] The righteousness of God both pardons the sinner and provides the life-force that breaks the bondage to sin.[170]

---

164. C. Hodge, *Romans*, 122. In the view of this book, this would be a demonstration of *injustice*. See chapter 2, Moral Objections.
165. J. Robinson, *Wrestling with Romans*, 48.
166. Ziesler, *Romans*, 113, emphasis added.
167. Bassler, "Divine Impartiality," 43.
168. Dunn, *Romans*, 183.
169. Dodd, *Romans*, 61.
170. Herrmann, "Righteousness," 53.

Appendix B

Atonement Fact versus Theory

THIS WORK HOPES TO achieve two ends: (1) enable its readers to be able to distinguish between fact and theory regarding the Atonement, and (2) present victorious substitution as a rational theory explaining the necessity of Christ's suffering and death based on Scripture. In addition to understanding Christ's substitutionary death in the context of ransom theory, the author hopes the reader comprehends the scope and power of Christ's victorious life as it lives in every Christian.

Something more, however, must be said about theory. The meaning of the Atonement is set forth clearly in Scripture. Yet God has not chosen to give full revelation concerning its mechanics, specifically "how" atonement is made. Atonement theories result from efforts to understand the "how." Gustaf Aulén plainly states that he does not use the word *theory* concerning the classic view because he believes it is rather a motif or theme that runs through Scripture.[1] Citing Aulén's example, J. I. Packer argues that the same can be said for the penal substitution view: "Penal-substitution has sometimes been explicated as a theory . . . but a doubt remains as to whether this way of understanding the theme is biblically right."[2] This book does not make such a claim, and the following attempts to distinguish *theory* and *fact* in the victorious substitution view of the Atonement.

1. Aulén, *Christus Victor*, 157.
2. Packer, "Cross," 26.

SCRIPTURAL *FACT*

The following are clearly not all the scriptural facts related to the Atonement but rather those that directly support the theoretical components of the victorious substitution theory.

1. One way Scripture expresses the Atonement is in terms of redemption (Rom 3:24; Eph 1:14; 4:30; Col 1:14; Heb 9:12).
2. Jesus says he came to give his life as a ransom (Mark 10:45).
3. Ransom is liberation from the powers of darkness and translation into the kingdom of God (Gal 1:4; Col 1:13; 1 Pet 2:9).
4. Humankind is purchased *for* God (Rev 5:9).
5. There is a great price paid (1 Cor 6:19–20).
6. The price paid is the blood of Christ (Rev 5:9).
7. Christ redeems humankind from the curse of the law, and in doing so became a curse (Gal 3:13).
8. Christ's death is sacrificial (1 Cor 5:7).
9. God makes a sacrifice (John 3:16) as well as receives a sacrifice (Heb 9:14).
10. Humankind is in bondage to sin (John 8:31–36; Rom 3:9, 7:14; Gal 3:22).
11. Jesus comes to free humankind from sin (Titus 2:14).
12. The result of sin is death (Rom 6:23).
13. Humankind is in bondage to death and the fear of death (Heb 2:14–15).
14. Christ comes to deliver humanity from death and the fear of death (Heb 2:14–18).
15. Satan had the "power of death" (Heb 2:14).
16. Christ calls the time when he is taken captive in Gethsemane "your [those who came to take him] hour—when darkness reigns" (Luke 22:53).
17. Christ comes to abolish death (2 Tim 1:10).
18. Jesus' death is vicarious (Isa 53:4–6; 2 Cor 5:14–15; 1 Pet 2:24; some would argue that this is not "fact").

19. Jesus' death is penal (Isa 53:4–6; Gal 3:13; some would argue this is not "fact").
20. Jesus' suffering and death is according to God's will (Isa 53:10; Luke 22:42).
21. Satan has power in the earth (1 John 5:19).
22. Satan has an array of forces hostile to God (Col 2:15; Eph 6:11–12).
23. Sinners live under the influence of Satan (1 John 3:8–12; John 8:44).
24. Christ comes to overcome Satan (John 12:31), to destroy Satan (Heb 2:14), and to destroy the works of Satan (1 John 3:8).
25. Christ's life is a battle against the forces of darkness (Luke 4).
26. Satan is involved in the betrayal (Luke 22:3) and crucifixion of Jesus (John 14:30).
27. Christ is victorious over principalities and powers (Col 2:15).
28. It is not possible for death to hold Christ (Acts 2:24).
29. Christ cancels the legal demands of the law (Col 2:14).
30. Christ is the end of the law "so that there may be righteousness" (Rom 10:4).
31. God "justifies the ungodly" (Rom 4:5).
32. Christ dies so that humanity can be reconciled to God (Rom 5:10).
33. In the end Christ will destroy all enemies (1 Cor 15:24–28; Col 2:15).

VICTORIOUS SUBSTITUTION THEORY—BASED ON THE PRECEDING SCRIPTURAL FACTS

It is difficult to call some of these statements theory, but some would disagree with each point.

1. The ransom price is paid to Satan.
2. Redemption through ransom is a necessity. God does not use force against his enemy because of his own justice, and Satan has a claim on humankind based on human choice and God's judgment against humanity's sin.

3. An accord is reached. Christ, in exchange for humankind, becomes a man and submits to suffering and death.
4. Christ wins every battle against the forces of darkness because he succumbs to no temptation, is always obedient to the Father, and is without sin.
5. Christ's sacrifice is the surrender of his life as a ransom as well as a perfect offering of his life to his Father.
6. Christ's becoming a ransom involves substitution and exchange. He takes humankind's place, enduring the full penalty for sin that humans deserve. In exchange, "whosoever will" is reconciled with God, free from eternal death as the penalty of sin, and free from the power of sin through the power of Christ's victorious life.
7. Christ takes humanity's place, enduring the due penalty for sin, but Satan, not God, inflicts the punishment on Christ.
8. Christ's death is according to God's will because through it he effects redemption. Because Christ is without sin, death cannot hold him. (Both of these statements are scriptural facts but Scripture does not specifically join them together.)
9. Satan loses everything. Humanity is free and Christ is resurrected.
10. Humans are free to choose reconciliation with God. This reconciliation involves establishing a relationship of fellowship rather than a contractual relationship. It does not involve punishment. Its two essential components are forgiveness and repentance.

Bibliography

Anselm of Canterbury, Saint. *Cur Deus Homo?* Translated by Edward S. Prout. Piccadilly: Religious Tract Society, 1886.
Arminius, Jacobus. *The Works of James Arminius.* Vol. 1. Translated by James Nichols. London: Longman, Hurt, Rees, Orme, Brown & Green, 1825.
Athanasius of Alexandria, Saint. *On the Incarnation.* Translated by John Behr. Yonkers, NY: St. Vladimir's Seminary Press, 2011.
———. *Orations of Saint Athanasius against the Arians.* London: Griffith, Farran, Okeden & Welsh, 1889.
Augustine. *On the Trinity, Books 8–15.* Edited by Gareth B. Matthews. Translated by Stephen McKenna. Cambridge: Cambridge University Press, 2002.
Aulén, Gustaf. *Christus Victor.* New York: Macmillan, 1951.
Bailey, Daniel Peter. "Jesus as the Mercy Seat: The Semantics and Theology of Paul's Use of Hilasterion in Romans 3:25." PhD diss., University of Cambridge, 1999.
Baillie, D. M. *God Was in Christ.* New York: Charles Scribner's Sons, 1948.
Barry, F. R. *The Atonement.* London: Hodder & Stoughton, 1968.
Barton, George A. "The Interpretation of the Epistle to the Romans." *Anglican Theological Review* 21 (April 1939) 81–93.
Bassler, Jouette M. "Divine Impartiality in Paul's Letter to the Romans." *Novum Testamentum* 26 (1984) 43–58.
Beare, Francis Wright. *The First Epistle of Peter.* Oxford: Basil Blackwell, 1947.
Best, Ernst. *The Letter of Paul to the Romans.* The Cambridge Bible Commentary on the New English Bible. Cambridge: Cambridge University Press, 1967.
Bloesch, Donald G. *Jesus Is Victor! Karl Barth's Doctrine of Salvation.* Nashville, TN: Abingdon, 1976.
Brown, C. G. "Objective and Subjective: An Assessment of R. C. Moberly's Atonement and Personality." *Scottish Journal of Theology* 25 (1972) 259–78.
Bruce, F. F. *The Letter of Paul to the Romans: An Introduction and Commentary.* Grand Rapids, MI: Eerdmans, 1985.
Brümmer, Vincent. "Atonement and Reconciliation." *Religious Studies* 28 (1992) 435–52.
Brunner, Emil. *The Mediator: A Study of the Central Doctrine of the Christian Faith.* Translated by Olive Wyon. New York: Macmillan, 1934.

Burnaby, John. *Christian Words and Christian Meanings*. New York: Harper & Brothers, 1955.

Burnet, Gilbert. *An Exposition of the Thirty-Nine Articles of the Church of England*. London: Printed by R. Roberts, 1699.

Bushnell, Horace. *Forgiveness and Law: Grounded in Principles, Interpreted by Human Analogies*. New York: Scribner, Armstrong & Co., 1874.

———. *The Vicarious Sacrifice: Grounded in Principles of Universal Obligation*. New York: Charles Scribner's Sons, 1866.

Calvin, John. *Calvin: Theological Treatises*. Translated by J. K. S. Reid. Library of Christian Classics, vol. 22. Philadelphia: Westminster, 1954.

———. *The Institutes of Christian Religion*. Edited by Tony Lane and Hilary Osborne. Translated by Robert Backhouse. London: Hodder & Stoughton, 1986.

Campbell, John McLeod. *The Nature of the Atonement and Its Relation to Remission of Sins and Eternal Life*. London: Macmillan, 1915.

Carruthers, Samuel W., ed. *The Westminster Confession of Faith: Being an Account of the Preparation and Printing of Its Seven Leading Editions, to Which Is Appended a Critical Text of the Confession*. Manchester, UK: Aikman, 1937.

Cave, Sydney. *The Doctrine of the Work of Christ*. Nashville, TN: Cokesbury, 1937.

Clark, Gordon H. *The Atonement*. Hobbs, NM: The Trinity Foundation, 1987.

Clark, Henry W. *The Cross and the Eternal Order: A Study of Atonement in Its Cosmic Significance*. New York: Macmillan, 1944.

Connell, J. Clement. "The Propitiatory Element in the Atonement." *Vox Evangelica* 4 (1965) 28–42.

Cranfield, C. E. B. *I & II Peter and Jude*. Torch Bible Commentaries, edited by John Marsh and Alan Richardson. London: SMC, 1960.

———. *Romans: A Shorter Commentary*. Grand Rapids, MI: Eerdmans, 1985.

Crawford, Robert G. "Is the Penal Theory of the Atonement Scriptural?" *Scottish Journal of Theology* 23 (1970) 257–72.

———. "A Parable of the Atonement." *Evangelical Quarterly* 50 (January 1978) 2–7.

Dale, R. W. *The Atonement*. London: Congregational Union of England & Wales, 1878.

Davids, Peter H. *The First Epistle of Peter*. The New International Commentary on the New Testament, series edited by Gordon Fee. Grand Rapids, MI: Eerdmans, 1990.

Davies, Glenn N. *Faith and Obedience in Romans: A Study in Romans 1–4*. Sheffield: Sheffield Academic Press, 1990.

Denney, James. *Studies in Theology*. London: Hodder & Stoughton, 1895.

Dodd, C. H. *The Epistle of Paul to the Romans*. The Moffatt NT Commentary 6. Edited by James Moffatt. London: Collins, 1959.

Dunn, James D. G. *Romans 1–8*. Word Biblical Commentary, vol. 38A, edited by Bruce Metzger, David A. Hubbard, and Glen W. Barker. Dallas: Word, 1988.

Dunn, James D. G. and Alan M. Suggate. *The Justice of God: A Fresh Look at the Old Doctrine of Justification by Faith*. Grand Rapids, MI: Eerdmans, 1993.

Eichrodt, Walther. *The Theology of the Old Testament*. Vol. 1. Translated by J. A. Baker. Philadelphia: Westminster, 1961.

Ellingworth, Paul. *The Epistle to the Hebrews: A Commentary on the Greek Text*. The New International Greek Testament Commentary. Edited by I. Howard Marshall and W. Ward Gasque. Grand Rapids, MI: Eerdmans, 1983.

Erickson, Millard J. *Christian Theology*. Vol. 2. Grand Rapids, MI: Baker, 1985.

Fiddes, Paul S. *Past Event and Present Salvation: The Christian Idea of Atonement.* Louisville, KY: Westminster John Knox, 1989.

Fitzmyer, Joseph A. *Romans.* Anchor Yale Bible Commentary, edited by William F. Albright and David N. Freedman, vol. 33. New York: Doubleday, 1993.

Forsyth, P. T. *Cruciality of the Cross.* London: Independent, 1955.

Franks, Robert S. *The Atonement.* London: Oxford University Press, 1934.

Fryer, Nico S. L. "The Meaning and Translation of *Hilasterion* in Romans 3:25." *Evangelical Quarterly* 59 (February 1987) 99–116.

Gerrish, Brian A. "Atonement and 'Saving Faith.'" *Theology Today* 17 (1960) 181–91.

Godbey, John Charles. "A Study of Faustus Socinus' 'De Jesu Christo Servatore.'" PhD diss., University of Chicago, 1968.

Gomes, Alan W. "De Jesu Christo Servatore: Faustus Socinus on the Satisfaction of Christ." *Westminster Theological Journal* 55 (February 1993) 209–31.

———. "Faustus Socinus' *De Jesu Christo Servatore*, Part III: Historical Introduction, Translation, and Critical Notes." PhD diss., Fuller Theological Seminary, 1990.

Goppelt, Leonhard. *Typos: The Typological Interpretation of the Old Testament in the New.* Translated by Donald H. Madvig. Grand Rapids, MI: Eerdmans, 1982.

Greathouse, William M. "Sanctification and the Christus Victor Motif in Wesleyan Theology." *Wesleyan Theological Journal* 7 (1972) 47–59.

Gregory of Nyssa, Saint. *The Catechetical Oration.* Edited by J. H. Strawley. London: Society for Promoting Christian Knowledge, 1917.

———. *Oratio Catechetica.* In *The Early Church Fathers: Gregory of Nyssa*, by Anthony Meredith. London: Routledge, 1999.

Grensted, L. W. *A Short History of the Doctrine of the Atonement.* Manchester, UK: Manchester University Press, 1920.

Grotius, Hugo. *A Defense of the Catholic Faith: Concerning the Satisfaction of Christ.* Andover, MA: Warren F. Draper, 1889. Microfilm, Perkins Library, Duke University, Durham, NC.

Grudem, Wayne. *Systematic Theology.* Grand Rapids, MI: Zondervan, 1994.

Gunton, Colin, E. *The Actuality of Atonement: A Study of Metaphor, Rationality and the Christian Tradition.* Edinburgh: T. & T. Clark, 1989.

Hart, Trevor A. "Anselm of Canterbury and John McLeod Campbell: Where Opposites Meet?" *Evangelical Quarterly* 62 (1990) 311–33.

Hays, Richard B. "Psalm 143 and the Logic of Romans 3." *Journal of Biblical Literature* 99 (1980) 107–15.

Hebblethwaite, Brian. "The Doctrine of the Atonement: Does It Make Moral Sense?" *Epworth Review* 19 (March 1992) 63–74.

Helm, Karl. "The Main Types of the Doctrine of the Atonement." *Lutheran Quarterly* 15 (1963) 250–65.

Herrmann, Johannes. "Righteousness," in *Theological Dictionary of the New Testament*, Vol. 3. Edited by Gerhard Kittel. Translated and edited by Geoffrey W. Bromiley. Grand Rapids, MI: Eerdmans, 1965.

Hicks, John Mark. "What Did Christ Accomplish on the Cross? Atonement in Campbell and Scott." *Lexington Theological Quarterly* 30 (March 1995) 145–70.

Hirsch, Emanuel. *Die Theologie des Andreas Osiander und ihre geschichtlichen Voraussetzungen.* Göttingen: Vandenhoeck & Ruprecht, 1919.

Hodge, Archibald Alexander. *The Atonement.* Grand Rapids, MI: Eerdmans, 1953.

Hodge, Charles. *Commentary on the Epistle to the Romans.* Philadelphia: Gregg & Elliot, 1835.

Hodges, H. A. *The Pattern of Atonement*. London: SCM, 1955.
Hodgson, Leonard. *The Doctrine of the Atonement*. New York: Charles Scribner's Sons, 1951.
Hunter, A. M. *Paul and His Predecessors*. Philadelphia: Westminster, 1961.
Irenaeus, Saint. *Against Heresies*. In vol. 1 of *The Ante-Nicene Fathers: The Writings of the Fathers down to AD 325*. Edited by Alexander Roberts and James Donaldson. Grand Rapids, MI: Eerdmans, 1978.

———. *Against Heresies*. In *The Writings of Irenaeus*, edited by Alexander Roberts and James Donaldson. Ante-Nicene Christian Library. Edinburgh: T. & T. Clark, 1868.

———. *The Demonstration of the Apostolic Preaching*. Translated by John Behr. Crestwood, NY: St. Vladimir's Seminary Press, 1997.

Jensen, Paul. "Forgiveness and Atonement." *Scottish Journal of Theology* 46 (1993) 141–59.
Jewett, Robert. *Letter to Pilgrims: A Commentary on the Epistle to the Hebrews*. New York: Pilgrim, 1981.
Johnson, Luke Timothy. *Reading Romans: A Literary and Theological Commentary*. New York: Crossroads, 1997.
Käsemann, Ernst. *Commentary on Romans*. Translated and edited by Geoffrey W. Bromiley. Grand Rapids, MI: Eerdmans, 1980.
Kehm, George H. "Calvin on Defilement and Sacrifice." *Interpretation* 31 (January 1977) 39–52.
Kleinknecht, Hermann, J. Fichtner, and G. Stahlin et al. *Wrath*. Bible Key Words from Gerhard Kittel's *Theologisches Wörterbuch zum Neuen Testament*. Translated by Dorothea M. Barton. Edited by P. R. Ackroyd. London: Adam & Charles Black, 1964.
Kümmel, W. G. "*Paresis* and *Endeixis*: A Contribution to the Understanding of the Pauline Doctrine of Justification." *Journal for Theology and the Church* 3 (1967) 1–13.
Lampe, G. W. H. "The Atonement: Law and Love." In *Soundings: Essays Concerning Christian Understanding*, edited by A. R. Vidler, 173–91. Cambridge: Cambridge University Press, 1966.
Lee, E. Kenneth. *A Study in Romans*. London: S.P.C.K., 1962.
Letham, Robert. *The Work of Christ*. Downers Grove, IL: InterVarsity, 1993.
Lewis, C. S. *Letters to Malcolm: Chiefly on Prayer*. New York: Harcourt Brace Jovanovich, 1963.

———. *Mere Christianity*. New York: Macmillan, 1943.

Loewe, William P. "Irenaeus' Soteriology: *Christus Victor* Revisited." *Anglican Theological Review* 67 (January 1985) 1–15.
Longenecker, Bruce W. "Pistis in Romans 3:25: Neglected Evidence for the 'Faithfulness of Christ'?" *New Testament Studies* 39 (1993) 478–80.
Lunceford, Joe Elbert. "An Historical and Exegetical Inquiry into the New Testament Meaning of the '*Ilaskomai*' Cognates." PhD diss., Baylor University, 1979.
Lyonnet, Stanislas and Leopold Sabourin. *Sin, Redemption, and Sacrifice: A Biblical and Patristic Study*. Rome: Biblical Institute Press, 1970.
MacDonald, George. *Discovering the Character of God*. Edited by Michael R. Phillips. Minneapolis: Bethany, 1989.
Macquarrie, John. *Principles of Christian Theology*. 2nd ed. New York: Charles Scribner's Sons, 1977.

Marshall, I. Howard. "The Death of Jesus in Recent New Testament Study." *Word & World* 3 (1983) 12–21.

Masterman, J. Howard. *The First Epistle of S. Peter*. London: Macmillan, 1900.

Mather, G. B. "The Atonement: Representative or Substitutionary?" *Canadian Journal of Theology* 4 (1958) 266–72.

McClendon, James W., Jr. *Doctrine: Systematic Theology*. Vol. 2. Nashville, TN: Abingdon, 1994.

McDonald, H. D. *The Atonement of the Death of Christ: In Faith, Revelation and History*. Grand Rapids, MI: Baker Book House, 1985.

Michaels, J. Ramsey. *1 Peter*. Word Biblical Commentary, vol. 49, edited by David A. Hubbard, and Glenn W. Barker. Waco, TX: Word, 1988.

Moo, Douglas J. *The Epistle to the Romans*. The New International Commentary on the New Testament, series edited by Gordon Fee. Grand Rapids, MI: Eerdmans, 1996.

Morris, Leon. *The Apostolic Preaching of the Cross*. Grand Rapids, MI: Eerdmans, 1960.

———. *The Cross in the New Testament*. Grand Rapids, MI: Eerdmans, 1965.

———. *The Epistle to the Romans*. Grand Rapids, MI: Eerdmans, 1988.

———. "Propitiation." In *New Bible Dictionary*. 2nd ed., 986. Wheaton, IL: Tyndale, 1982.

Murray, Andrew. *The Two Covenants*. Fort Washington, PA: Christian Literature Crusade, 1974.

Murray, John. *The Epistle to the Romans: The English Text with Introduction, Exposition and Notes: Chapters 1 to 8*. The New International Commentary on the New Testament 1. Edited by F. F. Bruce. Grand Rapids, MI: Eerdmans, 1993.

———. *Redemption Accomplished and Applied*. Grand Rapids, MI: Eerdmans, 1955.

Nee, Watchman. *The Life That Wins*. New York: Christian Fellowship, 1986.

Nygren, Anders. *Commentary on Romans*. Translated by Carl C. Rasmussen. Philadelphia: Muhlenberg, 1944.

O'Neil, J. C. *Paul's Letter to the Romans*. Harmondsworth, UK: Penguin, 1975.

Packer, J. I. "What Did the Cross Achieve?" *Tyndale Bulletin* 25 (1974) 3–45.

Pelikan, Jaroslav, ed. *Lectures on Galatians: Chapters 1–4*. Vol. 26 of *Luther's Works: The American Edition*. St. Louis: Concordia, 1963.

———. *Luther's Sermons I*. Vol. 51 of *Luther's Works: The American Edition*. St. Louis: Concordia, 1963.

Peters, Ted. "Atonement and the Final Scapegoat." *Perspectives in Religious Studies* 19 (1992) 151–81.

Price, James L. "God's Righteousness Shall Prevail." *Interpretation* 28 (March 1974) 259–80.

Prince, Derek. *Spiritual Conflict*. Sermons given by Derek Prince. Derek Prince Publications, 1971, six audiocassettes.

Quell, Gottfried, and Gottlob Schrenk. *Righteousness*. Bible Key Words from Gerhard Kittel's *Theologisches Wörterbuch zum Neuen Testament*. Translated by J. R. Coates. New York: Harper & Brothers, 1951.

Quick, Oliver Chase. *The Gospel of the New World*. London: Nisbet, 1945.

Rashdall, Hastings. *The Idea of Atonement in Christian Theology*. London: Macmillan, 1919.

Ridderbos, Herman N. *Paul: An Outline of His Theology*. Translated by John Richard de Witt. Grand Rapids, MI: Eerdmans, 1975.

Robinson, H. Wheeler. *Redemption and Revelation: In the Actuality of History*. London: Nisbet, 1942.

Robinson, John A. T. *Wrestling with Romans*. Philadelphia: Westminster, 1979.

Robinson, Norman L. *How Jesus Christ Saves Men: A Study of the Atonement*. London: James Clarke & Co., 1954.

Schreiner, Thomas R. *Romans*. Baker Exegetical Commentary on the New Testament. Grand Rapids, MI: Baker Academic, 1998.

Selwyn, Edward Gordon. *The First Epistle of St. Peter*. London: Macmillan, 1952.

Shakespeare, William. *Henry IV*. Edited by Barbara Mowat, Paul Werstine, Michael Poston, and Rebecca Niles. Folger Shakespeare Library. Accessed on April 5, 2024. Washington, DC: Folger Shakespeare Library.

———. *Richard II*. Edited by Barbara Mowat, Paul Werstine, Michael Poston, and Rebecca Niles. Folger Shakespeare Library. Accessed on April 5, 2024. Washington, DC: Folger Shakespeare Library.

Shedd, William G. T. *A Critical and Doctrinal Commentary upon the Epistle of St. Paul to the Romans*. Grand Rapids, MI: Zondervan, 1967.

Smith, David. *The Atonement in the Light of History and the Modern Spirit*. London: Hodder & Stoughton, 1918.

Snaith, Norman H. *The Distinctive Ideas of the Old Testament*. London: Epworth, 1944.

Songer, Harold S. "New Standing before God: Romans 3:21—5:21." *Review & Expositor* 73 (1974) 415–24.

Stauffer, Ethelbert. *New Testament Theology*. New York: Macmillan, 1955.

Stuart, Moses. *Commentary on the Epistle to the Romans: With a Translation and Various Excursus*. Andover, MA: Flagg & Gould, 1832.

Symonds, H. Edward. "Justification in Holy Scripture and in Later Theology." In *The Doctrine of Justification by Faith*, edited by G. W. H. Lampe, 69–80. London: A. R. Mowbray, 1954.

Taliaferro, Charles. "A Narnian Theory of the Atonement." *Scottish Journal of Theology* 41 (January 1988) 75–92.

Taylor, Vincent. "Great Texts Reconsidered." *Expository Times* 50 (1939) 295–300.

Tertullian. *Treatises on Penance: On Penitence and On Purity*. Translated by William P. Le Saint. Ancient Christian Writers: The Works of the Fathers in Translation, edited by Johannes Quasten and Walter Burghardt. Westminster, MD: Newman, 1959.

Vaughan, Curtis and Thomas D. Lea. *1, 2 Peter, Jude: Bible Study Commentary*. Grand Rapids, MI: Zondervan, 1988.

Wand, J. W. C., ed. *The General Epistles of St. Peter and St. Jude*. Westminster Commentaries. London: Methuen, 1934.

Wilson, William E. "Romans 3:25, 26." *Expository Times* 29 (1918) 472–73.

Winter, Bob R. "The Problem of Man's Salvation." *Restoration Quarterly* 2 (January 1958) 37–44.

Worrall, B. G. "Substitutionary Atonement in the Theology of James Denney." *Scottish Journal of Theology* 28 (1975) 341–57.

Young, Edward J. *The Book of Isaiah*. Vol. 3. Grand Rapids, MI: Eerdmans, 1972.

Young, Frances M. *Sacrifice and the Death of Christ*. London: Northumberland, 1975.

Young, Norman H. "C. H. Dodd, 'Hilaskesthai' and His Critics." *Evangelical Quarterly* 48 (1976) 67–78.

———. "'Hilaskesthai' and Related Words in the New Testament." *Evangelical Quarterly* 55 (1983) 169–76.

Yung, Hwa. "Theories of Atonement and the Mission of the Church." *Asia Journal of Theology* 3 (1989) 540–57.
Ziesler, John. *Paul's Letter to the Romans*. London: SCM, 1989.
———. "Salvation Proclaimed IX. Romans 3:21–26." *Expository Times* 93 (December 1982) 356–59.

www.ingramcontent.com/pod-product-compliance
Lightning Source LLC
Chambersburg PA
CBHW051637230426
43669CB00013B/2335